GET 'ER SIDEWAYS

Mike Banks
2018

MIKE BANKS

BANKS MOTOR COMPANY
Durant, OK

Published in the United States of America by

Banks Motor Company
502 Bryan Drive
Durant, OK 74701

www.banksmotorcompany.com
www.getersideways.com

Edited by Charity Banks

ISBN 978-1-7323508-0-9

All photos from the Banks Family Collection
All design and photography by Charity Banks

PRINTED IN THE UNITED STATES OF AMERICA
10 9 8 7 6 5 4 3 2 1
First Edition

This book is dedicated to all my friends and family. To the ones who were with me in these stories, thanks for the memories. To the others who have listened to these stories over the years, thanks for your patience. And to the ones who have always said "you should write a book," thanks for the encouragement.

Mike Banks

CONTENTS

NOTE FROM THE AUTHOR

There is nothing like the sound and feeling of two hot cars coming off the line together on a hot summer night, windows down on a narrow two lane road, the sounds of tires squalling and carburetors sucking air, feeling the tires break loose at the shift points. You can pay $100 to watch fuel funny cars and dragsters go over 300 MPH and threaten to break your ear drums, but you can't buy what I just described.

At the age of 16, I went on a hunt for the fastest car I could find. What I found was a 1967 Plymouth GTX with a 440 engine. The stories in this book have this car as a sort of home base. These things happened in, around, and sometimes because of this car. This old car became part of my identity and launched an interest which became both my hobby and my business and ultimately has become a family heirloom.

I sold this car as a young man starting a family. Decades later after an extensive search I was miraculously able to find it and get it back.

I hope I can portray to you with this book something that cannot be replicated today: what it felt like to own and operate a true American muscle car when they weren't expensive collectors' items, but were just being used the way Detroit intended. The impressions that these cars performance made on the people that were there and experienced them is the reason for their popularity today. They have become legends.

Just as I used to invite my friends to open the door of the old GTX so I could take them for an adrenaline-filled ride, I now invite you to open the cover of this book and get in.

--Mike Banks

PROLOGUE

T HE OLD RECLINER HAD SEEN BETTER days. It had been a Christmas present from my wife on our first Christmas as a married couple, and it had moved with us to our new house a few years later. But today it was time to say goodbye, and I loaded it into the back of my pickup to take to the dump. I backed up to the private dump ditch on a relative's private property, jumped up into the back of the truck, and grabbed the old recliner. It was not a big chair; it was the small variety that sold for $49.95, with only vinyl upholstery, but it was all we could afford at the time, and I loved this thoughtful gift from my young wife. Because of its small size, I was able to lift it over my head and prepared to throw it deep into the ditch, just for my own entertainment. Just as I got the chair over my head I heard a metallic clunk hit the bed of the pickup. I let fly with the chair and looked down to see a women's leather key fob, the kind that has a flap that you can fold the keys down in and snap the front closed. It had an embossed decorative pattern, and the words "Jesus is Love," and I recognized it immediately as belonging to my wife; it had gone missing years ago back in our trailer house days. As I picked it up and spread all of the keys out, I saw the front door key to our trailer house. Next there was a large rubber headed key with a VW emblem that had belonged to our VW Rabbit, but the next keys were the special ones: they were the original Chrysler corporation logo keys to my long gone, 1967 Plymouth GTX. Being young, and poor, and with a two month old child, we had sold it during one of the 1970's gas crises. This car had been instrumental in me meeting my wife and in it we had dated and fell in love. This was the car in our wedding album pictures, all adorned with toilet paper and shaving cream, with "just married" painted down the side and us smiling out the windows in our matching polyester, baby blue leisure suits. This also was the car that had quite a reputation, and the one that my friend would jump in the front seat and proclaim "Get 'er sideways!" Finding those old keys again brought back all of these wonderful memories.

Having these keys in my possession again was like having a symbolic piece of the GTX back. Several more years passed, and being a car nut, sometimes I would daydream about seeing a 1967 GTX at a car show and pulling out this old set of keys, putting them in and turning the lock. In my mind that would be a Cinderella being reunited with her glass slipper moment.

Now here I am in Illinois, a long way from my Oklahoma/Texas border home, pulling into a driveway surrounded by cornfields, and there sits the red, 1967 GTX I have come here to see. There it sat, backed up to a fence, facing the road. There was nobody there but my wife and daughters, who watched as I walked to the back of the car, pulled the old key fob out of my pocket, selected the round headed key, and stuck it in the trunk. I turned it ever so slowly, but at a certain spot there was a very lively pop, and the trunk sprang, just as though it was saying to that key, "Where have you been all these years?" You only have so many dreams come true in a lifetime, and I had just had one.

GET 'ER SIDEWAYS

THE BEGINNING

I F THERE IS AN UNDISCOVERED GENE FOR loving cars, I would be a good candidate for scientific research. My earliest memory of a favorite toy is a play car dash board with keys, and a horn that honked. Stories are also told of me ripping around the halls of our second story apartment building on my tricycle while slightly older children yelled, "Watch out for Mikey Banky, he'll run you over!"

Shortly, after having moved to a small house on my grandparents' property, I was the proud owner of a pedal car with the word "Flash" on the side. Flash did have one small shortcoming to my 3 year old mind: I had no keys to pretend I was starting it with. I voiced the complaint to my dad, who promptly found an old ignition switch and mounted it under the dashboard. I now had a set of keys to dangle.

I learned, while Flash was my daily driver, that if I got a run down a slight hill and jumped it off a one foot high rock ledge right behind the clothesline, I could make my Mom yell. First in fright, and then warning that I was going to hurt myself and to "Stop it!" Lesson learned. Reckless behavior in cars is an attention getter, especially to women. The chicks dig it.

As the normal progression of my age marched on, so did my vehicles of choice. After two or three hand-me-down beginner bicycles, I found myself looking at a new kind of a bicycle that had just hit the scene—the Stingray bicycle. These things looked so much more like a motorcycle than traditional bikes. I had to have one. This type of bike promoted doing stunts such as doing wheelies, jumping ramps and, one of my favorites, skidding around corners. Flat track motorcycles skidded around corners, dirt track cars skidded around corners, and *I* skidded around corners.

It's a well-known fact that a cool spectator feat is wasted if no one is watching. Enter this story, my little brother Steve. Having practiced coming down a pathway behind our house at speed and skidding around a 90 degree turn, I stationed Steve, who is five years younger than me, just beyond the curve, to watch me make this awesome dirt throwing turn. The end result was a trip to the emergency room for Steve, which left me at home in dread of the condition of Steve's chest and my rear end. You see, in my enthusiasm of putting on a good show, I had gotten up more speed than in my previous practice runs. As I got to the corner, I was going too fast to make the turn, and Steve lay in my only other pathway. The high rise handlebar picked him up and deposited him into the clothesline pole. Not the same clothesline as before, mind you, but one only a short distance away. It seems a lot of my early hot rodding occurred around clotheslines. Thankfully, he required no serious medical treatment. The doctor said he just had bruises. Steve and I learned what guardrails are for.

My brother is also the reason for my next interesting ride. Western Auto was the most important store for a young boy in our town because they had the market cornered on things like BB guns, ball gloves, and of course, bicycles. Their line of bicycle, the "Western Flyer", had just come out with a new model of sport type bicycles called the "Buzz Bike Eliminator." It was styled to mimic a rail dragster and even had a red line cheater slick on the back. I needed one of those! Here was my problem. I had a perfectly good bike, and I was not due for an upgrade. I was in a pickle. My brother had a nearly new beginner bicycle that he left laying behind a visitor's car in my Grandma's driveway, and it got run over. I was so put out by this. How could he be so irresponsible? After all, he was nearly five years old! To add insult to injury, his request for a replacement was none other than a Western Auto Buzz Bike Eliminator. Could this be happening to me? Thankfully and thoughtfully, my Dad came through like gangbusters and came home with not one but two new Eliminators. Now I had a drag bike!

Around this time, all of us neighborhood boys would ride our bikes in the evening. We would spend our time trying to perfect our bike trick abilities, the favorite trick being, of course, the wheelie. Now, I was never very good at wheelies. I could get a couple of pedals worth of distance, but that was about it. One of my most memorable wheelie experiences, and most disastrous, actually didn't involve a bicycle at all. It involved a shopping cart. A few years earlier, when Steve was a toddler, my dad worked in our small town grocery store. The store was located in an old downtown building, with old oiled hardwood floors. On this day

Mom, Steve, and I were in the store grocery shopping. Mom was pushing the cart and Steve was sitting in the cart's toddler seat, facing mom with his feet dangling out the back. We were nearly through with our shopping when mom remembered something she forgot a few aisles over. While she took literally 30 seconds to run back and get it, she mistakenly trusted me with Steve, and the full shopping cart. It was during these 30 seconds that I took the opportunity to give Steve the valuable experience of a shopping cart wheel stand, which as far as I knew was a brand new invention that I had just thought of. So I ran behind the cart pushing it and my brother in front of me. After a few feet when I felt we had reached the proper velocity, I jumped up on the bar running along the back of the cart to get the front wheels up. I could just see in my mind Steve and I traveling down the remainder of the aisle with our cart's wheels a foot off the ground and looking just like a funny car coming down a drag strip, with its front wheels dangling in the air. Well, it didn't happen that way at all. When I jumped on the cart, it flipped over backwards with my brother in it. Of course the full cart of groceries went everywhere with the canned goods making a terrible racket on the hardwood floor. To my horror it was my dad, not my mom, that came around the corner first. It seems he knew we were in the store at the time, and when he heard the crash somehow figured I might have had something to do with it. Rather than immediately deal with me, his first concern was to get the cart off my brother. I really don't remember anything past that point; I must have blocked it out. Fortunately, my brother wasn't seriously hurt in the incident, although I'm not sure he might not have grown to be a little taller had this not have happened. I guess we'll never know.

Beside wheelies, our second favorite thing to do was jump our bicycles. We would make ramps and find places where the sidewalks heaved and made a natural ramp. We had a ball! It was in this unofficial neighborhood bicycle gang setting that these next few events take place. I had a friend at school named Dick and his Grandma lived across the street from my house. She was going to watch him for the day, and he had brought his bicycle. So we had a day of exciting riding ahead of us. Because he didn't live in our neighborhood, he was not in our regular ramp building, sidewalk jumping crowd. So I decided to introduce him to the fun. As we began playing, I noticed a great raised sidewalk section at the entrance to his Grandma's driveway. The next few lines of the story vary from here depending on whether you are talking to him or me. My story is that I saw a great place to pop a wheelie, pointed it out to him and allowed him to go first. Dick's story is that I dared him to do it and made him go first. I guess that is forever lost to history, but the events from here would make a great scene from a comedy movie. Dick took off like Evel Knievel approaching the ramp at Caesar's Palace. He hit the raised portion of the sidewalk; his front wheel came up high in a picture perfect wheelie, and then abruptly fell off. With a terrified look on his face, he stayed on the bike until the front end came down with no wheel on it and the bare forks stuck in the ground. He flew over the handlebars, the bicycle stayed right there with the rear wheel in the air, still spinning, and the fork stuck in the ground. Dick hit the ground out in front of the bicycle, and was laying there screaming and crying when his Grandma came flying out of the house. You guessed it, another emergency room trip. While waiting for the results this time, I searched for his missing front wheel. I found it sticking upright wedged under the picnic table probably 100 ft. away. Thankfully, once again the return from the doctor showed no serious damage, just big knots and a few scrapes.

Now this was the era when choppers were the coolest motorcycles, and "Captain America," the chopper that Peter Fonda rode in *Easy rider* was the coolest of the cool. In an effort to look like a chopper, some of the boys were even cutting the aluminum legs off their mother's lawn chairs and making extended front forks (this worked about as well as you would imagine an aluminum lawn chair suspension system engineered by a 10 year old would). But there was a solution on the horizon. *Auto World Model Cars* was a catalogue for model car and slot car racing enthusiasts. Although this catalogue had been around for years, I had just recently stumbled onto my first copy on a trip to Kansas City with my parents, and I had gone bonkers over it. I was constantly building and modifying model cars so this was dreamland for me. My parents let me purchase a copy, I took it home, and began to pour over it. This catalogue had recently begun including bicycle accessories in their back section. "Auto World" was advertising a factory built, chrome, top fuel drag fork for my bicycle, for only $10. I had to have one of these! My only obstacle was I didn't have $10. During this time my dad had a carwash, and when dad would clean out the mud pits, it was my job to wheelbarrow out the mud to the edge of the property and dump it. On one of these many wheel barrow trips, I spotted a $20 bill in the weeds where I was dumping. When I took it back and showed it to dad, he let me keep it. I now had funding for my dream bicycle modification. I went directly to my "Auto World" catalogue and ordered that chrome plated drag fork, and I had enough money left over to order the tallest sissy bar I had ever seen, and an auto cutter to chop and channel model cars with. With these new bicycle modifications, I immediately moved to the top of the pack, with everyone asking to ride my bicycle. My ultimate confirmation came when the only person in a fifty mile radius that had a *real* chopper, and a ponytail to boot, walked by my bike and said "Hey! That's a cool bike!" Sadly, a miscalculation in speed and ramp height in an attempt to jump my mother's goldfish pond caused extensive damage to that bike.

Our bicycles were not only for fun but also general transportation. When I was in fourth grade my cousin Kim, who lived next door, started kindergarten, and I was trusted to bring her home from school on the back of my bicycle. One day when we got to the turn off to our homes, we found the city had freshly oiled our road. Not knowing what else to do, Kim and I continued on down the road to our houses. This fresh oil was a mess having just been put down hours before. The oil got all over the bicycle. The small front fender kept most of it off of me. The short turned up back fender did nothing to keep the oil off of Kim. That knobby back tire painted the back of little Kimmy pretty good; she looked like a crooked politician before they put the feathers on. Needless to say, my Aunt Mary was not very happy with me. This has become an often re-told family story, but I always think I get a bad rap. There was another way home, but it would have required Kim and me to ride down the main highway home. I had considered that, but was sure our parents would not want us out on that highway. In retrospect, I guess we could have dismounted and I could have pushed the bike home resulting in oil only on our shoes. Honestly, that thought never crossed my mind. I think I probably know why it didn't. A cycle guy don't push his ride, he rides it. Pushing it would be like the Lone Ranger leading his horse, Silver, instead of riding him. It's just not done.

HOT RODS

I HAVE ALWAYS BEEN FASCINATED BY HOT rods. I remember, as a preschooler, one of my aunt's friends was driving an early '60's Impala Super Sport, and it had what I know now to be a 4 speed transmission in the floor. I remember standing beside that car in a parking space on the town square and looking at that white ball on top of that shifter, while my mom and aunt and her friend visited. I was very interested in it. I knew it was different from any other car or truck I had seen. Now it wasn't the fact that the shifter stuck out of the floor; my granddad's pickup was like that. No, this was different; it was something more rare or exotic—it was sporty. I don't know why, but it caught my eye and it registered as cool.

I had a similar thing happen the first time my dad took me to a pool hall. The pool hall was located above one of the on-the-square businesses where we climbed a very steep staircase with noisy wooden steps, and with chipping plaster on the walls, to the smoke-filled pool hall. At the back of the pool hall were these huge pool tables like I had not seen before. The dark, rich, green color just looked like a miniature manicured lawn, but it was not the size of the table or the color of the cloth that got my attention; it was those fifteen cherry red solid colored balls, with no numbers on them, dominating the playing field, with a smattering of different colored number balls scattered around in the mix. I later found the name for this was a snooker table. Now I had seen pool tables with their striped and solid multi-colored balls before, but I had not seen these dark red snooker balls. Somehow it was a very powerful visual image for me. I have been a snooker fan ever since. As soon as I was old enough to go to the pool hall I began to play, and for the last twenty years I have had a snooker table in my home. And just like the snooker balls, somehow that 4 speed shifter imprinted on my mind as something neat, and continues to be a pleasing sight to me today.

The visual impact Hot Rods made on me continued when I first saw a '55 Chevrolet jacked up in the front, gasser style, with a straight axle. It was cool and different, and I loved for us to meet it coming down the street. I would twist around in the backseat and watch it 'til it went out of sight. My interest didn't end with the visuals. I remember hearing my dad and uncle talking about a car being hot or "souped-up" and a ¾ cam was mentioned. Now I didn't know what a camshaft was, let alone a ¾ one, but I was anxious to find out. Very few hot-rodder's today know what that archaic flat-head era term, ¾ cam, means either, but they know it was hotter than stock.

Model cars were a great learning tool and an outlet for my hot rod creativity. Model cars, the 1/24th scale normal sized ones, cost $2 when I started building them, which made them just right for a birthday gift, or a rare treat once in a while. I built many of the favorites from that era, like the Red Baron and the Tarantula Dragster, but my favorite thing to do was to modify them into drag cars. You see funny cars had just come on the scene at drag strips, and the magazine and comic books I was reading at the time were giving me lots of wild ideas for funny cars. So I took a 1/24th scale "Herbie the Love Bug" model kit, and altered it into a funny car. I had come up with a model race car technique on my own which served me well. For a while I would take the bodies from the $2 models, and replace their engines and tires with those from a larger scale $3 model. "Herbie the Love Bug" got this treatment, with a double blower hemi, set way back and sticking up as high as the roof, with a huge set of slicks in the rear, and the driver roll cage sticking out the sliding sunroof from the rear seat area. I didn't have to buy all of these model kits from the store. There was a kid in my neighborhood that had tons of model car kits in pieces, and he never seemed to finish anything, plus he was a very poor trader. So when I needed parts for a new project, I would gather up stuff I was no longer interested in and head for his house, much like going to a wrecking yard to find full size parts. After some intense trading and bargaining I would come home with a box full of good stuff for my projects. I once scored a 1968 Dodge Coronet highway patrol car kit from this kid. The '68 Coronet was the same body style as a '68 Super Bee. So I gave it the $3 funny car treatment, as well as keeping its patrol car lights and highway patrol shield decals on its door, along with a Dodge Super Bee tail stripe. I named and lettered it "Super Fuzz."

I mentioned getting inspiration from my hot rod magazines and comic book collection. This collection included hot rod cartoons, the full magazine size, plus Carlton Comics had several twelve cent comic book size series', such as Grand Prix, Dragon Wheels featuring Scott Jackson, and Hot Rods and Racing Cars with Clint Curtis. I also bought the big guy's *Hot Rod Magazine*, and had its posters splashed on my bedroom walls. The only specific one I remember was a two engine gas dragster called the "Freight Train." I remember as a kid always hearing the radio ad that began "Sunday! Sunday! Sunday! At Kansas City International Raceway!" I never got to go there, but it was something I always dreamed about.

I did have other interests as a child. I read Superman comics, Batman Comics and war comics and I played cowboys and wore out several BB guns, but the love of hot cars eventually came out on top.

UP ON TWO WHEELS

I T IS AN INTERESTING SUBJECT TO ME, THE how's and why's of the courses people take in their life: their likes, their dislikes, their choice of profession—how much is their environment, how much is heredity? Or is it just destiny?

I have often been asked if I remember my Great Uncle coming home from out of state riding a big old Harley Davidson, or sometimes an Indian, and I have to say I don't. That was either before my time or I was just too young to remember. If I actually witnessed this, maybe this was my implantation of an infatuation with motorcycles.

Something I do remember is my granddad, who had a scrap iron business, hauling in an old Harley Davidson that had burned in a fire. This Harley set at the top of a hill, leaned against a fence, and I remember plotting how I could get on it and coast it down the hill. I didn't factor in that my eight year old frame wouldn't facilitate my up righting the rusty 800 pound behemoth. Shortly after my failed attempt I was seeking help for my second attempt, when I found the truth of the statement, "loose lips sink ships" because my plan got sunk. It seems someone relayed the message to headquarters (my granddad) and the old Harley promptly became the victim of his cutting torch and was added to the iron pile. Oh how it pains me today to think of that old 1940's era Harley being cut to pieces.

Another memory is of a young man, who worked for my dad, parking his Allstate motorcycle (remember those sold by Sears and Roebuck) in our driveway while he was working each day. It was summertime and a big part of my day was making circles around that motorcycle. And a big part of mom's day was shooing me away from it.

I also remember watching a group of young guys who, on Sunday afternoon, would gather and climb a steep hill on the edge of our town on their motorcyles. They would make a circle and go over the hill again and again, and I couldn't get enough of it. I can also still recall the excitement I would feel if I got a glimpse of a real cool chopper traveling through our town, its rider adorned in some rebellious garb with long hair blowing in the wind. I can also remember my parents muttering "Hippies."

During that time period there was a drag strip about a half hour's drive from our town, and I would beg to go there, often with no success. The name of the drag strip was "Thunder Valley Raceway," as it sat between hills with the pavement utilizing the flatness of the bottom. In the rolling hills of north Missouri there were very few flat spots long enough for a drag race and a shut-down afterwards. This was to be a constant frustrating fact for me in the next few years with the shut-down portion often compromised—more on that later. Anyway, one lucky Saturday night as my family was returning from visiting someone, we traveled by "Thunder Valley Raceway." The races were still going on, but it was so late that the ticket booth was already shut down and vacated for the evening. Because of the topography of sitting between the hills many people parked their cars up on the hillside facing the strip, and watched from their cars, drive-in movie style. Not long after arriving, the announcer came over the loud speakers proclaiming that they had an exhibition run for the crowd's enjoyment. Then out of the pit area came a guy on a big loud powerful motorcycle. He brought it to the line and when the Christmas tree blinked down to green he did a huge wheelie and made a full power run, standing it straight up on its back wheel all the way to the finish line. I don't remember any other car or run that night, but I sure remember that motorcycle and that wheelie. I was hooked.

Mini bikes were the normal starter machine for a budding motorcycle enthusiast. My first round of anything two-wheeled and motorized went something like this. We were on a family vacation several hundred miles away to visit relatives and when we drove into town I spied a dirt track where Honda Mini Trail 70's could be rented. Now Honda Trail 70's, or Mini Trails as we called them, were the Holy Grail for boys my age of that era, and here was a chance to ride one. I immediately went into extreme nagging mode; I nagged like I had never nagged before. I figured the possible bad consequences of being this annoying were worth the risk; after all we would only be here a couple of days and what if I had to go home without getting to ride those Mini Trails—probably my only chance in the world. You

15

might laugh at that, but where I was from, and how little we traveled, I was probably right. I finally won out, and on the second day, just the men of the group, my dad, uncle, and granddad took me outside of town to the track. Arriving at the track we found the price to be fairly high: one dollar a lap, minimum 4 laps, but it was a fairly long track with lots of hills and curves. There was one stipulation: one wreck and you were done, no exceptions. I remember dad asking, "Do you know how to ride one of those?" I don't know for sure if this is the exact phrase being used back then but, the spirit of my answer, whatever it may have been, was "Don't worry Dad, I got this." Turns out second turn, fifty yards from the start, I'm done. Yep, I piled 'er up right over the handlebars. You see, I had actually contemplated while sitting on the starting line, taking it slow at first and getting the hang of it before going fast, but I nixed that plan, not thinking I could afford any part of those four laps being spent on diddling around, and not getting the full effect. So I had a very short ride.

Not long after this I got a mini bike of my own, I wasn't able to get a Honda trail 70, but I got what I thought was the next best thing. It was a Scat Cat mini bike with a 4 horsepower Clinton engine, but more importantly it had a torque convertor instead of a normal centrifugal clutch. This gave it much more take-off power without hindering its top speed, and it was a wheelie poppin' machine.

By this time my little brother got a really fast little go-kart. He was only six or not more than seven years old, and he was so light that a go-kart would fly with him on it. I remember at times seeing him lose it on our backyard track and go spinning through the yard like a NASCAR cup car sliding through the grass infield at 150 MPH. Our back yard was small and was located on the slope of a hill, and that is where our track was located. It had one high side and one low side connected by the corners. My dad worked just over the hill just a few blocks away and would come home for lunch. During this time our summer days were filled with mini bike and go-kart riding. We would ride until dad got home for lunch, and then wash up and eat. After lunch we would head back outside and my dad would say, "Now you boys don't race." We would then putter around the track like there was an invisible pace car driven by a grandma. When it was time for him to go back to work, we would watch him get in his truck and leave. Then as the tailgate of his pickup disappeared over the hill, it was as though an imaginary flagman dropped the green flag, and it was an afternoon of racing action until supper time. One of the coolest things I ever remember my dad saying was when a family member proclaimed "Joe, those boys are ruining your yard." Dad's response was "I can grow grass when they're gone from home."

LET THE GOOD TIMES ROLL

A S I WAS OUTGROWING THE MINI BIKE, I had the bug real bad for a Honda 100, especially a red and white one. They were so pretty. One of my classmates, Bill Goodin, had one and he was gracious enough to invite me to his farm for a sleep over and a chance to ride his brand new Honda. About five minutes after getting off the school bus Bill fired up the little Honda. Now I don't know whether the next thing that happened was a lapse in judgement on Bill's part, or perhaps I hadn't let Bill know of my extensive full size motorcycle experience, which was zero. At any rate Bill invited me to drive his motorcycle while he rode on the back. Remember, this was two decades before the movie *Dumb and Dumber* came out. So we were copying no one; we were the forerunners. We took off down Bill's gravel road and turned onto the blacktop. We were cruising along on the blacktop and everything was going well when Bill yelled in my ear and pointed, "Turn here!" Now things got a little complicated for my level of experience. I was managing the front brake as well as the rear brake and trying to downshift and turn at the same time. I ended up not getting slowed down enough before trying to turn, and the wheels slid out from under us on the gravel. We were turning right, and the bike slid out from under us to the left. I then went down face first, catching myself with my hands and Bill lit right on my back. Fortunately, neither Bill, myself, or the CB 100 were hurt very much at all.

I didn't end up getting a Honda 100, but instead a 1965 Honda CB 160 presented itself. It belonged to a friend of my dad's and after deciding to buy it, Dad said, "Well, can you ride it?" I told him "Yes!" with an attitude that said "Of course I can!" This time it turned out good and my confidence paid off. I was able to ride the CB 160 without incident, and it turned out to suit me so much better than a CB 100 would have. I had no way of knowing this, but CB 160's were kind of hot little numbers for their size, and were very successful in their displacement category in road racing. The CB 160 was a 2 cylinder compared to the CB 100 which was a 1 lunger. Also this particular bike had been bored out and had a slightly larger displacement. So it had a lot better performance than the 100 would have had. The first thing I did after getting it was to remove the baffles from the mufflers, and it was loud! You could hear it all over town (it was a small town). I also replaced the rear sprocket with one with more teeth to increase acceleration. This was all taking place just before dirt bikes hit the scene in a big way, and we used road bikes like these off road often; so the bigger sprocket helped.

This was a full sized 300 pound motorcycle and was quite a handful at first for an eighth grader. There was a learning curve, but I was an eager student and certainly enjoyed the practice. In retrospect, I actually think I felt more confident on that motorcycle than maybe any vehicle I have ever driven. I remember our school, which was built on a hill, had a long stairway leading from an upper parking lot to a lower one. When school wasn't in session, how I loved to ride down those stairs on the Honda. I should say that I can't imagine doing that today, but that would be lying. I believe if the stairs were still there and I had the old 160 in front of them, I would go down them even now.

During this time period I received a phone call from a girl who was in the class ahead of me at school. She introduced herself and said she babysat in our neighborhood and had noticed me riding my motorcycle. She then proceeded to ask me to accompany her to a school sponsored party that weekend. That party was my first date, and I believe, in a roundabout way, that motorcycle played a part in it.

The day finally arrived that I turned sixteen. At that time Missouri had no provision that would let you legally ride a motorcycle on the street when you were fourteen or fifteen like other states sometimes did. I, for the most part, had waited patiently. I did fudge a little but had only had one warning from the highway patrol in over two years of motorcycle ownership, so I had been pretty responsible. My birthday is in January, and I immediately got my driver's license to operate a car. I still remember how irritated the patrolmen wearing parkas were when they had to set out pylons and give me the motorcycle test in the north Missouri winter. Now I was legal.

"Let the good times roll." This is how I felt that spring, being finally turned loose on the roadways of America, in about a 25 mile radius anyway. This was also a line from the Kawasaki ads on TV, competing with "You meet the nicest people on a Honda" and "Yamaha, won't you fly me away." As I remember it, the good times did roll. As a devout reader of motorcycle magazines, I learned how to lay down over the tank and hand shift the old Honda without using the clutch or letting off on the throttle. This might sound ridiculous to some considering the size of this motorcycle, but the little Honda was really quick. With that lower gearing, it had a top speed of exactly 73 mph. However, it got there fast and I found it to be a match for some pretty fast cars for about a hundred yards, which was just right to embarrass them from a stop light in town.

Riding my motorcycle made mundane chores, like running errands or going to work, seem like fun. I still find that to be true today. I worked at a lake six miles from town, and would ride there and back, including coming to town for lunch, probably just to get the extra twelve miles seat time. My mom says she could hear me going back to work all out through the river bottom, wide open in every gear. To that I said, "Yep." On one trip back to work one of my friend's older brothers happened to be following right behind in his car when the wing nut holding the side covers of my motorcycle succumbed to the vibration. It came off, letting both the left and right side cover fall off, because they were held on with a common piece of threaded rod. My friend's brother Joe said, while kidding me, "I was following old Banks the other day and all of a sudden it looked like his motorcycle exploded. Parts were flying everywhere as I tried to dodge 'em."

Another memorable escapade that I remember doing on the bike is one that I am glad to be able to tell, without having to remember the involvement of the medical profession. I had a friend who was a very serious track and field athlete and did a lot of road work, both running and on his 10 speed bike. Sometimes I would be looking for him to go someplace with me, so I would go outside of town where he normally rode his bike until I found him. On finding him I would say, "Let's go" to wherever I had planned, and not wanting to wait for him to pedal the four or five miles back to town, he would pull his bicycle alongside the motorcycle and hang onto the seat with one hand, and his handlebars with the other, while I towed him back to town. We thought this was incredibly funny and once got up to 60 mph.

One glorious sunny Sunday afternoon I was out for a ride on the motorcycle. I came up to the main intersection of our town which consisted of a three way stop light—the only one in town. This intersection was the location of the only three major gas stations in town. At one of those stations I noticed a car I had not seen in town before. Now the town was very small, but not so small that I took notice of every strange car, but this car had two girls standing outside of it. That, I was more likely to notice. A couple of months before our church had gotten a new pastor and he had moved to north Missouri from Arizona. A lady in our church who wintered in Arizona had presented his name for consideration when our previous pastor had resigned. Now our new pastor had been talking for two months about his beautiful daughters back in Arizona, and had just recently told the church that he had convinced them to move from Arizona to our town. I remember saying to myself, "I bet that is those preacher's daughters." And I was right. One of those girls later said that on arriving in town, they had stopped at that filling station to ask directions to their parents' home. When they got out of the car, the first thing she noticed was that boy ripping through the intersection on an incredibly loud motorcycle. She said that it was so loud that she had turned around to see what it was. Little did she know that the kid on the loud motorcycle was going to be her husband.

LEARNING TO DRIVE

M Y LEARNING TO DRIVE A REAL CAR started early. My mom and dad had a 1955 Ford convertible, red and white, and I loved it. I called it "the bertle". I am told that I was very frustrated with not being able to see over the dash, and see the road ahead, when riding between my parents in the front seat of the car. Because of this, I always wanted to stand up and they were constantly making me sit down. You see, somehow my parents felt it was unsafe for me to stand up in the front seat as we drove. So to err on the side of caution, they took extreme safety measures and got me a Prince Albert tobacco can to sit on. Even with my tobacco can perch, this was still not my favorite spot. My favorite spot was sitting in Dad's lap and driving. This part I remember very well, and he let me quite often when we were out on the open highway, even sometimes taking his hands off the wheel to see how I could do as he coached me which way to turn "A little this way, a little that way. Oh! Watch out! You're going over the centerline!"

Not long after this, in my granddad's junkyard, among the junked cars, was a pea green Plymouth. I believe it was about a '47 model, and it actually ran. My dad would start it up and sit beside me in the middle, while I stood in the driver's seat. As he ran the pedals, I could drive anywhere I wanted, within the confines of the pasture. I thought "Now I am really driving!"

Next came the hayfield. Sometimes when shorthanded for a hay crew, I was pressed into service as a driver, while dad threw bales up on the truck on my side. He would put the old truck in granny low and let out on the clutch while sitting in the seat. Then he would climb out as I scooted over from the middle to take over. All I had to do was keep in the middle of the rows and not run over a bale, while remembering to keep my thumbs outside of the steering wheel. So if the tire fell into a gopher hole, my thumb or wrist would not be broken if the wheel spun wildly. Those who grew up on a farm driving tractors and old trucks in the field know what I'm talking about. By about eight or nine I was getting old enough to reach the pedals, and it was time for me to learn how to use the clutch. This was a time of intense bonding between my dad and me, but not so much in the Hallmark Family Channel kind of way, more like a modern reality show kind of way. I once threw him from standing, with his hands on the headache rack behind the cab, all the way to the rear of the truck, missing the 2 x 4 hay stakes at the back, and landing on his back on the ground. If this scene had of been filmed in a reality show, it would have required a lot of bleeping.

The next level was getting to drive on an actual road. Once a week we would take our trash off to the city dump in our 1953 Chevy pickup. The dump was on the edge of town and had a dead-end gravel road that led to it. After throwing the trash out, Dad would let me drive down that gravel road back to town. The one thing I have not been able to understand to this day is the place he chose to ride: he stood on the running board and held onto the side mirror. Maybe his strategy was that if things got dicey he could bail off.

During the next few years I would grab opportunities to drive when I could. Grandma would let me drive her Buick a few hundred yards to the car wash at the bottom of the hill to clean it for her, and occasionally Dad would let me drive when we were out in the country. One of those occasions, when I was about fourteen, stands out in my mind. On this day, my dad, my uncle, and my dad's good friend and I had gone quail hunting in my dad's 1966 Ford pickup. It was a single cab; so with us in our heavy hunting gear, we were pretty wedged in there. After hunting out one location and traveling to another one, the men decided on a stop at a country tavern, to warm up. Well the warm-up stop became quite lengthy, but I didn't mind as my time was filled at a coin operated pool table, and all the pop I wanted to drink. When they decided to leave, it was long past time to go to another farm to hunt. Even if there had been time, it would have been hard for them to figure out which of the two beads on the end of the shotgun barrel to put on the bird before pulling the trigger. Now, it always seemed to me that my dad was more agreeable when he had had a few. So I decided to capitalize on this and ask him if I could drive home. We were about fifteen miles from home, the last few miles being on a main highway and I usually only got to drive when it was just dad and me in the vehicle, so I was a little surprised when my dad agreed. So into the truck we piled. We went down a few gravel country roads with no traffic on them, and as we were about to pull out on the blacktop, my dad's friend made a statement that has become a verbal family heirloom. He said to my dad, and I quote "Well Joe, there's one thing for sure, you don't have to worry about some drunk running over him, because they're all in the cab with him." I got us home in one piece.

There was one thing left for my training to be complete. That was formal driver's education at school. You got a break in your insurance if you took it. We had one of our coaches for a classroom teacher, but the driving portion was delegated out to different teachers that had a free period. I drew our principal for a driving instructor. Our driving group consisted of me, a good friend of mine, a girl (poor thing), and one other boy. Our principal was a busy man, and since my friend, who was a country boy, and I knew how to drive, when it was our turn he would let us drive out on the highway to a nearby little town, or something like that while he did paperwork in the passenger's seat. Even though the speed limit was 70 mph, the principal had a rule that we were not to exceed 55 mph out on the open road. To entertain ourselves my friend and I had a game we played. We worked at getting that car, gradually, as far over 55 as we could, without the principal noticing. When the semester was over, I ended up with the record high score of 80 mph, which earned me a prize that day of a good butt chewing.

Bring on that driver's license.

SWEET 16

MY 16TH BIRTHDAY WAS BY FAR THE most anticipated event in my life up to that point. It also ranks right up there at the top as I look back over the years of my life. Now that might sound silly in comparison with huge things like getting married or the birth of children, but in my mind they are kind of a different category. You see those things just kind of come into the highway that is your life on entrance ramps, where as something like a specific age is somewhere you know you are going. The experience of reaching sixteen years of age is something I had wished for a long time. Even looking back, it was more exciting and fulfilling than any other milestone age, say eighteen or twenty one. The anticipation of it was greater and it seemed to deliver everything that it had promised.

That much anticipated birthday did finally arrive one January 29, and it found me sick in bed with a terrible flu, the chilling aching kind. That afternoon my mom came to my room and said, "Your dad has something he wants to show you." So I came out of my room, and mom motioned me toward our back door. I stuck my head out the door and there sat my first car. It was a 1953 Ford 2 door. I was so sick that I could only lean against the door facing—trying to stay out of the bitter cold—and admire it from afar, thank my parents, and then stumble back to bed.

It wasn't but a couple of days, though, that I was out in the new old Ford; I went to a basketball tournament being held at the high school. I soon found out that I had hurried my recovery from the flu, and had to make it an early evening because I felt awful. But it would not be long before the old Ford would become a happening place.

It is almost unbelievable today, but my dad had purchased this car for $95. I find it funny that the sum was $95, and not $100. I guess Dad must have really put the pressure on in the last moments of the negotiation. Now despite the low price, don't imagine this as some beat up clunker of a car. Cars over 20 years old just didn't command a lot of money back then and $95 was a lot more money back then too. My dad actually knew this particular Ford. His old FFA teacher had bought it new and it had lived in Dad's hometown its whole life. Dad had even ridden in it to and from FFA functions when he was in school.

My 1953 Ford was the Mainline model. This was the cheapest trim level for that year, which was perfect for me. Us hot rodders really didn't want a lot of chrome. It had a real straight body, with the only flaws being rust holes in the bottom of the quarter panels. This we knew how to easily remedy with some wadded-up newspapers jammed in the holes to support a thick layer of bondo, and then a coat of spray can paint to cover it up. This car was a particularly easy job because it was glorious black, the way Henry Ford meant cars to be. In my mind, the older a Ford product gets, the more it should be black. Even the interior of the car was in very good condition, adding an element to the sensory experience of a car: smell. I actually feel sorry for someone not old enough to go back in their memory and remember what an old car from the '30s through the '50s smelled like when you opened the door. Now I am talking about one with its original cloth interior, and it was especially strong if it had been sitting a long time without being opened. Much has been said about new car smell; you can even buy it in a bottle and spray it in your vehicle to make it seem newer when trying to sell it. I, and many others, can attest that there is another smell that is every bit as memorable: the very musty, but not unpleasant, smell of an old American car.

The drive train for this car was the brand new for 1953, valve-in-head straight 6. Had it been a V8, it would have been a flathead, but the valve-in-head engines debuted in '53 in 6 cylinders, and '54 for the V8. For a transmission, I had the standard 3 speed column shifter that we called "3 on the tree". This would have never been called that back in the '50's. After 4 speeds became popular in the '60's and were referred to as "4 on the floor", the less fortunate folks with a standard-column-shifted car were referred to by us kids as having "3 on the tree."

Rounding out the experience of driving an early '50's Ford was the wonderful, huge steering wheel. Right in the middle of that big old wheel was a badge proclaiming this to be Ford's 50th anniversary, 1903 to 1953. I found a used set of chrome reverse wheels and put those on the car, retaining the stock '53 Ford chrome cookie cutter hub caps in the middle. It was now perfect; all that was left was the driving.

As one of the first practical uses for the car, it was now my job to drive me and my brother to school, freeing mom from the task. I loved wheeling into school and parking it in the parking lot. The kids called it "Banks' old car," and many wanted to ride in it. The TV show *Happy Days* came out at the same time, making the '50's very popular, and the old Ford fit right in. On one of my first times to drive the car to school, it came a snowstorm and class was let out early. Our town was built on a big hill. My house and the schoolhouse were both located at the top of the hill, only several blocks from each other. As I tried to get my brother and I home, I found I could only make headway going downhill. All I managed to do was get my brother and me to the bottom of the hill, but no closer to my house than when I started. Since we were stranded, we decided to brave the elements and walked up the hill to our house. When we got home, I immediately called my dad and told him since my car didn't have snow tires, there was no way it would make it up that hill, so when he got home we would have to go together in his truck and tow it back home. I was amazed when, a few hours later, my dad drove the old Ford into the driveway. Since he had a set of keys to my car he had a friend drop him off at the car after work. Turns out, he was able to drive it right home. I saw then that I had a few things to learn about driving on slick roads.

We had so much fun in that old Ford. On the west side of town was the fairgrounds surrounded by an ancient horse race track that hadn't been used or maintained for decades. Us boys took the old '53 down there a few times and went around the track with it, sliding the corners. The '53 didn't offer much excitement in the area of acceleration, so we had to find other ways to compensate for that.

I once had a car load of kids, at least six of us, riding around in it one night. We weren't couples but were just friends riding around. There was a girl riding in the middle of the front seat beside me, and for some reason, she put her feet on the dash board. Not wanting her to disrespect my car that way, I kind of playfully said, "Hey! This is my car" kind of with the unsaid connotation that it might be old, but it is mine; please don't treat it that way. Her response was to, in spite, walk her feet right on up the windshield and onto the headliner. Then she stopped and I didn't think another thing about it. This had happened on a Saturday night. The next day my dad went out to move my car in the driveway, and when encountering me later that day, said "Son, I don't know what you're doing in that car, but I found girls' footprints on the dash, the windshield, and the roof. You better calm it down."

Now the old Ford had a few other rust problems, besides the rear fenders, that weren't visible, so we really didn't concern ourselves with them, but the biggest one was that it was a Fred Flintstone mobile. It had big holes in the floorboard. I found it quite startling, while sitting in a driveway with a girl, having a cat join us, coming up through the floorboard.

IF YOU LIKE IT, REVIEW IT

If you enjoyed reading Get 'Er Sideways
head over to amazon.com
and leave a review.

Also startling was the time my friend, Bill Kincaid, saw my car parked at my girlfriend's house. He had some guys let him off so he could hide in the backseat and scare me when I came out. It was very cold outside that night, probably near zero, and Kincaid assumed I wouldn't be in there long. When I finally did go home, I got in the old Ford and cranked it up, turning my head to look out the back glass to back out. I found the backseat to be filled with a 6' 2", 225 lb guy wearing a panda suite. The panda head spoke and said, "Banks, take me home. I'm freezing."

As I already mentioned, the '53—that's what we always called it, just the '53—wasn't much on performance. Dad always told me not to drive it fast because the idler arm was loose, so I never went over 85. You guessed it; that was as fast as it would run. I didn't do that but once or twice. I didn't do a lot of highway driving; I had an unseen perimeter that I was not to take it out of. I don't remember where my boundary lines were exactly, but all my memories in the '53 occur in a 10 mile radius of home. Another thing, it wouldn't peel out, but hey a guy has got to try. One day a friend and I were driving around and I decided to really rev it up and pop the clutch. I was hoping for a squeal of the tires, but what I got was a loud clunk and a terrible jerk. We opened the doors and got out, only to find both rear hubcaps had popped off because it had jerked so hard. We popped them back on and climbed back in the car. I gingerly let out on the clutch and the car moved as normal. I went on down the road and around two corners, and was up to about 55 mph when all of a sudden the back wheels locked up and we went skidding down the road. When we came to a stop, the car wouldn't budge. We had to leave it right there in the middle of the road. I got to a telephone and told my dad where it was, and he said, "Push it off the road and we'll come get it when I get off work. "I can't" I said "it won't move." So Dad and his buddy came and got it. I wasn't there when he came and got it and I didn't ask any questions because I didn't want to talk about it anymore than I had to. I had come as close to outright lying to my dad as I ever had before or since. You see, in our phone conversation he said, "You were getting on it when it happened, weren't you?" and my response was, "No, I was just driving down the road 55 and it locked up", not telling him getting on it was exactly what I had done five minutes earlier. With those kinds of skills I probably could have made a great politician, with one exception, I felt bad about it. It turns out I had busted the spider gears in the differential, more commonly referred to as the rear end.

Now there was a kid in my class at school that tinkered with cars and was also into woodworking. I once saw him come to school in a full-sized Ford car, about a '65 model with a big block in it and a very rare 3 x 2 barrel intake manifold. As nice a find as that old manifold and carburetors, and possibly the whole engine, would be today, the thing that sticks out in my mind is the wooden breather Andy had made out of 2x4's. Well anyway, Andy imagined himself as having a used auto parts business, and told me how he had a rear end for the '53 for $10. So the next Saturday, Dad and I travelled out in the country to Andy's house. I had imagined we would go down there, and Andy would have the rear end lying there, and we would pay him and leave with the part. When we rolled up to Andy's house, it kind of looked like a picture of the dust bowl days in Oklahoma, with the windows open and curtains blowing in and out with the wind. Across the gravel road from Andy's house was Andy's wrecking yard. It consisted of two old cars, one on its wheels and one on its top, but hey, that one on its top was a 1953 Ford. So Andy's dad came out, and he and my dad talked, and he told him that he would have to remove the rear end himself. Dad had his tool box in the truck, and he jumped up on the bottom of the old car and began taking out the part. When he was finished, I guess they had been watching from the house because when my dad came back over the barbed wire fence with the part, the old man came out of the house to meet him. Now, up to this point my classmate Andy was nowhere to be seen, but when my dad asked to pay him, the old man hollered toward the house and said, "How much for this rear end Andy?" To this Andy hollered back from the house, "Ten dollars Daddy." Then before Andy's dad could say anything, Andy hollered again, "Don't forget the sales tax daddy," to which his dad responded, "We'll wave the sales tax this time Andy." Now maybe you had to be there, and maybe you had to know Andy for this to be funny, but it was darn funny to me, the comedic content being: What was Andy doing in there that he couldn't come out... paperwork? At that time I had never been to the south where a grown boy calling his father Daddy is common. Also, the size of Andy's wrecking yard was comical, but that interchange about the sales tax, now that still tears me up.

Finding parts for the old '53 caused me to find some very interesting places. The idler arm was found at

Bones Lionberger's in Trenton, Missouri. Bones was a local legend who prided himself on having the most obscure items you can imagine, but his main business was auto parts. He was a character among characters. Those from that area who remember him and his place will remember his dogs. He had several of them; my guess would be eight to ten. On Bones' command, they would jump up on their respective stools, barking out songs in unison while Bones played the part of conductor. "Jingle Bells" was one of their favorites. Also famous was his coin glued to the floor which gave Bones the opportunity to goose whoever bent over to try and pick it up.

I also found a wrecking yard in a little community called Mill Grove, Missouri. This place had cars starting with Model T era up to the middle '50's, with many of them having trees growing up through them. My '53 model car was on the outer edge of the year models represented there. The place had not officially been open for years, but the old man who owned it lived there, and even though he was too sick and feeble to come outside, you could knock on the door and get permission to go out in the yard. After removing any parts you wanted, you could carry them back to his house, and he would price them to you and collect the money. I bought a starter off of him for the '53 for $5; it worked perfect. In this wrecking yard I learned what a Sunliner Ford was, with their transparent tops, and what Crown Victorias were. There was more than one of both.

Today, with shows like *American Pickers* being so popular, either of these places would have made a great episode, but the greatest one would have been the closed down Ford dealership in Cainsville, Missouri. It had closed down in the summer of 1955, and was untouched, with the banners for the new 1956 models hanging in the showroom. The closed down dealership was owned by a man who ran a gas station out of the front of it, and he collected Model T and Model A era Fords, and had two or three running examples. The parts department in this dealership was just as it was when they turned out the lights in 1955 on the last day of business. It still had the parts books racked up on the counter. The man who owned this place had no interest in selling parts, but my granddad knew him pretty well, and since we were not interested in any of the older stuff he was saving for himself, my dad, my granddad, and I were allowed in for a look around the parts department. I had been working after school and on Saturdays in a parts store, so I had a little foundation for how to look up parts in a parts book. The trouble was, although they had a fairly large inventory of parts for a dealership the size that it had been, they had not restocked newer stuff the last few years, as the business was waning so most things were too old for our '53 model. I can still see in my mind the upstairs loft with its brand new flat heads, stacked on their sides in a wooden rack made just for them, and brand new fenders hanging from the ceiling, as well as boxes of spark plugs that were huge, unlike any I have ever seen before or since. This town of Cainsville was my dad's hometown, and once had a coal mine that closed down, probably in the '20's. My granddad told a story about how, after the mine closed, the town used the mine shaft for a dump. He had helped tow old cars from the Model T era from this very dealerships back lot, down to the mine, and push them off in the mine shaft. He said that there were even a few that ran, and they drove them down there. Oh my! The only part I was able to buy for the old '53 was a new set of Ford piston rings; the owner sold them to us for $5. Thank you, sir.

Of all the fun I had in the old '53 Ford, and all of the attention it got, the most memorable feeling is what it felt like to have something that everyone in the family acknowledged was mine, and the freedom it gave me to travel within those 10 miles. Oh, but more than a vehicle, it was a place. I remember putting some sporting equipment in the trunk and just feeling like this was my own personal storage vault. The whole experience felt very grown up; and I was happy for it.

MOON RUNNERS

A BOUT THE TIME I WAS COMING OF AGE to drive, Hollywood flooded the movie screens with movies that contained car chase scenes. There was *Bullet* with Steve McQueen, *White Lightning* with Burt Reynolds, and there were a dozen other moonshiner-type movies. This influenced me and my friends greatly. I don't know if the school I went to was more susceptible to this kind of thing than normal or not, but I do remember that after the movie The *Blue Max* aired on TV as the movie of the week, that you could not open doors in our two, old multi-story school buildings, unless you knocked and the teacher opened it with a screw driver. The boys in the class ahead of me had started a game that the one that collected the most door knobs from the school would win the Blue Max. It seems we could be very creative in reenacting movie themes within our own world.

This is why we loved to play car chase. It was a very loose structured game that occurred when a friend of yours ran up on your bumper with his vehicle. If you accepted the challenge, you then tried to lose him, taking back alleys and sliding around corners. Winning the game was to get so far ahead that you could duck into a parking space or down an alley and shut off your lights, causing them to lose you, which meant you won. At this time my parents had a 1967 Ford LTD 4 door, and it was available to me to drive, especially if I had a date or needed to go outside of the '53 Ford's 10 mile limit. This is the car that I used most in the car chase game. I guess I thought I needed the 390 Cubes under the hood to outdistance the other competitors. This was all happening in the very first few months after I got my license, and I remember thinking that I need to know two things: how fast this car will run and what 100 mph feels like. So I took the car outside of town by myself, and got on top of a big hill where I could make sure there was nothing coming from the other direction. Since this was a two-lane road and I was not confident enough that I could keep the car in my lane, I straddled the center line and floor boarded it. The verdict was the LTD made 110 mph and it felt pretty good.

We would practice our car chase maneuvers in the daytime on weekends, as most car chases occurred at night. You see there was one variation to the game and that was called "bushwhacking." It went like this: there were two kinds of people on Friday and Saturday nights, those who had dates and those who didn't. The ones who had dates usually tried to find a secluded spot out in the country to go park. Those without dates were usually skoal-chewin', coon-huntin' types that if they found you, would get back and get a run, and run over your car from front to back on foot, or some such annoying behavior, meant to make you and your date miserable. So if you saw lights coming down a secluded dirt or gravel road, if you were smart, you had parked in such a way that you had an outlet; then the chase was on. We were very interested in honing our skill at taking corners at speed, and I learned something very interesting about a car: if you go around a corner hard enough, the outside front wheel will flex to the point of popping the hubcap off. So after losing the second hubcap, as with the footprints on the dash in the '53, my dad misconstrued what was going on and said, "You're going to have to quit going parking on these rutted old mud roads. You're knocking my hubcaps off." So my buddies learned to watch for where the hubcaps went in hard corners, and we would go back and get them later, after the chase was over. Fortunately, Dad's concern about my romantic life was a distraction from the way I was driving.

Once on a date with a very quiet little girl sitting next to me, and one of my friends in the backseat with his date, we were just cruising around town when a car chase player challenged us. Without thought, at the next intersection, I swung out and nailed it. The poor thing was thrown hard against the passenger's door, and she complained of a sore shoulder the rest of the night.

One of the most outlandish things I ever did in that LTD was one day we were out on the new highway that the Missouri Highway Department had just finished, coming into town from the east. Although it was only a two-lane, it was wide with wide shoulders and it was a big playground to us. On this particular day, while sitting at the western-most intersection of our town and facing Highway 136, I told my friend, "I'll bet I can pull out of this intersection and floor it and then turn in to the next intersection without hitting the brakes." Now I will have to add here that the LTD was a notorious dog for acceleration. I could run it through the quarter legally because it wouldn't spin the tires, and it wouldn't get over 70 MPH at the end. So even though I topped it out for a mile at 110, and it was faster than the 6 cyl '53 Ford, it was no hot rod. This was factored in to my self-imposed dare. We took off and I kept it floor-boarded all the way, and we were going way too fast to make a 90 degree turn, probably 40 to 50 mph. I know this now, but not then. Fortunately, this was a brand new concrete turn off, and it was wide. At first everything was going perfectly, and it was looking and feeling just like the car chases we were emulating. The car was laying way over and the tires were screaming, but something I hadn't counted on came into play. That was the pile of fine gravel and dust that had accumulated in the center of the intersection where the normal right and left traffic had pushed it to the part of the road where wheels didn't normally touch. When we hit that, we went completely sideways and began sliding down the road we had just turned onto. Now the owner and editor of our local newspaper was coming up that road in his Pinto wagon. He had seen us coming and had stopped his car, probably fifty feet down the road. So there he sat with us barreling toward him sideways with nothing he could do, and here we are sliding towards him with nothing I could do. I can tell you, if you're wondering, that this would not have been a little fender bender at the speed we were sliding. I would have wrapped the driver's side of that big Ford around the front end of that little Ford, probably totaling both. But lo and behold, a few feet before we hit him, the tires ran out of the gravel and caught, and I was able to steer out around him. His window was down and he stuck his head clear out of it, and hollered as we went by, "Ha Ha! You missed me!"

There was one other vehicle at my disposal in those earliest days of my driving, and that was Dad's '66 Ford pickup with a 352 and a granny low 4-speed. It was not very much of a hotrod, but you make do with what you got. Occasionally I would drive it to school, and since it was the only thing we had that would spin the tires, I would get out in front of the school and put it in compound low, and get it spinning, and then go to low. By this time, the tires would be so hot I could hit second and it would still spin for a while, with the white smoke rolling.

Maybe dad had gotten some wind of this (it, after all, was a small town) because one time he told me, "I don't want you to ever drag race my pickup. That's not the kind of transmission it has, and I don't want you tearing it up." Not long after this, one night a friend of mine was driving his dad's 454 Chevy pickup, and he challenged me to a drag race. Now I was in my Dad's LTD car. So I took the challenge, thinking maybe the car could out run this pickup, because pickups, even big block ones, weren't normally very good for drag racing. Well I was wrong, and the pickup beat us easily. That spring this guy's girlfriend at the time wrote in my yearbook, "Remember the night Ellsworth outran you with his pickup?" A few days, after getting my yearbook, I came in from school with my dad really hot about something. He said, "I thought I made it clear to you, I didn't want you drag racing my pickup" to which I responded, "I have never drag raced your pickup." He then said, "It says right here in your yearbook that Ellsworth out ran you with his pickup," and I said, "Aw

Dad, Don't worry, Ellsworth outran your car, not your pickup."

BIG EARL

R IGHT AROUND THE TIME THAT I WAS turning 16 there was a kid in town who came up with a 1967 Dodge Coronet R/T with a 440 magnum in it. This car was a bad mamba jamba and was a legend around our town for a short while. My friends and I called the guy that owned this car Big Earl (not because Earl was big but because his car had a big reputation, kind of like Big Daddy Don Garlits). Earl and I had been in the same class at school, and even received seven licks a piece from the music teacher in seventh grade.

My friend Ed and I very much wanted to see Earl's car run. Ed's dad had a 1970 Mercury ex-Missouri highway patrol car with a 428 super cobra jet engine. Ed used to impress people by sitting at a stop sign and stomping it, showing off how it would shift through 2nd and into 3rd gear, with the speedometer showing over 100 mph, and we hadn't moved but about 5 feet. Ed also used to take the same car downtown and backup to the side of a brick building, and throw the studs out of his dad's studded snow tires, by wildly spinning the back tires. The sparks would fly when the studs hit the bricks, and it looked like a machine gun in a WWII movie; it was fun while the studs lasted.

So we challenged Earl to a race. Now we had no thought of winning this race, because even though the old police car would really haul it on the open road, it was no match for a much lighter muscle car in a drag race. What we wanted was to see Earl's car perform; we just hoped we had enough of a car that Earl would even bother. Looking back, I imagine that Earl would have raced a wheelbarrow if someone had asked him.

I have often observed how things that happen when you are young and impressionable, remain large in your memory. Even though as you go through life and have much grander experiences, those early things that impressed you are not eclipsed; your mind tells you that you have seen much greater, but it still can't replicate the feeling of that early experience. Consequently, having a cool car is not about horsepower or miles per hour, but it's about the feelings at the time. I have heard men who know more about cars than I do, tell stories about the performance of some old car, that I know could not be totally true, and they do too if they would think about it, but that's how it felt. I really like Chuck Berry's song "Maybelline." In it, the Cadillac is doing about 95, and they were "bumper to bumper" and "side to side." To me that is cooler than hearing about 21st century $100,000 cars running 200 mph. I have been to the drag races and watched cars go 320 mph in a quarter mile, but none made an impression like this race with Big Earl.

Big Earl accepted and we went north of town—the place where people normally drag raced was commonly referred to as "north of town." We would travel north through the measured quarter mile, turning around at a gravel road that was roughly at the starting line, and then race back toward town. About six car lengths back toward town from the starting line was a mailbox, and it was considered the maximum you could spot a slower car. If your car was less of a match than that, what was the use? It was customary for the big dog to offer the underdog the amount of head start, and Earl offered us the max. "I'll spot you to the mailbox," he said.

We rolled out to the mailbox as had been agreed on. We had also agreed that Earl would flash his lights to signal the start of the race. Earl was in the outside lane, putting him to our left. In a few seconds Earls lights blinked and we were off. Earl's car seemed to literally eat up the pavement, catching us. I had turned sideways in Ed's passenger seat so I could watch them coming at us. Now Earl's bunch were pretty well lit, and as they came up on our rear fender, I could see Earl's friend Bill hanging out the right rear window with no shirt on, and waving his arms in the air over his head. Mufflers were not a priority for Earl, and that big 440 was roaring like a freight train. We had the good fortune that Earl hit second gear right beside us. The old R/T jumped sideways about three feet. The back tires broke loose and squalled. Bill had to grab onto the top of the door as the car nearly jumped out from under him. Ed and I had got what we came for. If it had cost a hundred dollars, it would have been worth every penny.

LOVE AT FIRST SIGHT

I WAS ON A USED CAR LOT IN TRENTON, Missouri, twenty-five miles from my home town, when I found myself no longer interested in the conversation that my dad was having with the used car dealer, or the car we had stopped to look at. So I was wandering around the back row of the car lot when I came upon a car nosed in, instead of facing out. I noticed it had a pair of chrome exhaust tips coming out from under the rear bumper, and I thought to myself "Well, that car at least has dual exhaust." Stopping to look down the side, I added to my conversation with myself, "Hey! It's also a two door hardtop! Maybe I ought to pay closer attention to this one..." As I walked by the window I noticed it had bucket seats, which surprised me because this was not a model of car that I was aware of. It didn't look particularly sporty to me, but I was already seeing three of the signs of a "hot car," and I was already on my way to the front to find out what really mattered—what was under the hood. As I rounded the front of the car I noticed the hood ornament sticking up, and at the bottom, the numbers 440. My next thought I may have proclaimed out loud. "Nooo..." I said to myself, meaning "Surely this engine compartment isn't filled with an honest to goodness, big block Chrysler 440! Maybe this is just the model number of the car, like a Dodge Coronet

440, or maybe someone put a hood ornament from another car on it." All the while I was going for the hood release. I grabbed the hood with both hands and lifted it. What the next couple of seconds felt like to me could have been taken straight out of a movie scene: beams of light bursting from the heavens and into the engine compartment, reflecting back in a show that would make most fireworks displays pale in comparison, as a chorus of trumpets blasted the soundtrack. This was something special. It took a couple of minutes for my mind to process what I had stumbled onto. This was indeed a 440 big block Chrysler, but this was not your garden variety 440 that commonly hauled grandmas around in their Chrysler Newports and New Yorkers. No, this one had factory chrome valve covers and big up and over factory cast iron high-performance exhaust manifolds. These were both evidence that it was what was commonly referred to as a 440 Magnum[1] . The engine was very visually impressive. First off it was huge; secondly, it was sporting a lot of chrome with a big chrome breather, in addition to the valve covers; and finally it was very clean. The chrome gleamed like someone had been very proud of it. The next thing I said was "Hey Dad! Come over here!"

The reason for us being there that day had started a couple of months earlier. With the oncoming of spring and warmer temperatures, I had been riding my motorcycle more and more. My dad had taken me aside

---

[1] In a Plymouth this engine was actually called a 440 Super Commando, with Dodge calling it the 440 Magnum. They were identical engines and most guys just referred to them all as 440 Magnums.

and quite out of the blue said to me "Mike, every time you leave the house on your motorcycle your mother is miserable until you get back. I'll make you a deal: if you will get rid of the motorcycle you can get any kind of car you want within our budget. I know you really like hot rods; so I won't stop you from getting a fast car." That was a deal I could live with! My parents could have easily forced me to get rid of the motorcycle with no compensation, and here was a chance to fulfill a lifelong dream. Hot Dog!

After that I began to focus all of my energy on finding my car. I only had one criteria and that was that it be the fastest one I could find. I didn't care what brand it was, and I didn't care what color it was. What kind of radio it had was of no importance to me. I just wanted to find the fastest car I could. Here is how this worked. I took the role of a scout and, along with my buddies, I would scout out these potential cars. Then I would bring my dad back on the weekend to view what we had found. You might ask how we were able to go to school and still look for cars during the week. It was simple. I had decided that me finding my dream car was well worth the sacrifice of an occasional day of classroom instruction, and I had a couple of buddies who were more than willing to go along with me for moral support. Those occasional days were in fact exactly one day a week. One of those buddies had a chiropractor appointment each Thursday twenty-five miles away. My other buddy and I would generously volunteer to go with him. Now he didn't need anyone to go with him, nor did his parents expect anyone to go with him. We figured since he had the note from home to be dismissed from school, that if caught we wouldn't be completely without excuse, but could claim we had gone along in case there was a medical emergency, and he was not able to drive himself home. This appointment was in a town to our south, and after a couple of weeks of going down there, we had scouted out that area for cars and were tired of waiting an hour on him while he was getting his treatment. So the next Thursday we all went east instead of south, and I don't think we ever went back to the chiropractor. I still remember Dave saying on some Thursdays, "Hey guys, I really need to go to that chiropractor. My back's been hurting." to which we would respond by calling him derogatory names and cause him to come along on the wonderful adventure that awaited us in used car lots some other direction.

We looked at and even drove a lot of cars. Looking back, I am amazed that car salesman would let three sixteen year old boys go out for a test drive by themselves in a car they had obviously chosen because of how hot it was, but they did. I remember driving a 340, 4 speed Plymouth Duster, and I remember a 1967 Mustang GT with a 390 in it—same type of car that Steve McQueen drove in Bullitt. Some of these cars I didn't like, usually because they weren't fast enough, and those I didn't bother dad with, but the ones I liked I would take Dad back to see. Once I remember he had brought a friend of his along on one of the Saturday trips. We were test driving a car; I was in the backseat. The friend was in the passenger's seat and Dad was driving. I remember him kicking the car into passing gear and exclaiming to his friend "This thing will run faster than I can think!"

One of the first cars I found was a 1969 Plymouth GTX. There was a banker that lived down by Jamesport, Missouri and he sometimes had a couple of repossessed cars from his bank in his front yard for sale. This particular GTX was a nice car. The '69 model GTXs all had a dark strip along the bottom of the doors and fenders, with a large GTX emblem down low in front of the back tires. It had the 440 engine and it was a four speed with a big ole pistol grip shifter. This was one of the first cars I drug my dad to look at, but after contacting the banker we found out the price was $1,400 and that was out of our price range.

I was already a big fan of Pontiac GTO's and looked at several. One of them we almost bought was a big blue '67 model with a 400 and a 4 speed with a Hurst pistol grip shifter. It had air shocks and was jacked up in the back with big tires and Cragar SS wheels. It had headers, and both looked and sounded great. It was already in the price range; so I hurried the thirty-five miles back home and told dad we needed to fast track this one. We went back at our first opportunity, and thankfully the GTO was still there. I liked the car and Dad liked the price, but as we drove it, we noticed it was missing, and just generally didn't run good. When we went back to the lot and told the salesman, he made a show of going to get his mechanic. Now this was a very small used car lot and the garage was little more than a shed. Out of this garage/shed comes this very toothy, loud mouth young guy. Now when I say toothy I think everyone knows the face type—someone with fairly prominent teeth and gums which are the most noticeable part of their face; some have big foreheads, some have big noses and some have big teeth. There is nothing wrong with having prominent teeth, and the only reason I remember this part is because this guy's teeth were not the color teeth should be. Let me put it this way, if he was a deer hunter he could smile all he wanted while hunting, because his teeth looked like Mossy Oak camo. So the guy with the teeth begins to very loudly say "So you want her to run better, huh? Give me a day and I'll have her pull the front wheels off the ground." This was a Saturday; so a deal was made for us to come back late Monday afternoon to check out the car again and purchase it, if it passed muster. Monday finally got there and I was pretty excited about the car now. Even at sixteen I was not so naïve that I thought this car could pull the front wheels off the ground, but both my dad and I were disappointed when we noticed the large volumes of blue smoke coming out the tailpipes when we cranked it up this time. Oh well, back to the drawing board.

So after many weeks of car hunting we find ourselves on this car lot in Trenton, Missouri where I have just called for my dad to come see what I have found. This lot had been under surveillance by me, along with every other car lot in town, for all of this time, and a few days before a 1969 Dodge Super Bee had shown up there. Now this Super Bee was double ugly, being a color between gold and pea green with ugly wheels, but hey, it was, after all, a muscle car, and needed to be checked out. This was the car Dad was talking to the dealer about when I had wandered off.

Dad came over and I showed him the gold GTX I had found. We looked at the car and asked the dealer about it. He said that this was a car they had just got in and had not had a chance to get it ready for sale. He quoted us a price of $900. We ended up leaving that day without even driving the car, to think about it and come back when it was ready for sale.

It wasn't long before we were back in Trenton, and noticed the 1967 GTX had been moved to the front row. We stopped and got out, and were walking around it when a young man, maybe 25 years old, stopped his car and got out. He asked us if we were interested in that car and we said "Yes!" He then just oddly hung around and finally said "What did the dealer ask you for it?" and my dad said "$900." To this the young man said "Tell him I said he could take $700." My dad then said, "Wait a minute. Do you own this car?" The young man said that he did and it was on consignment. My dad started to walk towards the small office of the car lot and the dealer came out to meet him. He told him what the young man had said, and it immediately infuriated the dealer, who said "…and he can get his &@#!&# car off my car lot!" He promptly took the keys out to the guy, chewed him out, and ran him off, making him pull his car out on the street.

We then began doing business directly with the owner. One of the first questions my dad asked him was "I guess this car is pretty fast?" I remember the guy saying "Oh, I wouldn't know. I never did that kind of stuff, like hot rodding it." Even as a kid I thought "Yea right!" After a few more questions, we took the car for a test drive. Our whole family was in there, Dad driving along with me, my mom, and my little brother. I can still vividly remember this car ride. My actions on this ride remind me of the kid in the movie *A Christmas Story* trying to convince his parents to let him have a Red Rider BB Gun. Even though I had looked at all of those neat cars, somehow I knew this was the one. And because of that, the seriousness of me getting this car caused me to be insecure about Dad not "vetoing" it because of how fast it was. I began to reason with Dad on how practical that this car was. Why, it was nearly as roomy inside as his and mom's LTD Ford, and that if we ever needed to it could do double duty as our family car. Heck, we could even take it on a vacation! All of this was going on as we made our way to Highway 65, going south of Trenton. The adjustment for the kick down rod that runs from the carburetor to the transmission was backed off to where the car didn't kick back into passing gear when it was floor boarded. So when my dad got on the highway and pressed the accelerator to the floor it didn't kick down a gear, making it less impressive than it should have been. My further insecurity caused me to say "Hey, this isn't even very fast." I can still see, perfectly, the look on my dad's face, as he turned his neck and looked at me. He said "This car is very fast!" and the look on his face said "Do you think I'm that stupid?" All the while, the four barrel was bawling and we were accelerating very rapidly.

When we got back my dad asked the guy some final questions and then applied his special set of skills. My dad was a shrewd bargainer, and he already knew it could have been bought for $700, with part of that having gone to the dealer. He also knew that the guy needed it gone or he would have to take it home. So, never one to be bashful, Dad offered him $500, and after a little bit of lip chewing, he agreed to take it. Shortly after, this guy's testimony that he "didn't know if the car was fast or not" proved false. Before the final negotiation, while my dad was going over the car with a fine tooth comb, the guy motioned quietly for me to walk down a few cars away with him, and he quietly told me that if my dad did buy this car for me, that I shouldn't take it to a certain nearby town. That they hated this car down there, and they would try to whip me over it. The guy said he paid for this car in one summer, street racing it there. Fortunately we were never whipped, but the screaming, cussing, motors revving, peeling out, and lewd hand gestures confirmed his story. It was a very infamous car each time we went down there.

Several months after I bought the car, I was driving down the street in Trenton in front of the Hy-Vee Food Store, when I noticed out in the parking lot two young women waving their arms wildly. I wondered what was going on, but never dreamed they were waving at me. When they got my attention they motioned for me to come over there. So I turned at the next driveway into the parking lot. The reason I described them as young women instead of two girls is, to my eye they were obviously not the age that I would describe as girls. They seemed much older than me. When I rolled to a stop one of them jerked open my right hand door and jumped into the passenger seat. She exclaimed loudly "This is my car!" While I sat there dumfounded, she opened the glove compartment and began rifling through whatever stuff I had in there. I was now wondering whether I was about to be kidnapped, or worse, or better. Finally she said "I used to date the guy who owned this car." She then looked at her girlfriend and said "Hey, this thing is fast!" and began telling her all about it. After realizing that they were not going to try to have their way with neither me nor the car, we chatted for a while; they thanked me for stopping, and went on their way.

I am so glad that I ended up with the GTX out of all the cars I looked at, but there is one car in particular that was my dad's favorite. It was a 1968 Ford Mustang. This was a car he found and had me come with him to take a look at it. It was as nice a used car as you can imagine. It only had 41,000 miles and was a one-owner trade in at the local Ford dealer. It was dad's favorite color, red, and had the premium red pony interior. It had a 302 V8 with an automatic. We took it on a test drive and I had to agree it was a very nice car. In fact, it was by far the nicest car we looked at during the whole process. The problem was I wasn't looking for a nice car. I was looking for a fast car. The price on this Mustang was also $1400, same as the banker's GTX. I think had I showed enthusiasm for it, Dad would have unleashed his Kung-Fu bargaining prowess on them to try and get it, but sensing my lack of enthusiasm he just said it was too high and we left. I agree with him. That was a nice sporty car, but I am so glad I didn't get it. I can just hear the conversation today, "Remember that dark headed kid from Princeton. What was his name? Oh yeah, Banks. I remember he had a low mileage used car."

WHAT I HAD FOUND

I N 1967 WHEN MOPAR DECIDED TO ENTER the badged muscle car market, their first example was a very serious competitor. Not only did they give it two very healthy engine options, but they also paid close attention to the suspension and geometry. Dodge and Plymouth had been very involved in Super Stock drag racing. They were famous for their altered wheelbase cars in the early 1960's which eventually evolved into the funny cars of today. Because of how odd the cars looked with their bodies appearing to be scooted backwards over the wheelbase, people at the drags started referring to them as those "funny looking cars." If you look at a side view photograph of a 1967 GTX, you can notice a subtle hint of that heritage, as the rear wheels are forward nearly to the back of the roof, and there is very little distance from the front wheel openings to the front bumper. Mopar was so serious about traction, that in the '67 GTX, they put one more leaf in the right hand rear leaf spring to help counteract the rotation direction that the differential turns, trying to lift that wheel off the ground.

As a sixteen year old kid I had no knowledge of how much these things could make a difference to a car's performance in a drag race. If someone had said I could have any car with no thought for cost, without driving them first, I would have surely, coming from a Ford family, chosen a 428 Cobra jet Mustang, thinking that this big beast of a Ford motor, in a little bitty Mustang, must have been the most awesome thing around. Little did I know that my GTX weighed less than the Mustang, and was rated at 375 hp compared to the 428 Cobra jet's 335 hp. It had that wonderful big old expanse of trunk hanging out over the back wheels, giving it better traction. No pony car—be it Mustang, Camaro, or 'Cuda—had that. If I had read a few more test reports, I would have also learned that elapsed times on my car were faster than the Mustang; but it still sounded cool to a kid, that you had to loosen a motor mount and lift the engine to change spark plugs in a 428 Mustang.

Total production of 1967 GTX's was around 12,000 compared to something like 81,000 Pontiac GTO's that same year. Ford Mustang's numbers were between 500,000 and 600,000 each year from '65 to '67. That's a lot of little horseys. Chevy also added about 221,000 Camaros to the mix in 1967. These numbers reveal that 1967 GTX's are a rare muscle car. Even Plymouth Road Runners, after their arrival, were in the 70,000 plus production range per year.

Even with their rarity, the '67 GTX's have made a big name for themselves. Richard Petty had his most successful year in NASCAR in one, winning 27 races. Sox and Martin ran a couple of them for '67 with their normal great success. Maybe the most impressive car is the one which has been featured in many magazines as the most successful street racer of all time, Jimmy Addison's Silver Bullitt, which was also a 1967 GTX. If you are not familiar with this car, give it a try on Google.

Even if you are a guy who doesn't buy that the Silver Bullitt was the fastest street car in the early '70's, there's no denying it is the most famous. For you pop culture fans, David Spade also drove a '67 GTX in the movie *Tommy Boy*; it was a convertible.

If you ordered the GTX in 1967 you only had two engine choices: a 440 cubic inch V8 with a 4 bbl carb, rated at 375 horsepower, or a 426 cubic inch V8 with dual 4 bbl carbs rated at 425 hp. Those who checked the box for the 426 hemi paid something like $800 extra and forfeited their warranty. Out of the 12,000 produced cars, only 733 came with the hemi option.

Hemis are one of, if not the most, legendary engines ever produced. To this day, every fuel dragster and fuel funny car runs a hemi engine, which can trace its roots to the very 426 hemi engine, and the same era that we have been talking about. With that said and that honor dually noted, back in the day a well-tuned 440 would sometimes embarrass a 426 hemi car on the street. The torque figures on a 426 hemi and the 440 magnum, the normal moniker given to the 440 super commando, were very close—490 for the hemi and 480 for the magnum. Torque is what you feel in the seat of your pants. So if you have felt a good running 440 come off the line hard, you have probably felt what a hemi could do, if not more. Street hemis were notorious for bogging coming off the line, and the two 4 barrels were very hard to keep in tune. Where the hemi shined was in a full quarter mile, as the big four barrels and bigger horsepower would really come on in the second half of the race. But much of the horsing around on the street was stoplight to stoplight, with bragging rights going to the spectators in each car and surrounding cars; so that made a 440 car a force to be reckoned with even for a street hemi. Race hemis were a different story in the hands of someone who knew how to tune them. I once heard a story about drag racers talking about hemis. These guys were running other brands and they said, "If a guy drove his hemi car to the strip, we could always beat him, but if it came in on a trailer, watch out."

One other observation in the realm of Mopardom (if that's a word), just as a well-tuned 440 could embarrass a slouchy hemi, you better not get too over-confident when your big ole 440 came up against a lowly 383 magnum car. They could sure surprise you. Tuned right and driven right, they would scream, and were more than enough to give a black eye to a slouchy 440.

GRANDDAD ORLEY

T HE FIRST PLACE I WENT AFTER GETTING the GTX home, was out to Lake Paho to show my friend Matt, who was one of the guys involved in going with me to scout out cars. Matt lived at the lake where his dad was the area manager. On arriving at the lake and driving past the spillway, I noticed my Granddad's pickup sitting alongside the road. My granddad was an avid fisherman, to the point that he had decals of bass fighting on a fishing line on the doors of his red 1955 Ford pickup. These had been added after his last paint job, which he administered with a three inch paintbrush. There was a small pool at the bottom of the spillway which was a favorite fishing spot of Granddad's, but it was still quite odd to run into him in the daytime, out here fishing. Granddad lived in Cainsville, fifteen miles away, and normally fished at night. I thought, "What luck, I can show my new car to Granddad Orley," and immediately pulled over and parked behind his truck. I crossed a foot bridge and went down a steep bank, where Granddad Orley was sitting on a bait bucket beside a friend. I walked up to him and said "Granddad, I got me a new car." At this point I was just waiting for him to say "Well, let's go see it," but his response was, "What kind did you get?" To this I responded "a 1967 Plymouth," leaving out the GTX part, figuring it wouldn't be important to him. His next words were, "Why would you ever want a Plymouth?" Granddad was a Ford man. I knew that, and I guess I should have known that he would not stop fishing and climb a steep hill to see a lowly Plymouth. One thing I had no way of knowing was that this would be one of the last times I ever saw my Granddad, as he was only to live a few more weeks. As I was just getting started in the world of driving, working on and trading cars, Granddad was finishing up a life of the same.

Granddad ran a filling station for years, beginning in the days when you pumped the gas by hand, up into a glass reservoir in the top of the pump, and then let it out into the tank of the vehicle. He was famous for pulling engines out, using a chain hoist hanging from a tree limb, and then overhauling that same motor while rolling it from side to side on the ground, and when he was done they always ran. Granddad loved to trade cars. As one story goes, there was a guy in town that had been hitting Granddad up to trade his car for Granddad's Model T, but Granddad wouldn't trade. One day, Granddad got his car stuck in a big mud hole, which were so common on the dirt roads of the day. While trying to get his car out of the mud hole, the guy who had been trying to trade with him came by and stopped and got out. Granddad asked him, "Do you still want to trade?" and the guy said that he did. On that note, Granddad went over and got in the other car. The other guy hollered, "Hey, aren't you going to help me get this out of the mud?" to which my granddad answered, "That's why I traded."

In later years, my family, with Granddad along, pulled into a local used car lot. This was a very small country car lot at an old man's house, in a one horse town. I don't even know if this town was big enough to be called a one horse town, maybe a one Shetland pony town. Anyway, we pulled in in our 1967 Ford LTD, and were looking at another later model Ford. Dad asked the dealer what he would allow him for his 1967 LTD, to which the dealer gave him a low-ball price. As dad protested, the dealer pointed to a 1966 Ford Galaxy 500, which was the same basic body style as our car, and proclaimed, "Why, there's the same car over there, and I would be glad to get $350 for it." To this my granddad spoke up and said, "Sold." Then the dealer began to back track, but Granddad said, "No, you said $350, and I'll take it." See, he had been walking around, and had looked at that car, while dad was talking to the dealer. The guy did finally honor his word, and sold Granddad the car. He told my dad, "Joe, you drive it home for me." So dad took it to his house, and we followed. For the next few weeks, when Granddad would come over for his weekly visit, he was still driving his old Ford Falcon. So Dad asked him, "Dad, why don't you drive your new car?" and granddad just made excuses, but when the truth finally came out, he had never driven a car with an automatic transmission. So my dad took him out and showed him how it worked, and he was fine after that.

I never saw anything but a Ford parked around Granddad's garage, but my dad told a story that when he was coming up on driving age, Granddad bought a 1937 Plymouth that was to be dad's first car. The car didn't run; so they pulled it home, and Granddad began to work on it. Coincidentally, their neighbor also had a 1937 Plymouth that didn't run that he was working on. Both men worked on those two cars for a couple of weeks with no success. While talking over their adjoining fence one evening, they decided on a swap. So the neighbor pulled his car to Granddad's yard, and Granddad pulled his car into the neighbor's yard. After working on them for another two weeks, they both pulled them to the junkyard. Maybe that's why he hated Plymouths.

LEARNING THE ROPES

I REALIZED THAT AFTER DRIVING A '53 FORD with a 6 cylinder that handling the GTX would be a lot different. So I took a couple of days just tooling around before trying to get on it. We had taken the car to a local mechanic and had it tuned up, had the kick down rod and secondaries on the carburetor adjusted, and it had really come alive. I finally decided the time had come to try it. I went outside of town by myself and turned around. I got faced around back towards town on a two lane highway, and I stomped it to the floor. Immediately the world started to spin, and I let off the gas and stomped on the brakes. When I came to a stop, I was on the shoulder on the opposite side of the road, headed the wrong direction. I remember thinking to myself, "This is going to take some practice."

Most real factory muscle cars came equipped with a limited slip differential, which was the case with my GTX. Chevrolet called it Posi Trac. Without going into detail of how a rear differential works, when you spin the tires on a car with a limited slip differential, they both spin. On a car with a regular differential, only one tire spins. The car with the regular differential usually stays pretty straight while spinning that one tire no matter how much power the car has. This makes it fairly easy to drive. On the other hand, on a car with limited slip, those two spinning rear tires causes the car to drift sideways and the more power the car has the more violently it does that. Once your car becomes crossed up with the back end trying to come around one side or the other, you have to be careful to keep your front wheels pointed where you want to go. If you follow the direction the car wants to go you will do a 360, more commonly known as a doughnut. Unless you are intending to do a doughnut, it is imperative you keep your front tires pointed down the road in front of you. Here's why: when the rear tires stop spinning and get a grip, your car is then going to be propelled rapidly wherever those front wheels are pointed. Even if you chicken out and get off the gas you still immediately are going to head where those front wheels are pointed. See, I learned something back there that day, or at least I had my first lesson.

The Tasty Freeze was our version of a Dairy Queen, and had actually been run by my grandparent's years earlier. Also, my mom had worked there when she was pregnant with me. The Tasty Freeze was the premier spot for burnouts, eclipsed only by the swimming pool when in season. On one early occasion before I had mastered handling the car, one of the scariest things that ever happened with the car, happened. I pulled out of the Tasty Freeze and nailed it, and immediately lost it. There was a self-service gas station directly across the road from the Tasty Freeze. It sat down off the road and had a small building behind the pumps. When I lost control, the car went down over the bank into the station, and I was able to regain control, and drive between the building and the pumps at way too fast a speed.

Another early-on-lesson with the car was learned shortly after exiting the Tasty Freeze. I bought a girl a large Coke, and as we left the drive-in, I was traveling behind a semi-truck at about 30 to 35 mph. The old GTX had a wicked passing gear kick-down, and at about this speed, if you were barely in third gear, would drop clear down to low if you floored it, and I did. Needless to say, my passenger was not ready for this, and most of that Coke went right down her tank top. Although she was very gracious, I doubt she was very impressed—lesson learned, G forces do not necessarily always impress girls.

HEY THIS THING DOES TRICKS

G ETTING TO KNOW THE CAPABILITIES OF my new ride was not all a lesson in how to drive, it was also fun and sometimes surprising.

One night, just before going home, I "got on it" for no particular reason. When I did, my glove box popped open, revealing my collection of 8-track tapes. I had been gifted an 8-track tape player from my grandparents, that had been given to them as a collective gift from their three children to go in their Pontiac Bonneville. At that time 8-tracks were fairly new and its eighty-dollar-plus price tag was quite expensive. After getting rid of the Bonneville they had given the tape player to me, so now my glove compartment was chocked full of 8-track tapes. When I got on it and the glove box popped open, the 8-tracks went all over the car. Since it was late I decided to wait until the next day to pick them up. The next day was Sunday but I didn't drive my car to church. It was common for me to use my parent's car for that, for the simple reason that I would stay out in the GTX the night before until it was so empty it was running on fumes. The next morning I had no confidence I could get the five or six blocks to the church and back. You see Princeton's gas stations all closed about 6 p.m. After that there was only one self-service station and it was the old type where you fed dollar bills into it, like is common at a car wash money changer today. For some reason this station, even though it had no attendant, closed at 11 p.m. My small circle of buddies always wanted to take the GTX when we ran around, so I would make them chip in for gas. Gas had recently gone from 29 cents per gallon to 60 cents per gallon. The old GTX held 19 gallons, and we would be careful to watch the time, hurrying back to that self-service filling station to get a second tank before it closed. By the end of the night that tank was also reduced to fumes. So, consequently it was Sunday afternoon before I gave my car interior any attention, but when I did, I found to my amazement that three or four of those 8-track tapes had ended up in the rear parcel shelf underneath the back glass. Awesome! I had discovered a new trick. In the annals of car legends there are many stories of people laying twenty, fifty, or even hundred dollar bills on the dash, and telling a passenger they can have it if they can grab it through the first two gears. I never tried this, nor did I ever see it done. I know for sure why I didn't try it: because I didn't have the twenty dollars to risk. For the rest of the time I owned that car, for any passenger I thought would appreciate it I would lay two or three 8-track tapes on the dash, stomp on the throttle, and throw them into the back window.

Another thing I found out about the car, was that it would cruise at 100 mph running only on the carburetor primaries—the first two barrels as most would call it—and if you floored the gas pedal from there, the opening of the secondary's of the 4 barrel would cause a significant kick in the rear end to the feel of the car. When I had someone who knew a little something about cars with me, I would cruise along at 100 mph, and then ask them, "Have you ever seen a car that would still kick back to passing gear at 100 mph?" Their answer was always "no," as it should have been, because automatic transmissions are made in such a way that they do not allow a car to kick back a gear at anywhere close to that speed, as it would over-rev the engine. I would then quickly stomp it wide open, opening the back two barrels of the carburetor, and the coinciding burst of power would usually convince them that it had, in fact, shifted back a gear into passing gear. Most cars would not run 100 mph cruising on two barrels, nor would they have that much acceleration left when pressing the throttle on down from already running 100 mph.

The GTX was a black mark laying machine and it would always lay two black marks. It would make very dark black marks at first, and then they would just gradually get lighter out to about a city block. After I started dating my wife-to-be, I would mark my territory by starting a block away and laying black marks past her house. One day I was going to her house, and at about the point I usually started my black marks, I saw her stopped on her 10 speed bike talking to a friend of mine. This made me mad that she was being chummy with this other guy. So after talking for just a second with them, I let the GTX roll out just a little bit, and then hit it, which would make it stand up instead of hunker down, and smoke the tires as I roared off. She later said that the guy she was talking to then ran out in the road and touched the dark patch of rubber and said, "I would love to have that car." I guess I won.

Once on a hot summer night we were coming back to Princeton, and it was about 10 o'clock at night. We were on a black top road, and I pulled out to pass a car. When I kicked the car into passing gear, the back tires broke loose and the car jumped sideways. I later thought this was really cool, but when it was happening it caused a second of terror until it straightened up.

The car had a set of chrome reverse wheels on it when I got it, and I ran them for a while after adding chrome spider center caps to them. One day I found out that a speed shop fifty miles away was running a special on E/T chrome five spoke wheels. They were blems or what we called leakers, meaning that they had come through production porous. The aluminum castings had pin holes so they could not be used with tubeless tires, but they were only $100 for a set of four. We dragged my dad down there and came home with a set. We purchased four inner tubes, and had the local D/X station put them on. I thought that these made the car look great, and I was really proud of them. Just a night or two after installing them, we were driving out in the country, when I had my first urge to get on it since installing the new wheels. After spinning the tires enough to scratch my itch, I let off the gas, and about ten feet later heard thump, thump, thump. I had not one but two flats on the rear. Apparently, the temperature must have been just right for optimum traction, and we had spun the rims inside the tires and cut off both rear valve stems. This is an anticipated problem on drag cars, and consequently, they often screw the beads of the tire to the rim. I have never before or since heard of this happening on a street car. These were not wide tires, but were ones that fit underneath the wheel wells without air shocks. This happening gives testimony to how good the old car could get a bite when conditions were right.

RED HOT PERSUASION

M Y COUSIN JOHN BANKS WAS VISITING our home with his dad from the Kansas City area, and I invited him to go out and run around for the evening in the GTX. We backed out of my driveway and went one block up Elm Street, and stopped at the stop sign on College Avenue. Immediately, a second generation Camaro, probably a '71, went by. It had a custom paint job of red metal flake, and on the quarter panel was lettered "RED HOT PERSUASION." It also sported an Iowa license plate. Following him, right on his rear bumper was a friend of mine, Rick Ellsworth, in his gold 1970 GTO. Right behind him was another friend, Matt Rongey, in his red 1968 Fairlane 500 convertible. So John and I fell in line behind them. As we went up College Avenue, Rick was running up on the guy and messing with him. The Camaro immediately made a couple of turns to get back to the main highway and headed out of town to the west, with Rick, Matt, and John and me right behind. The highway here was running through the river bottom, and then beyond that was a long climb to the top of the next hill. As soon as they got on the highway, all of the cars in front of me floored it and away we went. I looked ahead down the road and saw that there was no one coming. Then I looked over to my cousin and said, "I think I can get them all." We pulled out in the passing lane and blew by them, even though they were running about 100 mph at this point. By the time we got around them, we had eaten up the bottom land and were beginning to climb the hill, heading farther west. We kept it floored for a while and then let off and turned into a black top road, turned around, and headed back to town.

I assumed our excitement for the night was over, and that we had "peed" on enough tires to show this Iowegian hot rodder that this was our turf. Now this was all happening after dark, and as John and I cruised back to town, I saw a pair of headlights coming up behind me, and they were floating, exactly what it looks like when a car is running fast. I knew this was my friend Matt; his red convertible was a very fast car. It had a 390 engine and a 4 speed, and I had been in it more than once when the speedometer was past the 120 mph mark, and bouncing on the peg. I felt I knew what Matt was planning to do. He was getting a run to build up speed and pass me. Then he would tell the story that on the return to town, he had bested me. I stomped the pedal to the floor on the GTX just as Matt caught us and flew by, by two car lengths. Now the race was on. We began to eat up those two car lengths like we were reeling the convertible in on a fishing line. When we finally caught and passed him, we were back on the flat river bottom, and the town was coming up fast. As I let off the throttle, only then did I dare take my eyes off the road and glance down at the speedometer. One of the options that verify a 1967 GTX is really a GTX is that they came equipped with a 150 mph speedometer; lesser cars had the standard 120 mph speedo. When I looked down at it, we were decelerating rapidly, and I saw the needle of the speedometer fall back across 135. That was the fastest I ever drove the car. I don't know what it might have gotten up to before I let off. I also don't know how accurate the speedometer would have been at those speeds, but I do know that when my speedometer read 105, it was right on the money because I once had the Missouri Highway Patrol verify it. But that is another story.

THE TRANS AM

W HEN I FIRST BEGAN TO HEAR THE TERM muscle car being used, it was always preceded by the words mid-sixties. This was the early seventies, and even though a lot of the muscle car nameplates were still around, their big engine's compression ratios had been lowered, and they were choked down with smog devices. So a car magazine at the time would commonly make the statement that in a road test, some particular car's performance, although good by that day's standard, was definitely not up to par with a mid-sixties muscle car. For those of us die hard muscle car fans, who were willing to drive something that could only use ethyl gasoline, and a lot of it, when gasoline had doubled in price recently, we looked at the new badged muscle cars as posers, having the emblems and the hood scoops but not the horsepower. As they say in Texas, they were "all hat and no cattle."

While coming home from work one day in the old GTX, as I was sitting at a stop sign waiting to pull out on the highway, a car load of guys came by in a brand new Pontiac Trans Am. It was a gorgeous red car and they were by far the coolest new cars available at the time. I would still like to have one today. These guys were two or three years older than me and had already gotten out of high school. As they went by, one of the guys in the rear seat crooked his finger at me to "come on." So I decided to take them up on it. I had to wait for an oncoming car to pass before I could pull out, but after I did, I floored it to catch up with them. This place on the highway was a very long hill. They were running flat out but I easily caught them and began to run behind them. I had to stay in behind them for a little bit because of oncoming cars, but when they cleared, I pulled out and passed them and went on to town.

After arriving back at town a few miles away, I wasn't thinking much about it. I had only proven something I already knew well. When in the parking lot of a store I had pulled into, here came the Trans Am. "Hey Banks, how fast were we running?" one of the guys asked. By this time Pontiac was only putting 100 mph speedometers in Trans Ams. They later cut that back to 85, which was mandated by the government for a while, to discourage speeding and to conserve fuel. So they had not been able to tell how fast they were going. But thanks to the old GTX's 150 MPH speedo, I told them they were running 118 MPH when I passed them. I felt they were disappointed. I think they were hoping for something considerably faster.

HARRISON COUNTY

ARRISON COUNTY IS THE COUNTY JUST west of the one I grew up in and it was the county my dad grew up in. A friend that I ran around with a lot had also gone to school in this county until after eighth grade, when he moved to our town because it was larger and the school would give him better sports opportunities. Now, Harrison County was a little "woolier" than our county, and we always seemed a little closer to getting into mischief when we went there. Since there wasn't a lot to do in our town, we usually went either south to the next town which had a movie theater, as well as a drive-in and so forth, or we went west to Harrison County whose county seat also had these things. The small towns were also very familiar to my friend Ed and me because of our family ties there. We would occasionally go to a basketball game or tournament in one of these small towns. We had no interest in their basketball teams, but were hoping to meet girls there. Besides movies and basketball games, our main destinations were the county fairs in the summer time. The main draw of county fairs was also the local girls. Now the thing about meeting girls that are strangers is that you have to be willing to begin a conversation with said girl. There was one pitfall to this process; a lot of times these girls already had boyfriends, and sometimes you were unlucky enough that these boyfriends were not far away. They might actually walk up while you were obviously flirting with their girl or girls. Here's where the GTX came in; we considered it our security blanket, knowing that if we could make it back to it we could outrun anyone back to our home territory. I remember one instance of high tailing it on foot across the parking lot of a fair ground with my keys in hand.

Another time we were sitting on the town square of one of those little Harrison county towns, and considered ourselves very fortunate to have two very pretty girls being very friendly; one was leaning in the passenger side window talking to Ed, and the other was leaning in my window talking to me. The GTX was sitting there idling, and I switched it off to save fuel. I used to joke that I had to turn it off at gas stations so it wouldn't get ahead of the pump. The minute I turned it off, Ed said very forcefully, "Crank it back up!" To which I responded, "Hey, we're getting low on gas!" He then leaned his head towards me, and as quietly as he could, told me whose girlfriend the girl I was talking to was, and he's a guy we should be afraid of. He then looked over his shoulder and said, "If his car comes around that corner, I want this thing to be running!"

On one of our excursions we had met a couple of girls that we later took on dates. These girls lived in another one of Harrison County's small towns. This town had long passed its heyday, and had no businesses left just dilapidated buildings on what was once the town square. On leaving one of their houses very late one night, while crossing that town square to get back to the highway, a car came towards us from the opposite direction and stopped abruptly when he got along beside us, obviously wanting to talk to us. We both rolled down our windows. I could see there were two guys inside the car and they were older than us, definitely not high school boys. The driver then asked me, "Are you Mike Banks? And I said, "Yes." He then said, "I've been looking for you for a month. Is that the Plymouth that is supposed to be so fast?" My response was, "I guess it is." He then said "Let's just see how fast it is." Now I also had heard about him. There was a bridge around these parts that guys raced across. It was very short for a drag race, not even an eighth mile. This 1969 Road Runner he was driving, legend had it, had outrun a 750 Honda across that bridge. Honda 750's were fast motorcycles, and normally a car was no match for a big, fast motorcycle in a very short distance, making this a very impressive feat.

I agreed to race him and we went outside of town. We went a couple of miles out through the river bottom. This area of north Missouri is known as the rolling hills area, and that topography does not lend itself very well to drag racing. So the river bottom made for a convenient place to race. There were a series of bridges out through the bottom, and two of them were supposed to be exactly a quarter of a mile apart; so it was the place in eastern Harrison County to drag race. We would be racing back towards the little town and just before it, the bottom ground ended and the road climbed a low hill and curved hard to the left. We went out and turned around, and like a dumb kid I let him have the right hand lane, making me get in the left lane facing oncoming traffic.

Fortunately, it was very late and if there were any oncoming lights, we would be able to see them all the way back to town. Ed had his window down, and as we lined up, I yelled over to the guy above the noise of the engines, "How do you want to start?" There were several ways to start a drag race. Sometimes it would be agreed that one guy would honk his horn or blink his lights, or sometimes a passenger in one of the cars would actually get out and flag with a flashlight or a handkerchief. He looked over at me and yelled back, "What kind of transmission do you have?" Not quite as dumb about this, I tugged on my column-mounted automatic shifter and said, "It's just an automatic on the column." His car was a big bad 4 speed, and had wide tires on the back. People who told stories about this car claimed he would roll backwards in reverse and dump the clutch, jerking the front wheels a few inches off the ground. I am always a little skeptical about those stories. Anyway, between my column-shifted automatic and my narrow tires, he very confidently said, "Aw, when you're ready, just take off." Now I didn't know what the outcome of this race would be, but one thing I did know is that if he was underestimating how the old GTX would come off the line, he had another thing coming. I have never driven or ridden in a street car that came out of the hole any harder than it did. I actually think its success against other muscle cars was primarily for that very reason. Looking back now, it was probably a fortunate coincidence of just the right gear ratio, weight, and horsepower, along with the compound of my cheap rear tires, and some tired old leaf springs. I had learned if I cleaned and heated my tires with a short burnout, put my left foot on the brake, and brought the rpms up to load the torque converter, that when I floored it off the line, it would transfer its weight. The front suspension would raise, and the rear of the car would hunker down, and it was gone. If you went back and looked afterwards, it had laid two very long black marks, but you never could have told it from inside the car. If you were to nail it just rolling along at 10 mph, it would stand up in the rear and smoke the tires. Shortly after telling me, "Just take off any time you're ready," I did.

The old GTX was in great form. It must have liked the temperature and the texture of the asphalt that night, because it felt like it leapt instead of rolled that first car length. This put us ahead of the Road Runner with our rear bumper just a few feet ahead of his front bumper, and the race was on. When we got to the next bridge, which should have signaled the end of the quarter mile and the race, we were still in that relationship to one another. The normal thing would have been for us both to let off and he let me pull in in front of him, but he didn't. My thinking was if I let off and pulled in behind him, his story would be that he outran me. So on across the bottom we went, flat out. My guess is we raced for at least a mile, maybe more. I have no idea what the speedometer got up to, as I had plenty to do beside look down at it. The trouble was the town and that curve were quickly approaching. Even though I had been ahead the whole time, it would have been too dangerous to have whipped over in front of him at that speed, with no more distance than was between us. I did finally get ahead enough to pull over in front of him, and I really don't know if I finally began to pull ahead, or if he for the sake of safety, let off. That car gave the GTX the best race of any that I raced. Ed had been to a very important track meet that day, and had won a first place medal that he was wearing on its ribbon around his neck. I remember seeing him in the front seat shaking that medal and saying, "We both won first place today!"

GETTING ON IT

"**H**EY, BANKS! GET ON IT!" WAS something I heard frequently when driving the GTX. I could count on hearing that yelled to me anytime I was pulling out of a parking lot or driving slowly by a group of young people who knew me. If I was in a neighboring town where people may not have known my name they would just yell "Get on it!" If they were too far away or I had my windows rolled up where I couldn't have heard them yell, they would simply substitute the universal hand motion for "getting on it" by holding one arm in the air and rotating the hand to symbolize spinning tires. And often times the hand motion accompanied the yelling for a more dramatic plea.

Driving a muscle car as a teenager automatically entered you into a competitive group where you were expected to perform. Even if you didn't have a "real" muscle car, loud mufflers and wide tires advertised that you wanted to be associated with this group too. I always equate this scenario to Johnny Cash's song "Don't Take your Guns to Town." As the young boy in the song strapped on his newly acquired fast draw holsters and six gun set and goes out the door, his mother begs "Don't take your guns to town, son. Leave your guns at home, Bill. Don't take your guns to town." This wise mother knew that by sporting the equipment he was, in effect, signing up for the competition, which in his case was to see who the fastest gun fighter was, with the results being life or death.

In the competitive arena of the '60's and '70's muscle car scene, there were two distinct arenas of competition. The first arena was the drag race. Drag races were the equivalent of an old west gunfight in the middle of the street, you either won or lost. Your hot rod reputation was on the line and it could be killed or wounded. But just like the gunfights of the old west, actual street races were not an everyday occurrence, but there was lots of "muscle car flexing" that went on in between

That leads us to the second arena of competition if you "brought your muscle car to town, Bill": Getting on it. Getting on it was an art form. It was an unofficial competition judged by those watching, either as passengers or bystanders. Your status on the baddest cars in town list relied heavily on these exhibitions and however well you "scored" in the minds of your viewers either raised or lowered your standings. Many cars that I remember as being really fast cars I never actually rode in or saw them race, but I saw them get on it on one or more occasions, and it made a big impression on me. When I was a small boy I spent a lot of time at the public swimming pool, and I remember the older guys circling the pool and we would stop what we were doing and watch intently, just hoping that at least one of them would get on it when they pulled out to leave. They seldom disappointed us.

Getting on it was very simple. As you left a parking lot, a side street, or a stop light you nailed it, stomped on it, or floored it, whichever terminology was appropriate for your crowd. Now the test was on. Very similar to bull riding, where the better the bull performs in trying to throw you off, the better your score will be if you ride him, the same was true here. The stouter and harder to handle your car was, the better your imaginary score was considered to be. A successful run was one in which the car, while trying to go sideways, was controlled by the driver with as much tire smoke as possible while the engine roared and the tires squealed. The object for the driver was to never lift your foot off the throttle. To have to lift to regain control was the equivalent of being bucked off the bull before the eight second buzzer. To stay in it was a full ride; the tougher the bull the better the score. The GTX was always a handful to drive when you got on it. In a rodeo it would have been the bull to draw.

The risk in these horsepower and testosterone rich exhibitions was losing it. Losing it is a phrase that you don't hear very often today but it was very common to us back then. Losing it simply meant losing control of the car, and the car then going where it wanted to go instead of where you wanted it to go. Losing it was very serious when an immovable object like a pole or a tree lay in the path that the car wanted to go. Thankfully for all the times I ever got on it in the GTX, the only harm that was ever done was to the tread of the back tires.

To me, to drive around in a muscle car without getting on it, would be like walking around in a gymnasium with a basketball in your hand and not shooting a basket once in a while. For every time I ever raced the GTX I got on it hundreds of times, many of those times just for my own enjoyment, I didn't even require spectators. Likewise, the reason my friends always wanted to take the GTX when we were going somewhere wasn't because of its comfortable seats or its sleek appearance. They wanted the carnival ride experience that it offered a few times each evening when I dropped the hammer on it. My good friend David Gentry would open the passenger door on the old GTX and as he was sliding in he would pat the dash and say "Get 'er Sideways!"

When the movie *American Graffiti* came out I was so excited about a movie that was full of hot cars and drag racing that I went to see it several times. The last couple of times we went to see it, we left the theater five minutes before the movie ended. We went around the back of the building to the parking lot and fired up the GTX. We then came up the side street beside the theater. After a good crowd had gathered on the sidewalk exiting the movie we would do a burnout in front of the theater and get 'er sideways for the folks. We figured someone needed to supply this kind of entertainment and we were more than glad to do it.

MAGGIE MAY

1 967 PLYMOUTH GTX'S HAD AN INTERIOR option which was listed on the build sheet as "console delete." If a car was ordered as console delete and if it was an automatic, the shifter was moved to the steering column and the center console was left out. In the space between the front seats where the console would normally be, a folding armrest was substituted in its place. When the top piece was folded down it was an armrest, but when it was folded up it made what most people called a jump seat, about ten inches wide. Just before school started back my junior year in high school, I found the one who was to become the permanent occupant for that little seat.

My friend Matt and I were in the aforementioned Tasty Freeze and had ordered our food. We then turned around to the juke box a few feet behind us to play some songs. Matt pulled out a quarter and put in the slot. Just then, before he had a chance to make any selections, a girl walked up and pushed the buttons selecting songs herself. As we stood there in disbelief, she looked at me and said, "I hear that you have the fastest car in town," to which I responded either "Yeah," "Yes," "Probably," or "uh huh." I don't recall exactly my response but I do recall the feeling which was slightly above being told I would receive that year's Nobel peace prize. You see I had a very fast car, and to find out that this girl had acknowledged that guys were calling it "the fastest car in town" was music to my ears. She then said gesturing back over her shoulder to a booth occupied with another girl, "My sister and I would like to take a ride in it."

Now these were those very same preacher's daughters that a week or so ago I had noticed while riding my motorcycle. Yea, I hadn't gotten rid of the motorcycle yet, but I had agreed to it. And I was not riding it very much because I was distracted by the GTX. Even though I had met and shaken hands with these girls that first Sunday at church, I had had no contact with them since. Now I had a dilemma. We were not in the GTX, we were in Matt's car. When I was with my buddies we were always in the GTX, but not tonight. We had arranged for the GTX to go in the shop for an engine rebuild in a couple of days, and I had decided to not drive it until then. I was afraid I might have the misfortune of damaging the engine just days before it was rebuilt. The guy we bought it from at 73,000 miles, said he had overhauled it at 49,000 miles and now it needed it again, as it used oil and smoked, but none of that seemed to slow it down.

We agreed to take them for a ride, and went home to get the car. When we pulled up at the Tasty Freeze, the older sister, Jeana, the one who had punched the juke box buttons, crawled in the backseat with my friend Matt. Her younger sister, Lynn, got in the front seat with me, but didn't get as close as the jump seat –yet.

We rode around for a while and drove out into the country towards the lake. I attempted to make a big turn through some trees to turn around, but in the dark I didn't notice a small tree, about six inches in diameter, that I had just driven by. When I cramped my wheels left, I crashed into it with my door. I was in no way hot rodding. We were going walking speed, but never the less, it put a huge dent in the door requiring replacement. I was very distraught by this and headed back to town, dropped everyone off, and went home.

At this point Lynn had seen my motorcycle and the GTX. So the next day I decided to take her the old '53 Ford. Yea, I still had that too, although technically its owner was now dad. He hadn't sold it either, and I could drive it whenever I wanted. So off to Lynn's house I went and I took her riding around in it. The next day I took her my parent's car as well. As you can see, there was a pattern developing here, but I still had a green '66 Ford pickup to go.

After the parade of vehicles and our time riding around together, Lynn and I were hitting it off pretty well. So, I asked her for an official date. Her answer was that she would get back to me with her answer. Now this might sound odd seeing as how we had already been out together a few times. It wasn't that she didn't know if she liked me. I learned later that she had shown interest in me which is why her sister had set the whole thing up at the Tasty Freeze. Her sister was already seeing a guy in town and he and his friends are the ones that told her about my car. The problem was our age difference. I was sixteen and beginning my junior year in high school. She was twenty-one and soon to be twenty-two in a couple of months. So when the deadline for her to accept or reject my request for an official, "let the whole wide world see" date came, she actually accepted.

Lynn's parents seemed to like me and had already mentioned me in phone conversations back to Arizona before she had moved. However, they were not so excited about us becoming romantically involved. After that first date on a Saturday night, the next morning was back to school Sunday at church, and her dad made it a point to come up and ask me, "What grade will you be in this year, Mike?" Little did they know that for the next couple of years they were going to be serenaded by a big block Mopar with burnt out glass pack mufflers setting idling in their driveway at midnight. The neighbors across the street from Lynn's house said when I was in Lynn's driveway with the GTX and they were in their living room they would assign a family member to hold their palm against the picture window that faced Lynn's house to stop it from vibrating.

Lynn sang and played the guitar and had actually had some opportunities to begin a professional career, but had opted out of what she knew that lifestyle would be like. She had been quite popular locally back in Arizona, and sang at weddings and local celebrations, and was even asked back there from Missouri to sing. No one in our town, of course, knew this, but her dad didn't hesitate to get her to sing at some of his speaking engagements at other Churches. One of these ended up being our second date. I was her official chauffer and guitar carrier.

On that second date, we traveled south only a few miles to the extremely small town of Spickard, Mo. Spickard was a special place for us car guys because the highway leading into it from the north went through some bottom ground and was straight and flat as a board, a rarity in our part of the world. We called it the "Spickard Flats." Even though it was flat and straight, it was a terribly narrow two lane road with the notorious lip along the outside, infamous for causing drivers to wreck if they inadvertently ran up on them by accident. Coming back after her singing, I was showing off winding the car out on the Spickard Flats. I enjoyed the feeling a little too long and stayed in it until it was too late to properly slow down for the corner at the end. I braked as hard and as long as I could, scrubbing off as much speed as possible, knowing if I was still on the brake in the curve I could not keep the car from sliding. I then let off the brake and barely made it around the corner, with the tires protesting. I think that was Lynn's initiation to many more exciting driving adventures.

Lynn came to Princeton from the West; the very hip, modern and progressive Phoenix Valley in Arizona. She arrived in the not quite as hip Midwest. Lynn was not a hippie, but she had been around real hippies and I had not. Lynn's attire had a very western hippie influence. Starting at her feet she wore what she called "water buffalos" which were a type of sandal that you soaked in water overnight before wearing them for the first time, then put them on wet so they would conform to your foot. She assured me they were very comfortable. Heading north from there was usually a pair of cutoff shorts topped by a halter top. She carried an Indian blanket purse that looked sort of like a prayer rug, and she sometimes pulled her hair up in a bandana. Besides the short skirts of the day she often wore a long sundress with those same sandals. See what I mean? It looked to this north Missouri boy like I was dating a little hippie, but I must have loved it. Shortly after we started dating Lynn got a new purse and retired the Indian blanket one. I asked her if I could have the old purse, she looked at me kind of funny but gave it to me. I put it up on a shelf in my closet thinking if this one gets away I'm gonna have something to remember her by.

We had taken the GTX to a body shop in Bethany, Missouri twenty-seven miles away, to have a used door installed and painted to repair the damage we had done to the GTX the first night I had given Lynn and her sister a ride. When we got the call that it was done, I asked Lynn to go with me the next morning to get it, and drive one of the cars back. After we got back to Princeton, I took Lynn back to her driveway. The sun was shining very brightly into the car and it reminded me of a line from a Rod Stewart song which was wildly popular at the time, "Morning sun when it's in your face really shows your age, aw but that don't worry me none, in my eyes you're everything." From that day on my nickname for her has been Maggie.

BARBECUE BEEF AND MOSQUITOS

T HAT FIRST DATE WITH LYNN WAS TO A drive-in movie, and the GTX was our chariot. If there is one thing that keeps me glad I am not a younger man, it is that I would have hated to miss the era of drive-in movies. The drive-in movie had a feeling that is hard to explain to someone who never experienced them when they were "the place to be." From people hiding in trunks to get in free, to the dusty line of cars full of bleary-eyed people leaving up in the morning hours, and everything in between, there was an excitement about it. I still remember the advertisement for the snack bar that came on before the movie and at the intermission. It was the same ad and pitchman, no matter what drive-in you were at. There was that wonderful picture of a kind of orange colored bar-b-que beef being scooped into a sandwich, and even though the last time you had it, it wasn't too good, you just had to have one tonight. You might ask someone, "How would you like to try and watch a movie on a hot and sweaty summer night, while sitting in a car with the windows down on sticky vinyl seats, while listening to a crackly mono speaker, while fighting off mosquitos?" This doesn't sound very appealing, but a family picnic or camping trip can also be described this way, and they are still very enjoyable for many people. I can tell you a drive-in was an experience worth the inconvenience.

Lynn and I had three different drive-ins we frequented, each about as far away as the other, one to the south, one to the west, and one in southern Iowa to the north. The one to the west was very rustic and you actually parked your car on grass, with gravel being only on the lanes between the rows. This drive-in sat in a low area and the mosquitos were legion. There was a guy with a mosquito fogger on his back that walked around between the cars during the movie. On especially hot nights, after the engine cooled down enough, we would sometimes climb up on the hood and lean back against the windshield to get a little breeze to help stay cool, but we had to wait a good bit for the old 440 to cool off, because that hood was about egg frying temperature right after you turned it off.

Once while we were at a drive-in, I spied two rows in front of us a couple of kids on their first date for both of them. I knew both of them well, and they were a couple of years behind me in school. This particular boy was real good natured, and just as upperclassmen do, I had teased him some, but not in a bad way; I really liked him. He had borrowed his dad's four wheel drive pickup for the date, and it sat very high off the ground. I noticed she was sitting very close to him, and that they were "hugged up" so to speak. I told Lynn to "watch this" and I proceeded to crawl, commando-style, the two rows to their truck, so as not to be detected. My plan was simply to startle them. As I got beside the truck, I decided that if the door was unlocked, the best way to startle them was to jerk it open. When I jerked the door open, he proceeded to fall right out on the ground, and I had a great laugh at his expense. Look under drive-ins in the book *How to Win Friends and Influence People.* This method might be there.

Even though Lynn weighed 98 pounds, she had a voracious appetite and was capable of downing a large supreme pizza by herself. Pizza Hut was a fairly new restaurant chain for our neck of the woods, and it was our favorite place to eat while on dates. My last two summers at home I worked at Lake Paho, a Missouri conservation commission lake outside of Princeton, as a laborer. This was my, and my other high school buddies that worked there, official title because there was no job title called "goofing off". I met Lynn right at the end of my first summer's work there and had amassed a summertime fortune of something over seven hundred dollars, which normally would have been plenty to take me through the winter. Sometime around late December I asked dad for some money to go on a date. His response was, "Use your own money," to which I replied, "I'm out." Between the GTX's appetite for gas (no buddies to help pay now) and Lynn's appetite for Pizza, romancing this older woman had already taken my life's savings. A "We can't believe what you just said" moment ensued with my mom and dad, but I had a good relationship with my parents, so we recovered quickly.

From the first date on Lynn and I were pretty much inseparable. It was not like we dated a couple of times a week; we were together every night, many times at my house or hers. Although we made no mention of it then, looking back, we both agree that we probably knew that each other was "the one" in the first two weeks of dating. From my standpoint, besides being very physically attracted to her from the start, I immediately found out she was also very pleasing to be around. I might not have been able to give you an explanation why, I just knew that she was, and that she was the one for me. Looking back now, I know what word I would pick to define her: real. Lynn was real. She didn't play games. She was very confident, and her life wasn't dictated by insecurities as so many young peoples are. She didn't have a group of friends that she was constantly looking over her shoulder for approval from. She wasn't shallow, consumed by the latest fads or fashion. She was not selfish, either in deed or conversation, always wanting to hear what you had to say rather than what she had to say. And last but definitely not least, she was fearless. Lynn is hands down the most fearless person I have ever known, and that is someone you want in your corner in life. I don't think we ever thought of it in those terms, but I think we were finding out that we were good for one another, and were, in fact, meant to be together. It is hard to explain, but even after all I just said, it was a year before I actually considered marriage. Looking back, the best explanation I could give is subconsciously, I can see I was there, but my mind had yet to catch up. If this were a romance novel, I guess my heart was already there, but my head wasn't. As a sixteen year old I had not considered marriage at all, which is understandable. Now within the course of a year, I found myself with an old gold Plymouth and a girl of my own.

SNOW DAYS

W ITH LYNN'S GROWING UP IN TEXAS and then Arizona, It was fun watching her get acclimated to north Missouri weather — which she never did. Lynn weighed 98 pounds when we met and had 10 weight Arizona blood for operating in hot conditions. At family gatherings my granddad would always try to run her through the buffet line more than once to get her fattened up. I think we did get her up to a whopping 103 before we were married. But she was still constantly freezing between September and May.

I loved the winter and especially snow and ice. In my grade school years we lived in the middle of one of the biggest hills in town, and I became an avid sledding enthusiast. Mentioning sledding in Princeton would be inconsiderate without giving the proper respect to the steepest, and by far the most popular hill in town: Axtel Hill. It was named after Dr. Byron Axtel and his hospital that sat at the top of it. In times past sometimes they would open a fire hydrant at the top of the hill to create a place to slide when there was no precipitation, but for the most part, a normal Mercer county winter provided plenty of slick weather. Axtel hill was very steep and all forms of sleds could be commonly seen on it, but for the older guys, car hoods were the most fun.

My most memorable sledding experience occurred with several of my friends out at Lake Paho. By this time we were old enough to drive, and several of us went out to the lake to try sliding down the dam. I should not have to convince anyone that a dam is a formidable venue for sled riding. Because of their function they are incredibly steep. There were several of us out there, at least eight to ten. After going down the dam individually for a while, we came up with a plan for more excitement. We had with us three of the longer style conventional sleds that up to three children can sit upon at one time, or an adult sized person can easily lie down on. We laid these three down side by side on the top of the dam. Then the three largest guys lay down on them to be the drivers. On top of those three, three more took their positions crossways on top of the ones already on the sleds. After that, the remaining two or three boys pushed the other six as fast as they could over the edge and piled on as we were going. We had probably 1500 lbs. on those 3 sleds as we barreled down the dam. At the bottom of the dam, just as it leveled out, there was a little bump of a hill about three to four feet high. It ran the length of the dam and probably was there to divert the rain water to either end, as it ran down the back of the dam. We hit that hill and went air born and landed on the other side in a pile of arms and legs and sleds. No one was hurt and we loved it. Everyone was screaming, "Let's do it again," but when we grabbed the sleds to go back up the hill they were all busted. The phrase that has been true for many things I have experienced fits here perfectly: it was fun while it lasted.

Lynn and I spent a lot of time at my house with my mom and dad and little brother. One time, while spending time at my house the snow had gotten really deep, and so as not to risk getting stuck I decided to walk Lynn home. As we were walking along all bundled up, I fell over backwards beside the sidewalk and moved my arms up over my head and back down repeatedly, all the time moving my legs together and apart. Lynn stood there dumfounded thinking I was having a seizure, and wondering if she was going to have to go call an ambulance. It turns out this Arizona girl had never seen anyone make a snow angel before.

To coin a phrase a teacher used once to explain why I was being sent to the office, ice and snow was a great opportunity for "general messing around." Most of the time when it got slick, my buddies and I got out on the road as soon as possible doing donuts, and seeing who could climb Axtel hill without having to back down. Donuts for some boys were a mainstay even when it's dry. On any given Saturday night, you could bet before the night was over someone would be out in the intersection of Hwy 136 and 65 in front of the DX station doing donuts—some even to the point of blowing out a tire. I, on the other hand, only did doughnuts on slick streets, seeing no need to do them in dry conditions. The GTX would smoke its tires and lay black marks without cramping the wheels in a circle. In horsepower as in life, there are the haves and the have nots.

Lynn had a terrible time walking on ice. In fact, even standing on it, whether it was trying to get from church to the car on Sunday or from a house to a car anywhere, she was usually completely out of control flailing her arms and yelling things like "whoa!" until someone, usually me, got there to grab her.

Walking was one thing, driving was another. One day I was following Lynn while she was driving her Volkswagen and there were some patches of ice on the roads, still left over from a storm a few days before. Following behind Lynn I was shocked whenever she completely ran a stop sign at a major intersection. She didn't even slow down. While I was processing this and carefully braking and stopping at the stop sign myself, I noticed Lynn a few yards on through the intersection jump out of her car and stand there with a very shocked look on her face. I drove down to her and she exclaimed, "My brakes went out!" For a split second I believed her. Then I looked back at the patch of ice that covered the intersection. I asked her a few questions to get to the bottom of her brake problem. Me: "Did you notice that ice back there at the stop sign?" Lynn: "Is that ice?" Me: "Yep, how did you get stopped right here?" Lynn: "Well the brakes started working again." Me: "uhuh."

Lynn and I were driving in front of the courthouse in Princeton one Saturday and town was full. We were in my parent's big Ford and there was snow packed and ice was covering the road on the square. All of a sudden the car did a 360 degree spin. There were cars on both sides of the road, as well as in front of me slightly to the right parked around the bandstand. I did what I could with the steering wheel trying to steer with the spin, and when we came clear around, we continued on without hitting anything or coming to a stop. Lynn said, "Wow that was some fancy driving. Your hands were just a blur." I think she thought I had done it on purpose, and as tempting as that was, I had to tell her I was out of control. It just turned out good.

Lynn also had a problem with the topography of North Missouri compared to the Phoenix valley's flatness. She moved to Princeton with an almost new 10 speed bike, but found she had to push her bike uphill and ride it downhill. When she informed me of this dilemma I asked her what gear she was trying to go up the hills in, and she gave me a blank stare. It seems in Arizona one gear had sufficed, and she had never learned how to shift it.

Maybe the scariest thing that ever happened to Lynn and me in the GTX didn't involve hot rodding or slick roads, but it did involve inclement weather. The movie theater in Trenton, 25 miles away, was showing *Gone with the Wind*, and Lynn really wanted to see it. I wasn't too excited to see a really old, really long movie, but I didn't want to keep Lynn from seeing it. The theater showed the film with an intermission in the middle. During the intermission Lynn went to the restroom. When she came back, she said "Mike, maybe we ought to go ahead and go home. I saw out in the lobby that it is getting really foggy outside." We left immediately but when we got out on the road away from the lights of town, we met with a fog that I didn't know was even possible. I have never to this day experienced fog like this, and I have never talked to anyone who has. It took us several hours to travel the 25 miles back to Princeton, and the scary part was we had no idea where we were until we came into the lights of Princeton. We were not able to see even to the ditches on the side of the road, so we were unable to see any land marks. There were several large landmarks that I thought we would be able to recognize when we went by, but we were not able to see anything. I drove the whole way with my window open with my head stuck out looking almost straight down at the broken white lines on the road, and would feel panicky when one stopped, making sure to steer straight the few feet until we came upon the next one. Early on I had thought of letting Lynn drive while I led her by walking in front of the car. We dropped that idea because of how dangerous it would be, and I didn't know if she could see me. It was very hard for me to see the hood ornament on The GTX. After hours of this, we finally came into Princeton, and I dropped Lynn off at her house. The next two days my eyes were a mess. They were turned wrong side out from straining to see in that fog.

FUN AND GAMES

M Y FRIEND MATT HAD AN OVERACTIVE sense of humor and was also very creative. The things that Matt would come up with would make an interesting and hilarious book in and of themselves. There are a couple of things car related, that he was particularly famous for. Matt lived out at Lake Paho six miles from town. He made that trip into town and back at least a couple of times a day, if not more. The road between his house and town was new and wide. It was also the best one in the county. Matt drove a 1968 Ford Fairlane 500 convertible. One of his signature moves was to make it look like his car was empty with no driver in it. On his way to or from town he would lean completely over in the seat. The dashboard in this particular model of car had some ridges and valleys on the top edge of it where gauges were located. Matt would put his eyeball right at one of those indentations, as he drove down the highway meeting cars. Now these were not usually people he knew, they were mostly strangers. He thought it great fun, and did this for his own personal enjoyment. If per chance he should meet someone he actually knew, then that was just a big bonus. He was hoping that the approaching car in view would be saying to themselves or their passengers, "Can you see anybody in that car?" As they got closer and finally met, he would lay completely over where they could not possibly see him, just holding his wheel straight while driving blind and hoping for the best. I can't tell you how many times I met Matt's empty car, both on the highway and in town.

Matt and I came up with another variation of this trick. Since Matt had already mastered lying over in the seat and driving, we came up with the idea of me driving his car while sitting in the backseat. I would roll the back window down and put my left elbow on it, and then reach up with my right arm and drive the car. Everyone in town knew Matt's car was a four speed. Matt, while lying in the seat, would run the throttle, the clutch, and the brakes and shift the gears. We would drive around town like this for long periods of time. Our favorite thing to do was come up to our only intersection in town with a traffic light, which was also a gathering place for young people at the surrounding gas stations. Then, when we'd take off from the stop light, we would get on it doing a burnout, and Matt would hit second gear hard, getting rubber while I drove from the backseat.

Even more famous than that were Matt's cop turns. As I mentioned earlier, we had been influenced by the movies and we loved to play car chase. Matt had taught himself to do cop turns like they do in the movies, where they slam on the brakes, cramp the steering wheel, and slide down the road sideways. Then as the car swings completely around, stomp the gas, causing the car to be going backwards while the car's rear tires are spinning forward. When they finally get traction, the car takes off the opposite direction than it had started. Matt had perfected this to where he would do it running 60 mph, and he loved to do it unexpectedly when you were just riding with him carrying on a conversation. It made you think you were having a terrible car wreck.

One of Matt's brothers had a 1971 Mercury Cougar. This was Matt's car of choice for the cop turns because it was an automatic, so he didn't have to deal with the clutch during the procedure. One time, with Lynn and me in the car with him, Matt did this, and that car was rolled over so hard on its suspension, that it felt like if the window had been down I could have drug my elbow on the pavement. Lynn was so mad she told Matt she would never ride with him again, and she was good to her word. A funny side note to all of this was that my dad and Matt's dad were friends, and they often talked about their cars. Matt's dad told my dad "Joe, there is something wrong with that Cougar. It keeps breaking off right front shocks. I don't know what it could be." Dad sucked it up and didn't tell on Matt even though he knew what was behind the broken shock mystery.

There were a couple of other games that my friends and I entertained ourselves with. On the south side of town on Highway 65, there was a roadside park that set on a big hill, a couple of miles or so from town. I don't know where this game originated, as it had been handed down to us, but the rules were as follows. You would take off from the roadside park heading towards town from a standing start. You were then allowed to get up as much speed as possible until you reached this particular road sign that was at least a quarter mile away. At the sign you had to slip your car into neutral and begin to coast towards town. This took you down the big hill, around a pretty good corner, under the railroad bridge, past the swimming pool, and headed for the beloved Tasty Freeze. At the swimming pool you had started to climb the big hill Princeton was built on, and at the very top was our one and only blinking stop light. The goal was to roll all the way to the stop light and over the hill, and then continue down the other side. As far as I know nobody ever did it. I could get between the Tasty Freeze and the intersection, which means I would have coasted about 2 ½ miles, but still lacked probably 100 yards or more to the top. I could get that far because I could get to well over 100 MPH before going into neutral at the road sign, but that made the corner at the bottom of the hill a bit of a clincher. If you were sitting in the Tasty Freeze and saw a car barely roll to a stop just before it passed the driveway, you knew someone was playing the game.

Another game was the three man weave. We only did this a few times. If you were ever on a basketball team, you probably did this drill in practice. It is an exercise to learn how to fast break. Three players start at one end of the court at the baseline and run towards the other end. The one with the basketball throws it to the player next to him, and then runs behind him. When the ball gets to the side of the court, that guy throws it the other direction, and the ball moves side to side, as the players weave around each other. I worked at the lake in the summer time with my friend Danny and my friend Bill. We were in the same class, and had been on the basketball team together for years. One evening, going home from work in our cars, just being a nut, Bill passed me on the wrong side. We were quite impressed with the new road the state of Missouri had built us, with big wide shoulders. I don't know how it happened, but we all three just started doing the three man weave, using the two lanes of traffic and both shoulders. After that first time, we found it great fun to catch an oncoming car way down in the bottom. While we were coming down the hill we would start doing the weave while they were a mile away, and come at them, then forming a single line in our lane just before we met the approaching car. The last time we did it, when we got to the approaching car, it was a local judge. Although we never got in any trouble for it, we drew on what little brain cells that were actually functioning in our heads, and decided we had been lucky, and that we would not do that again.

BUGS

W HILE WE WERE DATING, LYNN'S DAD came back from a trip to their relatives that lived in Oklahoma, towing A VW Bug that he had brought home for Lynn. As Lynn's mother said, this was just like a big toy for me. Technically my first car was a Bug, although I never got to drive it. My dad and I bought it, and a parts car, at Pea Ridge Auto Salvage, over by Mount Moriah, Missouri. We had my uncle come up from Kansas City and paint it for us, but Dad sold it before I ever got to drive it. Later, my friend Ed had a VW Bug that he terrorized two counties in, sometimes with me inside. Ed was fascinated by the places he could go with the Bug that other cars couldn't go. These included up the sidewalks in Cainsville, which had awnings on them, but the Bug fit between the awnings and the store. I can still see the old ladies jumping back inside the Hy-Vee grocery store, as Ed drove up the east-side sidewalk on a Saturday afternoon. This car was also used to drive around a certain girl's house from front yard to back, making several circuits in the middle of the night, while flashing his lights, honking his horn, and flapping his doors open and closed. Any guy playing a guitar and serenading his girl below her window had nothing on Ed. He once pulled the emergency brake while driving down the road at 50 mph just to see what it would do. The answer was that it spun around uncontrollably until it came to a stop. Ed once tried to cut through a couple of yards in our town while going from one road to the other. One of these yards belonged to one of our high school teachers. This was not the first time he had done this, but he didn't know they had plowed their garden since he had been through last, and he got stuck in it. Fortunately, I was not with him that time.

Now I had my own Bug to play with. One Sunday afternoon Lynn and I were riding around in her Beetle, and we went up on the square at Princeton. There was not one car parked around either the bandstand or in front of the stores; the only other car was a guy entertaining his girlfriend by driving down the south-side sidewalk. I guess driving on the sidewalks had kind of become a thing at that time. This feat was more impressive than Ed's though, because he was in a big Pontiac, not a little VW. As he was easing his car down the west steps of the sidewalk, I began making circles around the bandstand, just keeping the wheels on the Bug cramped, and going faster and faster. This was too much provocation, and he fell in behind me and the race was on. We made several rounds around the bandstand to the point where I was getting dizzy, and Lynn was starting to become less than entertained by our fun. The Volkswagen was leaning very heavily, and I could see in the rear view mirror that his car was really heeled over, when all of a sudden he spun out. The car made several rotations and just stopped, and kind of quivered on its suspension. It looked a lot like a dirt track spin out.

Fortunately, they didn't hit anything; no harm was done, and more fun was had than a Sunday afternoon picnic.

It was also my responsibility to maintain the Volkswagen. I once pushed down on the clutch and it broke off. To this Lynn's mom said, "You broke your toy, didn't you?"

We were in Chillicothe, Missouri shopping one time, and as I drove by a wrecking yard, I saw a wrecked Beetle sitting out front. It looked as though they had just got it in. I stopped and got out and looked inside, and saw that it had a pristine interior. Lynn's interior was shot. I made a deal to buy the interior, and also borrow some wrenches from them in the deal. I removed her interior and replaced it with the one from the wrecked car, and we went back to Princeton in style.

Bugs were often picked on when they were left parked somewhere and their owner was not around, especially on the school grounds. Our favorite thing was to pick up or drag the Bug to someplace it was obviously not supposed to be, or, ideally, between two immovable objects that were narrow enough that you couldn't get the doors open. One similar story which is a favorite in my memory happened not to a Bug, but another really small car; a Toyota. Our school had hired a new girls PE and basketball coach, and it was her first year teaching so she was quickly given the nickname "Rookie," which stuck big time. Rookie had a great personality and just immediately hit it off with all of us, especially anyone involved with basketball. Rookie was from our neighboring state to the north, Iowa. Iowa played five person girls basketball while Missouri was still playing the old fashioned six girl basketball, consequently making the Iowa girls play basketball more like we boys did. Rookie would often play pickup basketball with us boys in the gym and she was the first woman I ever saw shoot a jump shot. I was impressed. Like high school boys are apt to, we teased and pulled pranks on her often and she was a great sport about it. Rookie was the one that drove the Toyota and we were constantly picking it up and setting it over the sidewalk that her parking space butted up against, making it look like she was a terrible driver, and causing the grade school kids and their teachers to have to walk around it to get to the playground at recess. One day Rookie came to us boys and said "Boys, please stop putting my car over the sidewalk. Mr. Shelton (the principal) has asked me to please quit parking my car over the sidewalk and I didn't tell him it was you guys doing it because I didn't want to get you in trouble." Yes, she was that nice! Well to us the comedy value of the uncomfortable exchange between her and the principal way outweighed any threat of "getting in trouble." So sure enough, the very next day, over the sidewalk Rookie's car went. After that Rookie, knowing that reasoning with us was hopeless, she simply traded work vehicles with her husband who drove a 1967 ¾ ton Ford pickup, and parked it in the same parking spot where she normally parked her Toyota, without ever saying a word to us boys. It takes approximately 17 high school aged boys to pick up a mid-sixties ¾ ton pickup and carry it approximately 20 feet and then set it over a sidewalk. Just a little bit of trivia I learned in high school.

THE HIGHWAY BARN

O N THE NORTH SIDE OF OUR LITTLE town there was a flat straight section in the highway that was just barely longer than a quarter of a mile. On its north end the highway fell off down a big hill, and on the south side it made a large curve. Just before the curve on the south end sat the Missouri State Highway Department barn, where all of their equipment was stored. It consisted of a large building and a gravel yard with gravel, sand, and salt for the roads. This was the popular spot for drag racing, and was referred to as either north of town or "the highway barn." So if you challenged somebody to drag race you might say, "How about we go north of town?" Or if you were bored cruising around, you might say, "Hey, let's go out to the highway barn and see if anything is happening." I was never the challenger in a street race, and I also never lost one. I also didn't race everyone that wanted to race me. Most of these races were proposed, not by the guy that owned the car, but by someone else. So if I had agreed, they would have gone and found that guy, and said, "Hey, Banks wants to race you" making me the challenger. I have always been the kind of person that when being manipulated or forced into something, my response is an automatic no.

On one occasion though, I was approached just right. A car load of older guys—by older I mean just out of high school and probably three years older than me— pulled up beside Lynn and me in the Tasty Freeze parking lot. They were on Lynn's side of the car; she rolled down her window so I could talk across the car to them. They began with a very gentle approach. They said, "Hey Banks, why don't you race us? We know you don't usually race anybody, but we would really just like to see your car run; we hear it's pretty fast and there won't be anyone up there, just us up there, so why not?" I did feel some obligation since these were older guys, and they were being so respectful, so I agreed. Their car was a 1970 Dodge Super Bee, dark green in color, and it had aftermarket lace decals applied to the quarter panels adjacent to the bumblebee stripes, which was real popular at the time. It was also jacked up in the back with very large tires.

When we arrived at the highway barn, there were probably twenty cars in the parking lot. The guys who had been in the car were across the highway on the grass with the hood up. They were taking the header mufflers off and removing the breather. It seems they had told everyone that they were going to get a race with me, and this group had gathered while they went down into town to find me. Lynn decided to sit this one out; so she stayed behind in the parking lot while my friend Matt happily volunteered to ride shotgun. When their race preparations were completed, we both went to the north end of the designated quarter; then on a horn honk from them we took off. I never saw them after that, and when the race was over I went back to get Lynn. The Super Bee never even came back, but just continued on south, back towards town. Lynn said that when we came by them, the crowd cheered and the consensus was that I was about six car lengths ahead.

On another occasion Matt and I were in his convertible when we were challenged to a drag race by a classmate of ours who had a 1970 GTO 400 automatic. We went north of town for the contest. It didn't go well for Matt and me, as the GTO beat us handily. It looked to me like he had bested us by as much as six car lengths. I was kind of shocked by this, thinking the Ford would have made a better showing, but it was kind of high geared, and drag racing was not the best race type for it. We all pulled in at the highway barn, and Matt and I asked everyone to hang around for a minute, while we went back to town and got the GTX. This was exactly the type of provocation that could inspire me to race. We went back up to the starting line and went at it again. This time the GTO was beaten by about the same distance that it had won the race before. This came in real handy because it spared Matt and I having to race one another.

Even though I didn't race people there all the time, I did frequent the north of town quarter mile often for solo runs. My wife tells everyone that we ran the car through the quarter every Sunday after church. I did this for the sheer enjoyment of it, and to keep tabs on its level of tune and performance. The car always read exactly 105 mph on the speedometer; it was super consistent. If it didn't reach 105 I looked for the problem. The problem was almost always that a plug wire had come off and it was running on seven cylinders. I only ever used the cheap plug wires, and the 440 hi-performance exhaust manifolds were notorious for burning up plug wires. The amazing thing was that the car ran so strong I could never feel it had a cylinder down; I always had to learn it by the speedometer. One time I ran through the quarter and got a lower mph reading than normal, but when I checked under the hood, this time a plug wire had not come off, and I was worried. It was a couple of days before I remembered that on a recent spell of slick weather, I had piled several heavy items, including my entire set of barbell weights, in the trunk for better traction and hadn't taken them out.

This story always reminds me of something that happened to a friend of mine. He had his car, a '63 or '64 Chevy with a six cylinder engine, parked at the school while he was gone to a track meet. Another friend of ours who lived across the street from the school noticed his car was backed up to a pile of sand that our janitors had there for some reason or another. He also knew where this guy hid his spare keys; so for a prank he opened his trunk and shoveled the pile of sand into the trunk. When the guy who owned the car arrived back after dark, he didn't notice how the back of the car was sitting low, but he did notice that his car could barely make it over the hills to his house fifteen miles away. After shoveling it out and threatening his friend with what he would do if he ever did that again, he dropped it. In a couple of weeks the car was sitting in the same spot when the other guy was taking out two big bags of garbage. So he decided to put them into the trunk. I think it was about a week before the stink got the best of him.

One of my friends had a Missouri State Highway patrol trooper as a brother-in-law. My friend told me that on one Sunday dinner, the highway patrolmen said in front of the whole family, "That car of Mike's is pretty fast, isn't it?" Because his parents were at the table, my friend wouldn't admit to it, and said, "I wouldn't know." The patrolman then countered saying, "I saw you and Mike run it through the quarter the other day, and I clocked it at 105. That's as fast as I have ever clocked anybody up there." There were two troopers who were headquartered in our town. On occasion, one would hide in the highway barn while the other would hide in his car behind it. When they caught a regular speeder on the highway, or hit the jackpot of one or two hot rodders running through the quarter, the man in the car would chase them and ticket them. We had run through the quarter while the chase car was out ticketing another driver. Many times car speedometers are not very accurate, but my friend's story provided me with an official certification on mine.

A few years back, I was back in Princeton for a visit in a late model Dodge pickup. It was a crew cab and there were six of us in it. I was showing my family around town, and I went north of town to show them where we used to race. Since I had to turn around anyway, when I did I floored it and began to run it through the quarter. Now this was not a Hemi Dodge; it was the regular little 4.7 liter V8, and it had six adults in it. As we hit 85 mph, we had not reached the finish line yet at our old racing spot. I felt uncomfortable trying to negotiate the upcoming curve if I didn't begin to brake now; so I didn't stay in it to the end. As I chickened out, I thought of the possibly hundreds of times that I had kept my foot to the floor and gone at that curve at 105.

THUNDER VALLEY RACEWAY

SOMETIME IN MY SECOND SUMMER WITH the car, after having nothing but success with its performance on the street, I decided to truly put it to the test by taking it to the drag strip and pitting it against similar cars. Thunder Valley Raceway was the closest drag strip to us. So after a new set of points and resetting the timing, it was off to the drag strip on Saturday night. I drove the car over, with Lynn in position on the jump seat perch beside me. Dad followed in his pickup in case I broke something and he had to tow it home. On paying the entry fee and entering the pits, the first stop was the tech inspection, which for the stock class that the car would be in, was not very demanding. They made sure things like a battery hold-down was in place, so that if you got on your top the battery wouldn't fall and short out. Any factory safety items that were appropriate for the year model had to be in place—in this case only lap belts. The car couldn't be leaking oil or any other fluids, plus just a general check for overall common sense things like bald tires or loose lug nuts. You don't have to be a genius to drag race your car, so somebody's got to check this stuff. If you passed tech, the next stop was the scales where the car was weighed with the driver in it. Now is where it got interesting; this was pre-bracket racing days, for our part of the country at least. The cars at this track were handicapped by a points system, and then staged on the starting line, with the slower car physically set in front of the faster car the appropriate number of car lengths dictated by their handicap. To start out with, there were six different main classes: showroom stock (my class), showroom optional, formula stock, hot rod, competition, and finally cycles. The two street car classes were the showroom stock and showroom optional. To qualify for showroom stock, your car could not have tube headers; it had to have street tires and a stock suspension and ride height. The next class up allowed open headers, drag slicks up to ten inches wide, electric fuel pump, rear spring shackles, and a few other items.

After you fell into one of the general classes, there were four things that you were given points for that determined your handicap. First was cubic inch displacement (420 and up was the top category) and my 440 received only one point for this. Item number two was carburetion. It was zero for multiple carbs, one for 4 barrels, two for 2 barrels, and three for 1 barrel. I got a one for 4 barrels. The third category was weight: 4,101 lbs. and over for car and driver was the top weight class and I received a score of six for that. The final category was transmission, and because Mopar torque flights were so effective, there was a special notation that they received a zero, like a floor shifted 4 speed, where other automatics got a one or a two. So the GTX now had a handicap assigned to it of eight: engine one, carb one, weight six, and transmission zero, totaling eight. The first qualifying run was not for qualifying at all, as that would be done by the handicaps painted on the window, but was actually just a test and tune run. As I came out of the staging area, I noticed the water boxes on both sides of the strip. Now like Jethro Bodine on the Beverly Hillbillies who often said, "Uncle Jed, I been doin' some studying on this," I too had been doing some studying, and I had decided I needed to stay out of those water boxes. They were for cars with slicks to get them started spinning and to clean them; my tires had tread on them in which the water could get trapped, and then drain out on the starting line. So I pulled my car between the two water boxes. The starter, without looking, gave me a "let 'er rip!" arm twirl over his shoulder, and I started my burnout. Now even though I had never been on a drag strip in my life, if there was one thing in the world that I was a well-seasoned pro at, it was doing burn outs in this car. Just as it always did, the GTX started to get a little sideways, which was no problem. I had it well under control, but just at that moment, the starter turned around and saw me coming at him sideways, and he thought I was out of control. He jumped and ran out of the way. When I got stopped, he charged up to my window and most of what he led off with I won't repeat, but the last part I remember well. He said, "If I ever look up and see that little gold car of yours coming at me again, you are out of here for life." After making my run I was surprised that at the end of the track the shutdown area was not completely paved, and even in my street car, I fell off on dirt at probably 50 mph. I'll bet that could get pretty exciting in a really fast dragster.

After the test run, it was now time to race. As we came up through the staging lanes, the track officials would point to who they wanted in each lane. They paired me with a 1968 Dodge Charger, and like mine, it was a 440 car. A '68 Charger was what the bad guys drove in the movie Bullitt. So I was going to get to see how The GTX would stack up against the Bullitt car. It also had an 8 circled on the side glass and windshield, both which were identical to my handicap. So it would be a heads up race. The yellows blinked down as I held my left foot on the brake and loaded the torque converter with just the right amount of throttle that it didn't try to spin. Remember I had done this part a lot. I was careful and just as the last yellow was fully lit, I stomped it to the floor releasing the brake at the same time. Man that drag strip was a lot better to get a bite on than the street. I was gone. The Charger disappeared from peripheral vision immediately, and it was an easy win. These were single eliminations, so the Charger was out for the night. My next time up I drew a '68 or '69 Ford Torino with the big 428 cobra-jet. It was a red car and had a seven handicap, so I had to spot him one car length. As we came to the line, I decided I would do exactly what I did the last time as it had turned out pretty well. Just as I had hoped, this was another easy win. The final round came down to me and a guy who I found out was a regular at this drag strip, and he had of all things, a 1973 or '74 Dodge Monaco, safety bumpers and all. It carried a handicap of fifteen, meaning I would have to spot him seven car lengths and that in an only 1/8th mile race. Even before the race, people started coming up to me when they found out who would be in the final round. They said he always cheated and the car was really a 360 that he billed as a 318, causing him to get three undeserved extra handicap points. As we came to the line, I thought to myself, "Don't red light and you have this in the bag."

This car I was up against was such a dog in my opinion, that I would have no problem overcoming the seven car lengths, especially after how badly I had just beaten those two real muscle cars. So I changed my strategy this time, and I waited until the bottom light glowed green before I took off. When I caught him, my front bumper was right at the back of his front wheel as we went across the finish line. I had just been a little over confident.

After the race we hung around to watch the other classes. I didn't know anyone else there that night except my family. In a little while some guys came up to my dad and me, and said that I had run a faster time than the winner of the showroom optional class, the guys with open headers and slicks. They wondered if I would agree to a grudge race after the big classes finished, and we agreed to it.

As the evening wore on, the crowd got drunker and more rowdy, and my dad and I didn't know that a "grudge race" is a common term. in drag racing; it sounded somewhat antagonistic to us, and Dad voiced his concern about this race. We speculated that they had asked me first and then approached this guy that had won the bigger class, so he had to race to defend his honor. If I beat him and embarrassed him, there might be trouble, so we decided to leave. As we were leaving, we were on the gravel road that wound behind the timing tower and I had the windows down, because even though it was midnight, it was a hot night. I heard the announcer come over the loud speaker and say, "You guys stick around. After the final race in the competition eliminator (which was the highest class), we've got a grudge match between the show room optional winner and that little gold and white GTX that was so fast in the showroom stock class." Once again the old car had made quite an impression on people, and that wasn't the first time I had heard it called that little Plymouth that was so fast, but this time it was from a drag race announcer.

I never went back there. I had confirmed for myself that my car definitely stacked up to the competition, and to me, drag racing was not about whether or not you could catch your grandma's unleaded gas tugboat, if she got to start at half-track. Although that makes me sound bitter, I wasn't. That's the way the competition was set up, and I understand that. It's just that my interest is all about who has the fastest car in a heads up race. That's why I've never understood guys who've been boasting about their car being the fastest and how they are going to outrun someone. Then when it finally comes time to race, they demand to be spotted. Hey, at that point we already know who has the fastest car, and if the guy wanting to be spotted knew that, why did he even want to race. If their bragging was correct, it would go something like, "Yea, that guy thinks he has the fastest car, but I bet he couldn't beat mine by more than fifty feet."

YE OLDE AUTO SHOPPE

A T EACH LEVEL OF MY SCHOOLING I HAD a favorite class. In grade school it was P.E. where we got to do things like play dodgeball and field hockey in the gym when the weather was bad— getting to beat each other's shins with hard plastic hockey sticks was better than scoring a goal any day. In junior high, basketball practice happened during the school day as a class period, making it an easy choice. But my favorite class in high school was, hands down, auto mechanics class.

A few years back, Princeton had built an addition on to the building where the wood shop was housed, and had started an auto mechanics class. They put a sign over the door that read YE OLDE AUTO SHOPPE. This class was available for juniors and seniors only. I so wanted to take it as a junior but my schedule wouldn't allow it— seems they had some kind of nonsense going on that certain classes awarded you credits, and you had to have a certain amount of credits for them to let you out of there with the piece of paper. If not, you just wasted 12 years. So I had to wait until I was a senior to take it.

Auto mechanics was also taught by one of my favorite teachers, Mr. Bill Prichard. By the time I became a senior I had a long history with Mr. Prichard, because he was also the industrial arts teacher known by most people by the simpler title "wood shop." I had been taking Mr. Prichard's wood shop classes since junior high. Mr. Prichard was one of the few teachers that you didn't mess with, or assume their bark was worse than their bite, because under the right circumstance, he would sure lay the wood to you. As you might have guessed, my friends and I were somewhat ornery. So a teacher like Mr. Prichard offered us a challenge. If you wanted to impress your friends with a prank or any kind of shenanigans, doing it in some sweet old ladies class might get you a chuckle, kind of an honorable mention, if you will. Doing it in Bill Prichard's class was like going off the high dive or the advanced run on a ski course; you could really get hurt, and we all knew which end it was that would be hurting, but if you pulled it off and stuck the landing, that mischief could become legend.

Once when we were underclassmen, Mr. Prichard had a student teacher under him for a semester. Mr. Prichard would take the opportunity a lot of times, to leave the classroom with the student teacher. When he did, it would get out of hand because our class could get wild. Mr. Prichard also taught drafting in the classroom side of the wood shop, although I never took that class. The drafting class had these little cloth bags filled with something; they were called eraser bags, and they were lying all over the tables in the class room. We were constantly beaning each other up beside the head with them. One day, as soon as Mr. Prichard left to go to the teachers' lounge, the student teacher got our attention, and he made a deal with us. He said, "Hey guys, managing this class is for my grade in college, and I really need it to be good. So, here's the deal. I will let you do whatever you want, except leaving or hurting one another. Just before it's time for Mr. Prichard to come back, I will alert you, and I expect you to be sitting quietly at your desks studying your books when he comes back." Sometime into the class period, I took a sheet of notebook paper and cut it lengthways in strips about an inch wide. I then scotch taped the pieces together, and on the last piece, I took a pair of scissors and drew the paper across the blade, like ladies do when they curl ribbons when gift wrapping packages. On the other end, I attached another piece of scotch tape. It was so wild in there that it was easy to sneak up behind the student teacher and attach this tail to the back of his belt with the tape; it was perfect. It reached nearly to the ground and the curled portion bounced when he walked. As he promised, the student teacher alerted us when it was time for Mr. Prichard to arrive back, so we all took our seats. Shortly, Mr. Prichard came through the door. He stood there facing the student teacher. He called him by his first name and said, "How were they, Dave?" and the student teacher answered "They were good." Now Mr. Prichard was nobody's dummy, he knew us, and was well aware of how we normally acted. So he further questioned the student teacher, as he gestured to us, sitting there with our faces in our books. "So they have been like this the whole class period, huh?" The student teacher then lied again and said, "Yep." Just then the student teacher turned to walk away. Mr. Prichard then very smugly said, "Hey, that's a nice tail you got there, Dave."

Thankfully, Bill Prichard was not a book learning type of mechanics teacher, but was the hands-on type of teacher, and after a short week or so of orientation in our books, we were out in the shop working on vehicles that townsfolk and students wanted repaired. There were no limitations. We worked on antique cars and current vehicles. We did both mechanical work and body work; some boys even brought in tractors to be worked on. By far, the thing that we spent the most time on was engine overhauls, and that familiarity with the internal combustion engine, has been a great foundation for me. Besides Mrs. Tudor teaching me to read in first grade, and Mrs. Graves teaching me to add and subtract in second grade, the things I got exposed to in this class have been the most instrumental in my career. Mr. Prichard had a nickname for me; he always called me "Banky." I remember one exchange between us like it was yesterday. By the time I was a senior, Mr. Prichard had become our principal, as well as teaching his shop classes. One morning in first hour, he came to the door of our class and called me out in the hall. He told me that they had a school bus's clutch go out on that morning's bus route, and that they needed it repaired before school let out that afternoon. The school had a mechanic for their buses, but he wanted me to go down to the bus barn and help him, so the job could go faster, and just do whatever the mechanic told me to do. The class he was pulling me out of was a class that I didn't feel like I was doing too well in, and this particular day we were having a test. I felt like missing this might be the final straw for the grade in this teacher's mind. So even though I would much rather be under that bus than in a class, I said, "Hey, I'm not doing too good in this class," and Mr.

Prichard's comforting words were, "I'll take care of your grade Banky." And he did.

Along with learning a great deal, we also had a lot of fun. We learned things like: if a guy was lying on his back on a creeper under a fender, and you whacked the top of that fender hard with the side of your fist, you could dislodge a bunch of caked on mud. And when he rolled out from under the car, coughing and spitting, he would be solid dirt except for the whites of his eyes.

In auto mechanics class we would usually be assigned a major project in groups of three or four to work on. David Gentry, Danny McClain, Denny Powers, and I often made up such a team. Once we were overhauling the 292 Y block Ford V8 in Mr. Prichard's own early '60's Ford pickup. After getting the engine torn down and power washed, while breaking the glaze in the cylinder walls with a hone, we found a crack in one of the cylinders. Mr. Prichard said he had a '58 Ford station wagon out at his house that had this same engine in it. He wanted us to get the engine out of it, and use that block instead of the cracked one. I agreed to bring my dad's pickup to school the next day and during shop class, go outside of town the mile or so to Mr. Prichard's house and acreage, get the old station wagon, and pull it to town. When we got to the farm and tried to push the car, we found out the brakes were locked up on it from years of sitting, but we overcame this problem by taking a sledge hammer to the wheels until the brake shoes broke loose from the drums. Of course, this also meant that the car had no working brakes. I had learned from my dad pulling old tractors and vehicles with no brakes, to hook the log chain to the pickup, then run it through a piece of steel pipe a few feet long, wrap it around the frame of the towed vehicle, then go back through the pipe with it, pull it tight, and hook it to the pickup again. With this accomplished the towed vehicle could neither get loose or run into the vehicle towing it, even though it had no brakes. And if you weren't concerned about where the pipe contacted the pickup's bumper or the towed vehicles front end, you were good. We got the car hooked up, and Denny Powers was elected to steer. The rest of us piled into the cab of my dad's truck and took off for town. As I have said before, our town was built on a big hill. There was a succession of hills surrounding it, and I was not in the habit of driving slowly or easily. As we went down the big hill leading from the Prichard's farm towards Princeton, we noticed Powers up in the window waving his arms wildly. Someone voiced, "What does Powers want?" and someone else answered, "I think he wants you to slow down," but our consensus was, "Aw, he's fine," and we continued on at the same speed. When we got back to the school, Powers jumped out of the car and chewed us out for going so fast. He might have mentioned something about how scary it was with the old car's front end wobbling. We just blew him off. A few days later after we had pulled the engine out of the car, it was time to take it back out to the country. I brought dad's truck to school again, and when it came time to leave, we said, "Powers get in there and drive," to which he said, "No way, not after the way you pulled me last time!" I hate to admit it, but I think at this point there might have been some promises made to Powers that what had happened before would not happen again. As politicians often voice when confronted with something they said in the past, my memory fails me in what was actually said, but at any rate, powers climbed in behind the wheel again. My dad's pickup was a '66 Ford with a 352 and a four speed, and it had plenty of pulling power. As we came down the hill in front of the Tasty Freeze, heading east out of Princeton on 136, I floor boarded the truck. There was a railroad bridge at the bottom of the hill, and I estimate we were probably running 80 mph when we crossed that bridge. The three of us in the cab of the truck were laughing our heads off. Back in the station wagon, Powers looked like a clown that had just popped out of a jack-in-the box, wobbling around and waving his arms with a horrified look on his face. When we got to our destination, I pulled the car down the driveway on through the barnyard, and back into the pasture where we had gotten it from. The Prichard's house sat on a hill, with the land falling off steeply on either side. Mr. Prichard had told us when we took the car back, to put it down over the hill to the east side, where he had some old derelict Volkswagen bugs sitting. Surprisingly, when we got out of the truck, Powers was pretty quiet. I guess he either thought it was useless to berate us, or he might have just been addled. At any rate, we told him to stay in there as we rolled the car over the hill. He said, "How am I supposed to stop it?" We said, "Just run it into the side of that old Volkswagen." We thought that would be great fun to watch. When we pushed Powers over the hill, we ran behind the car getting up as much speed as possible so as to get the maximum effect of our miniature demolition derby. We had already calculated that Mr. Prichard would not be very proud of us crashing into one of his old bugs. We decided we'd tell him it got away from Powers somehow, and it was an accident. It turns out we got Powers going so fast that he was afraid to hit the VW, because he might hurt himself. The hill was very steep, and just beyond the bugs, was a cross fence with a pond on the other side. Powers decided that he would turn the old station wagon sharply, and turn back up the hill to stop it before going through the fence into the pond. The old car was light, not having a motor in it, and as he made a sharp left turn on this steep incline the left side wheels, both front and back, came up in the air. This is no exaggeration; you could have walked under them. For a split second the car hung there right at the tipping point, and I remember thinking, "Oh no, we have killed Powers." Fortunately, just before it went over, its momentum stopped and it fell back on its wheels. I for one breathed a sigh of relief.

I don't want you to think from this story that we ever intended to hurt anyone; everything we did was for comedy's sake. And Powers wasn't someone we picked on; among our group of buddies in our class everyone got their turn, and often it was me. The way we treated each other was like a game of musical chairs; if the music stopped and you were the one standing there...well, you know what I mean. Everyone gave as good as they got. Imagine it this way: if there were 6 guys standing outside the back door of the schoolhouse with pre-prepared snow balls, pretty much whoever came out that door next was going to get it, even if you were a nice guy like Powers with a four speed GTO.

On another occasion, Rick Ellsworth and I were alone in the auto mechanics shop when the high school basketball coach came in. He told us that he wanted us to take a floor jack down to the teachers' parking lot, jack up the junior high math teacher's car, and put it on blocks with the rear tires barely clearing the ground. We were all about this kind of stuff, and could very well have come up with it on our own, but Griz (that was our nickname for the coach) had caught us at a slack time. We gladly went the 150 feet or so down to the parking lot, and had the deed done in no time. This was towards the end of the day, Griz had told a lot of the men teachers what he had done, and they were stationed around at strategic spots around the parking lot to watch the fun. The math teacher was a very serious kind of a guy, probably why Griz chose him. He came out, got in his car, cranked it, put it in gear, turned around, and looked over his shoulder. He let out on his clutch, and nothing happened; he didn't move. Then just for good measure, he put it in first gear, and let out on the clutch with the same result. He then got out of the car, looking very frustrated, and hollered at someone else who came over, and ultimately found the problem. He was furious. His face turned beet red; the veins popped out on his neck; and he stormed up the hill and straight to the superintendent's office. Ellsworth and I had been leaning on the doorway of the shop building, watching the math teacher's response, and gazing around at small groups of men busting a gut as they peeked around the edges of buildings and vehicles. When the teacher headed for the Superintendent's office, Ellsworth and I conferred that we were not taking the fall for this, and that if need be, we would readily throw Griz under the bus without hesitation, for putting us up to it. The superintendent came over to the auto shop, where by now he found Ellsworth and me busily working. He asked us to take a floor jack down to the parking lot and get the math teacher's car off of the blocks, to which we acted shocked.

We then pulled the same jack that we had used before down the hill, and saved the day. Looking back, I would imagine even the Superintendent knew what was going on.

During the last period of our last day of school as seniors, there were several of us standing around the door of the auto shop when Mr. Prichard walked up. Gentry said "Hey, Bill! I guess it's okay to call you Bill, now that we're out of school, right?" To this Mr. Prichard responded "Yeah, I guess that's right. Just remember there are a lot of things I've been waiting to call you too."

THE COPS

I CAME OUT OF MY ROOM FOR BREAKFAST one morning and my dad was waiting for me at the kitchen table. He said to me, "How much was your ticket for?" I said, "What?" He said, "The ticket you got last night, how much was it for?" I then said, "I don't know what you're talking about." His response to that was, "Don't lie to me. I saw the cop turn his lights on and get after you." I just stood there dumfounded as I absolutely had no idea what he was talking about. So the best I could muster was, "Where did you see this at?" My dad said, "Downtown at the post office." Now I was really confused. Finally my dad started to explain what he saw, and why he was in our small town post office in the middle of the night. Mom and Dad had some friends that they ran around with that had three daughters; the oldest girl was an early teenager. The mother and the girls were alone at night during the week, as the father worked out of town and only came home on weekends. They had been having trouble with a prowler doing things like scratching on their screens, and turning their water hose on at night, but it never happened when the dad was at home. The husband and my dad had come up with a plan that my dad and another buddy would stake out the house during a week night, hoping to catch the prowler when he didn't expect it. They had not let anyone know, especially any kids, in case word might get out alerting the perpetrator. The house that the family lived in was across the street from the post office, and my dad and his friend knew the postmaster well enough that he agreed to let them sit in the post office to watch the house they were staking out. The house actually was kind of diagonally across the street from the post office, but the Chevrolet garage was directly across the street. It was in this parking lot that the night watchman, our version of a city cop, had backed his patrol car into.

Now let me bring you up to date on our side of the story. Lynn and I were having a quiet uneventful evening, cruising around town and trying to burn our expected quota of gasoline for the day, to help the oil companies of course, when Dave flagged us down. Dave, as he explained to us, was being harassed by two guys in another car, and they were threatening to whip him. When we came up, they had roared off and I considered the incident over. We sat and chatted a while with Dave through our rolled down car windows. When we finished talking, Dave left and said he was headed home. Soon after Dave drove off, I caught a glimpse of those two guys who were bothering him as they crossed an intersection a couple of streets down. They had been hiding a couple of blocks away waiting for him to leave. Dave was headed one direction and Lynn and I were headed the opposite direction, and of course these guys were headed Dave's direction; so I had to get the GTX turned around. Dave lived south of town several miles on the highway, and then on down gravel roads. I was worried these guys would get him out in the country on his way home. This all occurred in the general quadrant of town that my Dad and the night watchman were in. When I got turned around, both Dave's car and his tormentor's car had quite a head start on me. As I came around the block to head their direction, I roared right past the post office and the cop. I went one block and turned right for about three blocks, going by the Methodist, Baptist and First Christian Churches, running at least 80 mph; fortunately, it was also past midnight. We made a jog right, and then an immediate left, down what is referred to as Wildcat Hill past my grandparents' house. This route up through town was Main Street which intersects with Highway 65 at the bottom of Wildcat Hill; there we turned south on the highway. Meanwhile back at the post office, Dad and his friend had watched as Lynn and I roared by the night watchman, and he turned on his lights and pursued us.

It actually ended quite uneventful. Lynn and I caught up to the guys chasing Dave and passed them, and got between them and him. They immediately backed off, and we followed Dave down to his turn off. I absolutely never knew the policeman was back there, and had I ever seen his lights, I would have stopped. We had outrun a cop without even knowing it.

Lynn and I had one more interesting encounter with the GTX and the police. Back then it was not uncommon for us to just be traveling to or from a movie, or anywhere, and me to be driving 90 or 100 mph. We were coming home from Trenton in the middle of the day one time, and I was going up a hill running about 90. I was meeting a big line of cars, and in them was a Missouri State Highway patrol cruiser. He could obviously tell I was flying, because the speed limit by this time was 55mph. I watched in the rear view mirror as his car dove for the shoulder. There were cars behind him and he had to wait for them to come by him before he could make his U-turn to come after me. When I saw him go to the shoulder I floor boarded the GTX. I knew you could really get in trouble for outrunning a cop. My thought was he already knew I was going really fast, but not how fast. So if I opened up and made it over the next hill before he could get turned around, he might not ever get close enough for me to see his lights; he could not know for sure I even knew he turned around. The patrol car was a big Chrysler and it also had a 440 in it, but it was much heavier than the GTX. The road in this section of our county was a succession of rolling hills for miles, and we made it over several of them without seeing the patrolmen. We then came to a little bit of a plateau where there was no immediate hill to get over. There was a main blacktop road that intersected the highway, at this point to the right. It was at least a quarter of a mile down it, if not more, to the first hill. If we continued on the direction we were going, we would soon be into town. I chose to take the blacktop turn-off, hoping I could cover the distance to the first hill before the patrolmen reached that spot. If not, it was completely open country and he could easily spot us going down the road. To my amazement, we made it over that first hill on the blacktop with still no flashing lights in the rear view mirror. We went down that road for several miles, and then meandered around on gravel roads, just killing time for probably an hour. We didn't want to go back to the highway or town in case we might run into the patrolman. After this lengthy time, we finally went back the way we had come. As we approached the intersecting highway, I spotted the patrol car sitting in the roadside park that was at the intersection of these two roads and I thought "Oh no! We have had it." To my surprise he let us go right past him and made no move to stop us. He seemed to be saying to me, "You didn't fool me; I know exactly where you went and I will get you another day."

THE GOAT

B ACK IN AUTO MECHANICS CLASS, I WAS in need of a project. My dad found the perfect one for me. It was a 1967 Pontiac GTO with only a little over 60,000 miles on it. It was a project because it had been in an accident and had damage to both the front end and the right rear quarter panel. The great part was we only had to give a couple of hundred dollars for it. Pontiac GTO was, and is, at the top of my list for muscle cars. We had a family friend that bought a red '66 model GTO brand new. I remember when the GTO Judge came out, our local GM dealer got one in and I would make my mom drive by everyday on the way home from school so I could see that orange Judge setting on the corner of the dealer's lot. That route from school to home continued until the day it sold.

We began working on the GTO under Mr. Prichard's supervision. He showed us how to use a hammer and dolly to straighten sheet metal, and how to use a torch and wet rag to shrink places where the metal had become stretched. During this time I would sometimes take a day off school to scour wrecking yards for parts. Mr. Prichard noticed that after a serious one day "illness," I would often return back to class with an arm load of parts for the GTO. He once told my dad when visiting with him on the street, "I am going to catch Mike in a wrecking yard some school day."

I remember one frustrating occurrence in a wrecking yard in Bethany, Missouri that I frequented. It had a '67 GTO that I had been revisiting for parts. Fortunately the damage on both ends of my GTO was fairly light. On the front end, I had purchased a used fender on one side already, but the front bumper was slightly askew. This wrecking yard in Bethany's GTO donor car had a pristine front bumper that I had priced already, and they had quoted me a price of twenty five dollars. I couldn't afford it that day; so I had been saving up for it. A few weeks later when I rounded up the money for the bumper, I went back to the wrecking yard. When I went out in the yard I could not find the GTO. I went back inside and asked the counter man where the GTO was. He said, "Oh we crushed it last week." This really frustrated me, that rather than make a deal with me on that bumper, they just wasted it instead.

I logged a lot of hours in wrecking yards and saw a lot of colorful junkyard employees, but some of the most memorable ones were the dogs. In those days most junkyard's security measures were dogs, and when Jim Croce sang that "Bad Bad Leroy Brown" was meaner than a junkyard dog, we knew for sure what ole Leroy's disposition was—at least those of us that frequented junkyards. An example of this is something I saw in a wrecking yard in Trenton, Missouri. The first time I ever went to this yard, before allowing me to browse through the cars, they warned me that there was a dog chained to a tree in the middle of the yard, and said, "Don't under any circumstances get within the reach of his chain."

They also pointed to another scraggly dog which was loose. They said, "That one will try to sneak up and bite you, but not if you're looking at him; so keep an eye on him." This made for a very tense shopping experience for a young lad such as myself, but somebody had to do it. When I finally came upon the dog at the tree, I had already had to stare down the scraggly one a couple of times. This one was something to behold. He was chained to the tree with a small log chain, and he was big and black and mean, a perfect specimen for a horror movie. When you got where he could see you, he would lunge at the log chain so hard it would turn him over backwards sometimes, all the while baring his teeth. He wanted you bad! After seeing him up close, I finished rather quickly and went back to the office. Before I left I asked a few questions about that dog. They said they had purchased the wrecking yard a while back, and he came with it already chained to the tree. I asked how they fed him, and they said that they threw his food inside the chain. I guess they pushed in water with a stick. I didn't ask. As I turned to leave I noticed a huge German police dog lying in a corner, and he looked too torn up to still be alive. I said, "What's wrong with him." They said, "He got too close to the chain."

The GTO we had been working on was a gold car with a black vinyl top. We decided we wanted a different color; so I let Lynn pick the color. She chose a medium blue metallic, which after being painted, was indiscernible from a factory '67 GTO color. Then it came time to paint. This was the first time I had ever touched a paint gun. Unbeknownst to Mr. Prichard, I had gotten some verbal instruction from someone I knew who was attending body school. He told me not be afraid to hold the gun close and lay the paint on pretty heavily. As I started to paint, Mr. Prichard was watching over my shoulder and he said, "Watch out Banky. You're going to run it," but after watching for a few seconds, he said, "I'm gonna leave you alone. You're doing a better job than I do" and it did turn out great. The car was already equipped with the factory Pontiac rally wheels, and it was gorgeous.

For a few weeks I was in tall cotton. I was a senior in high school and I owned both a 1967 GTX and a 1967 GTO. For a young muscle car aficionado, it couldn't get much better than this. We had so much fun driving the GTO that we transferred the tags and the insurance from my GTX over to it, and it became my car for a short time. Lynn was more comfortable driving the GTO than the GTX, especially hot rodding it. It wasn't quite the handful that the GTX was when you got on it. Lynn wasn't a tomboy but she also wasn't a frou-frou girl setting around and filing her fingernails and constantly checking her makeup. She never gave me a hard time about my hot rodding and in fact seemed to love it. When I first started dating Lynn, my friends and I were shocked at how the skinny little preacher's daughter could handle a car. The first time it happened we were driving around in Matt's 4 speed car. Lynn asked us to let her drive. Matt asked her if she could drive a stick shift, to which she gave a resounding, "Yes!" Matt and I were having a conversation and not paying close attention. Lynn got in the driver's seat, dropped the clutch and peeled out, wound it up, and speed shifted to second, breaking the tires loose. We were impressed. It turns out, back in Arizona she had a 1966 Mustang GT 289 4 speed. I have always been sad that I never got to see it.

Once when Lynn was driving the GTO with me in the passenger's seat, we were headed north towards Iowa when a Corvette came up behind us. He ran right on our bumper until a passing zone, and then blew around us. Immediately Lynn pushed the GTO foot feed down and stayed with him. We were running 100 mph right behind the Corvette. I had a general rule of thumb, in those days at least when I was in the GTX, about playing with Corvettes. If they had rubber covered painted safety bumpers, I knew they were '73 or newer and were no match for my car, but if they had small chrome regular bumpers although we could handle most small blocks of that age, we might be unlucky enough to encounter a 427 car, which would mean we had bit off more than we could chew. This car that we were behind had small chrome bumpers. As we came over a hill and there was a clear road ahead, I told Lynn, "Well, see if you can get him." Lynn thought better of it and backed off, which was probably a better idea than mine was. But I had given her a vote of confidence that I was willing to ride with her over 100 mph, in the passing lane beside another car on a hilly two lane highway. Going back again to Rod Stewarts Lyrics from Maggie May, "in my eyes you're everything".

I had a memorable experience driving alone one day in the GTO. It was equipped with an automatic in the console with a Hurst dual gate shifter, more commonly referred to as a "his and hers shifter". This meant that if you kept the gear selector in the right hand gate, in the normal PRNDL positions, and selected what gear you wanted, the car did the rest. But if you pulled the shifter towards you into the "his" position, then you controlled the shift points of the forward gears, which was better for racing. Also, there were built in stops so you could not accidentally hit reverse or park while speed shifting. One day on College Avenue in Princeton, I took off from a stop sign headed towards the high school and floored it. Thinking I had it in the left gate, I slammed the shifter forward into second gear, but instead of going into second, it went all the way forward into park. I had the shifter in the "hers" side. The back tires immediately locked up, throwing my chest into the steering wheel, and I skidded to a stop in the middle of the road hunched over the steering wheel. It turns out it did no harm to the car. Apparently GM automatics have a very strong parking pawl.

My GTO project could not have had a happier ending. Its purpose from the start was to eventually sell it and make a profit, for which I had a specific purpose in mind. I had become very fond of it and wanted to see it go to someone who would appreciate it. Mine and Lynn's good friend, Dave Gentry was that guy. This is the same Dave that had sacrificed his spinal health and gave up his chiropractor visits, when the search for the fastest car in the kingdom required it. Dave was always a more than willing participant to any thrill the GTX could give us once the gas pedal hit the floorboard, and was the one who coined the phrase "Get 'er Sideways!" Dave had even helped work on the GTO in auto mechanics shop. He was a trusted friend and a top notch car guy.

Up until this point Dave had been a repressed hot rodder. The car his family had steered him towards was a beautiful Ford with a non-factory metal flake purple paint job, and a pretty sedate 302 two barrel under the hood. Dave missed his calling by not being a comedian. I have often been in that "beautiful" Ford. Did I mention it was ski boat or possibly dune buggy purple metal flake? Yea, I guess I did. Anyway he would stomp on the accelerator, and as absolutely nothing happened, he would slap it on the dash repeatedly while yelling, "Run mother bear, run!"

When Dave decided to buy the GTO it was quite a step up from his Ford snooze mobile. The GTO was no slouch; in fact it also registered 105 in the quarter, and I tried it several times. Dave and I also drag raced it and the GTX a few times. The GTX always handled it. I think the main difference in the two cars is it just didn't get out of the hole as strong as the GTX. I think Dave and I both loved that car.

CAR TUNES

MUSIC MAY BE THE MOST EFFECTIVE stimulant for the emotions that there is. Hearing a familiar song can awaken, or change the direction of a person's emotions, very much like breaking a vile of smelling salts awakens one who has lost consciousness. Hearing a song takes you immediately back in time to when that song was most relevant in your life. It can remind you of loved ones, friends and past romances and it can bring back memories like driving to school each morning or attending a concert. Remembering people or special events can also cause the songs that went with them to come back to your heart. When I think about the events that make up this book, the things that happened in, around, and sometimes because of the GTX, and my relationships with Lynn and my friends, and my teenage years in general, those memories definitely come with a sound track.

Along those lines, many of the things I recall about running around in fast cars in my teenage years have songs interwoven in the memories. For instance, my friend Matt with the Fairlane 500 convertible had inherited a Tommy James and the Shondells eight track tape from one of his older brothers. I loved that tape and we liked to listen to "Crystal Blue Persuasion" and

"Crimson and Clover," but by far the favorite was "Mony Mony." That song was like pushing a secret button that made the accelerator go to the floor, and I remember seeing the speedometer needle bouncing on the peg at the bottom of the speedometer, while "Mony Mony" blared in the speakers, accompanied by the big block Ford playing its own tune through the twin Walker continental mufflers.

My all-time favorite driving song was "Radar Love." I remember being in the old GTX after dropping off a date and coming home across a river bottom, listening to "Radar Love" while cruising along at a hundred and five, and just like the line in the song, "the road has got me hypnotized," I almost realized too late to slow down for an approaching turn.

For those of you who are not aficionados of fast cars and their accompanying songs, I want you to know that there are two categories of songs that are pertinent to a car guy, gearhead, or whatever you want to call us. These two categories are car songs and driving songs. The first category of car songs is simply by definition songs about cars. One of the earliest and most famous is "Hot Rod Lincoln." This song is very familiar to most people with interests similar to mine. It was written in 1955 by a guy named Charlie Ryan, and was covered by many artists including Commander Cody and his Lost Planet Airmen in the early 1970's. What a lot of people don't know is that this song was actually an answer to an earlier song written in late 1950 or early '51 by a man named Arkie Shibley. His song was about two guys, one in a Ford and another in Mercury, who raced for miles through small towns in southern California, and neither could get the best of the other; they stayed side by side. At the end of that song both drivers were shown up when they were passed by a kid in a souped-up Model A. If you are familiar with "Hot Rod Lincoln," you will remember that Hot Rod Lincoln starts out with the line "You've heard the story of the hot rod race, that fatal day, when the Ford and the Mercury went out to play. Well this is the inside story, and I'm here to say, I was the kid that was a drivin' that Model A."

After that, the early '60's surfing and drag racing crowd became a hotbed of car songs, with literally hundreds recorded by many obscure bands, but by far the most popular were the hits of the Beach Boys like "Little Deuce Coupe" and "Giddy Up Giddy Up 409." It was about the legendary Chevrolet 409 engine of the early '60's. I have a friend about ten years older than I who told me a story about a high school buddy of his whose family had lots of money. My friend and some other guys went down into Texas with this boy, to pick up, as the line in the song says, his brand new 409. According to my friend, as they were preparing to drive off, the salesman was standing beside the car telling the kid to take it easy until the break-in period was over. As soon as the guy quit talking, the kid peeled out, throwing gravel all over the salesman.

I liked the Beach Boys song "Get Around" because it had the line in it "Well, we always take my car 'cause it's never been beat." The Beach Boys had another song called "Shut Down," which is a story about a drag race between a 1963 Corvette with fuel injection, and a 1963 super stock Dodge with a cross ram 413. In the song the 'Vette wins. In later years a magazine supposedly did a reenactment pitting two cars the same year and equipment as these cars in a drag race, with quite different results. "Little Old Lady from Pasadena" was a Jan and Dean song that was also recorded by the Beach Boys, and last but not least, who can forget "Little GTO" by Ronnie and the Daytona's.

Now driving songs are a whole different category. These are songs which are favorites of people for whom driving is much more than a means to get from point A to point B, but is, in fact, their favorite pastime. I am not talking about the hundreds if not thousands of songs that make for enjoyable listening on an afternoon drive or a road trip. What I am defining as a driving song, are songs that raise adrenaline levels in a driver; they are songs that have a direct connection to your right foot. Maybe I can let lines from some of my favorites explain it to you. They are songs that "get your motor running" and make you want to "head out on the highway." They make you want to try stuff like "last car to pass and here I go, and the line of cars go down real slow." These songs are for those with the attitude "put me on a highway and show me a sign, and take it to the limit one more time." Every hot rodder feels like that even though "the Cadillac was moving on an open road, that nothing can outrun my V8 Ford." Sometimes this inspiration comes from a song that is not even about cars. Sometimes you just feel like a "737 coming out of the sky, gonna take me down to Memphis on a midnight ride. I wanna move." Who knows what "Wake me shake me Mony Mony" means, but "it feels good. Yeah it feels good." If you are having trouble plugging into this, maybe you need to experience it firsthand, so "Why don't you come with me little girl on a magic carpet ride?"

Here are a few of my favorite driving songs:

"Radar Love" by Golden Earing

"Mony Mony" by Tommy James and the Shondells

"Magic Carpet Ride" by Steppenwolf

"Born to be Wild" by Steppenwolf

"Maybellene" by Chuck Berry

"Helen Wheels" by Paul McCartney and Wings

"Take it to the Limit" by The Eagles

"Traveling Band" by Credence Clearwater Revival

It seems pertinent here to shift gears a little bit while on the subject of entertainment, from music in and about cars, to movies about cars. I would like to share with you a few of my favorite movies from the time, ones I enjoyed and the ones I feel captured the essence of the time and the car culture the best.

American Graffiti. Certainly my favorite and named by many guys my age as the best car movie ever. George Lucas, who is a car guy, made the movie about the cars, the cruising, and the music that accompanied them in his youth. Nothing bad about it, all good.

Two Lane Blacktop. Don't try to watch with your wife or girlfriend. She will think it is slow, boring, and stupid, and might wonder the same things about you. But it's got a couple of great cars. It's the story of two young guy's and it pits the work of their hands, represented by a '55 Chevrolet hot rod, against the Detroit establishment, represented by a new GTO, and an old guy who drove it who was a liar and a fake. I loved both cars. By the way, the '55 is the same car from *American Graffiti.* Also, one scene was filmed in Boswell, Oklahoma.

Bullitt. Steve McQueen, who was the real deal as far as a car and motorcycle guy, has the leading role in this. This is hands down the best car chase scene ever filmed. It features two fast cars, and is real driving and filming with no computer generated junk. At one point in the filming, a car hit a camera and you can see it in the film. The bad guys are in a 1968 Dodge Charger with a 440 magnum. McQueen is chasing them in a 1968 Mustang GT with a 390 high performance engine. The only unrealistic part is the Mustang being able to catch up to the Dodge on the open road. I have driven both 390 Mustang GT's and B-body Mopars with 440's. I know who wins. Turn the show off after the car chase. You will feel about the rest of the show like your wife did about Two Lane Blacktop.

Vanishing Point. How can you not like a movie with one prop, a 1970 Dodge Challenger with a 440 magnum in it. Great, late '60's early '70's culture. I remember everybody in school talking about the surprise ending.

Corky. A bad movie with Tony Blake in it. Has a great street race scene before the opening credits. It is a hard to find movie. Watch the first scene on YouTube, and call it good.

Dirty Mary and Crazy Larry. A movie about this wild couple being chased by the cops the whole show, and Larry outrunning them in a big block Mopar. (Do you see a pattern here?) It has another surprise ending.

Thunderbolt and Lightfoot. Pontiac Trans Am, and did Clint Eastwood ever star in a bad movie? Watch for the guy with the bunnies.

GOIN' TO THE CHAPEL

I N THE LATE FALL OF THE NEXT YEAR, some 14 months after our meeting, I asked Lynn to marry me. The GTX was the setting for this event, and just like Lynn and myself, we all three were entering into a transition period—us from boyfriend and girlfriend to man and wife, and the GTX was going to transition from hauling around fun loving kids to young adults with a purpose other than fun.

The first order of business was to go find the ring. This was the purpose for the money earned from the sale of the 1967 GTO. On the trip to a larger town to find the ring, I made a left-hand turn out of the right-hand lane, Lynn immediately said, "Mike! You can't do that!" Which showed that although I had become quite adept at handling the GTX while sideways, I had a few things to learn about driving in a town with more than one blinking red light? This was not the first time I had heard, "Mike! You can't do that!" from Lynn concerning traffic laws. In Trenton they had recently put a new section of highway 65 through the east side of town, and even though it was a two lane road, it was built more like a modern divided road and had acceleration ramps leading up onto the roadway. These were the only ramps like this near our hometown, and every time we left Trenton going back to Princeton I would floor the GTX at the bottom of the ramp. It would just reach 100mph at the top where I would then let off and merge into the northbound traffic. The first few times I did this Lynn would say, "Mike! You can't do that!" and my response was "it's an acceleration ramp, and I am accelerating." To my memory, I did it every time we ever went up it.

This was my senior year in high school and Lynn had a job at a local grocery store as a checker. Lynn's day off was Tuesday and by this time I had pretty much adopted a 4 day school week myself, also taking Tuesdays off. Even though the car had been found, and there was no longer a need to locate parts for the GTO, I had a new mission. Besides preparing for a wedding which was mostly all Lynn, ever since the movie *American Graffiti* I thought I needed a deuce coupe, and in those days it was not unreal to imagine finding a fairly complete old car in a field. We called it "vintage tin." It seems like most of my searches took me into southern Iowa. I guess having gone the other three directions, looking for the fastest car I could find, and then parts for the GTO, I decided to go north this time. Although I am sorry to say there is no Deuce coupe in my history, at least not at the time of this writing, I did find some very cool stuff.

Once in the little town of Seymour, Iowa, I was driving around town and noticed some old cars sitting around a building. The doors were open on this building, and when I stopped, a very elderly gentleman came out. We began to chat about old cars and he invited me in to see some of his old cars in this building. This man was a retired doctor who really loved cars. His building was not like ones you see with tile on the floor, and decorations around. It was just an old sheet iron building with a lot of junk strewn around, and some very valuable cars in it. The thing I remember is I got to sit in the seat of a 1937 Cord boat-tail Speedster. The old fellow told me how it was front wheel drive with an aluminum V8 engine, and had an electronically shifted 4 speed transmission. I can still see in my mind the little chrome knob that you used to select the next gear. It was very small, like a drawer pull on a desk. The Doctor told me that after you selected your next gear with the little knob, you then stomped the clutch and the car automatically shifted. How cool! Also impressive to me were the eight large diameter exhaust pipes coming out of the hood cowling on each side –something that I had only seen in books. I even took my dad back there a few days later, and we once again enjoyed visiting with the old doctor.

Another time Gentry and I were in Lamoni, Iowa when we found a guy who had a lot of hot rod stuff. When we were about ready to leave, he took us out to a little old garage like the ones that were popular in model T days. He swung open the wooden garage doors, and backed inside was a yellow '70 Challenger R/T 440 6bbl with a 4 speed. He was frustrated with it because it had a rod knocking. He said that he would sell it "as is" for $700. Imagine that.

About this time, Lynn's sister was dating a guy who was going to body school and we had the opportunity to get the GTX painted. Ever since that incident with the driver's door, the paint on that door had not quite matched. It was just a shade of gold off the original. The car also had rust in the back quarter panels and the driver's floor board was rusted out. We left the car at the school for a week and it came out looking great.

That spring Lynn wanted me to meet her extended family in Oklahoma and Texas. She also wanted to go there to shop for fabric for her bridesmaid dresses, because of better availability and the fact her cousins from there were actually going to be the bridesmaids. We borrowed my Mom and Dad's nearly new bright red Ford LTD for the trip. Lynn's mom went with us and we figured it would be more comfortable and less noisy for her than the Plymouth. The LTD had a set of ET 5 spoke mags that Dad had put on it, and it was really sharp and flashy for the time. This was my first time to ever drive in traffic in a big city, and it was also my first time to drive on a long trip. Divided highways, or "four lanes" as we called them, were also new to me. On arriving at our destination, we began to drive around in north Texas. We were in Denison, Texas, and I had gotten used to the divided roads. We happened to be in an older section of town, and I pulled up to a stop sign in the left lane, thinking it was a divided road. When the light turned green, here came all of the cars right at me. We were on a two lane. As Lynn and her mom made whooping noises, that you can't understand unless you are a part of that family, I looked to my left and I was right in front of a drive thru liquor store. I quickly turned left as the cars approached, went right under the awning and passed the drive thru window then made a right and stopped at the same light I had just been at—crises averted.

When we got back home from Oklahoma, Lynn focused on finishing up our wedding plans and I focused on finishing up high school. I was scheduled to graduate May twentieth and our wedding was scheduled for June twenty-sixth. So I was a single adult for approximately 36 days.

I had got a job at an auto parts store in Trenton, Missouri a couple of weeks before the wedding, and my boss graciously let me off early on Friday, because it was the day of the rehearsal dinner. He also, of course, let me have Saturday off as well. I was truly thankful for this even though it was a small amount of time, having a job and being responsible was very important to me. No longer than I had worked there, I didn't have the attitude that they owed it to me. On that Friday I had run my route delivering parts to country mechanics in my own car, working my way towards Princeton. When I was finished I was off for the weekend. I remember driving along a ridge after the last delivery in the old GTX and truly feeling I was on top of the world.

As the wedding approached, I had a grand plan for involving the GTX in the festivities. When we came out of the Church to leave, I had planned a tire smoking, window rattling, burnout on our departure. The night before the wedding, after the rehearsal dinner, Lynn left with her bridesmaids, so some of my buddies and I went out running around. We guys decided that Gentry and I should drag race the GTX, and the GTO, one more time for posterity's sake before I became an old married man. We headed out of town north, and instead of waiting till we got out of town, we floored it in both cars and went right up through town at probably 80 to 90 mph. When we got to the north end of our favorite old quarter mile spot, we pulled in beside each other and immediately we saw red flashing lights coming our way. The highway patrolman pulled right in behind us. While we were receiving our respective tickets, Lynn and her carload of bridesmaids came by. Imagine them looking for me at the highway barn. I heard later how upset Lynn was thinking they might put me in jail, and we wouldn't get to be married the next day. Thankfully, in the wild, wild Midwest of that day and time, drag racing was not a jail offense. That pretty much threw cold water on my burn out plans the next day, I felt like that would be tempting fate. Also there were cars lining both sides of the street going both directions with just one very narrow lane between them. If I had been dumb enough to still try it, I am afraid the GTX would have looked like a ball in the pinball machine bouncing off those cars .

Our friends made sure the GTX was properly decorated with toilet paper and shaving cream. We had already made arrangements to take it to dad and mom's house and trade it for their car to take on the honeymoon. Dad was going to clean the car up for us. It turns out the sun was hot that afternoon and the shaving cream stained the fresh paint on the car. It wasn't real noticeable but for the rest of the time, until we sold the car, at just the right angle you could still read "just married" on the hood.

NEWLYWEDS

W E WENT ON OUR HONEYMOON TO Liberty, Missouri only a couple of hours away. We were married on a Saturday, and I had to be back at work on Monday morning. We came home from Liberty to our own home in Trenton, a trailer house we had rented a couple of weeks before, as soon as I had got the job. Lynn had gotten a job as secretary at a loan company in town. We had our trailer house with her VW and the GTX in the driveway, and a 250 Yamaha that I had recently bought sitting on the patio. Life was good.

We were married on June twenty-sixth, and on the Fourth of July we went back to Princeton for the annual celebration and watermelon feed. This was the first time I had gotten to be around my buddies since I had been married, and it was only about six weeks since we graduated. Some of them told me how lucky they thought I was, and that gave me a great feeling of satisfaction.

I never would let any of my friends drive the GTX, and there was never much of a reason for Lynn to drive it when we were dating, but now that we were an old married couple, it was just our family car. One day I was behind the parts counter at work and Lynn called. It was her day off and she was calling from a store in the shopping center across the street from where I was. She said, "Look out the window at the parking lot in front of the clothing store," and when I did I saw the GTX sitting there with a huge dent in the door. A lady had backed into it in the parking lot and ruined the same door that we had already replaced when we were first dating.

Not long after this, we were on our way one evening to a church function for youth at the new church we had just joined in our new town. The picnic was at a lake maybe thirty miles away, and the pastor had asked me to speak to the kids. It was a big hurry for us to get off work and make it to the lake for the start of the meeting. As we were traveling through the country in the GTX on a road unfamiliar to me, we came around a corner and there sat a '67 satellite with a pristine driver's door. The car was sitting behind a house beside a shed, and it obviously didn't look as though it had been driven for a while. I stopped immediately and went up and knocked on the door. A lady came to the door and I asked her if she would consider selling the door off the old car, and she said "Yes." I then asked her what she might want for it. She said, "Would you give five dollars for it?" and I quickly agreed. Even though this was very reasonable, I was just excited that I could afford it. In that day and time an old car like that was probably not worth over fifty dollars for the whole thing. I opened my trunk and got out my tool box and had the door off in no time. I was able to sit it behind the front seats in the back floor board. We then went on to the church function and arrived just a tiny bit late, but hey, we had a five dollar door.

We only lived in Trenton four months before moving to Southern Oklahoma. Lynn's parents had already moved there, and this was the area where both her mother and father had grown up. Surprisingly this was my decision not Lynn's; she only went along with it. She actually had me out looking at houses with a realtor because she wanted to put down roots, and not throw our money away renting when we could be buying. When I told her I thought we should move to Oklahoma she was agreeable to my leadership in our new family, but had to get her mind right because she had never lived in rural Oklahoma, but in Dallas, Texas and Arizona; both were very progressive. Going to Oklahoma to visit her grandparents was like going back in time, and it was hard for her to imagine living there. One thing about it was if she needed a transition time between her Arizona life and rural Oklahoma, two years in Princeton came in very handy.

When we called our landlord to tell him we were leaving, he said, "I was just going to call and tell you that that I have sold my trailer house and you are going to have to move."

Lynn's dad brought a truck and small trailer along with his brother-in-law and one of his niece's husbands to take our household stuff and my Yamaha, back to Oklahoma. Lynn and I spent the last couple of nights in Missouri at Mom and Dad's house in Princeton. I remember sitting in the driveway there and attaching a trailer hitch to the rear bumper of the GTX so we could tow her VW. We still had the homemade tow bar that Lynn's dad had someone make for it, when he pulled it to Princeton from Oklahoma a couple of years before.

Early in the morning we said goodbye to my mom and dad and little brother, and took off. Just as we got to Kansas City the Plymouth started missing. I thought "Oh no, what kind of problem are we going to have to deal with?" but upon opening the hood I found that it was only a plug wire that had fallen off, and I replaced it and we continued on. The GTX got 14 mpg towing that VW, and it was completely full of clothing and small household Items. We were using the little car like a suitcase. 14 mpg is also exactly what my car normally got on the highway; so it basically didn't even know the Volkswagen was back there. Although that does not sound like bad fuel mileage, that was for sensible highway driving; when you were hot rodding it I could swear you could see the fuel gauge go down before your eyes.

Does this little guy look like he'd
run over anybody?

I was thrilled when my Dad installed
an ignition switch in my beloved
"Flash" so I could play-start it. Now I
had keys of my own!

My little brother Steve. Wasn't he a cutie? We are all thankful he survived my childhood.

Steve was always my more than willing side kick to whatever new stunt I was trying to pull off. Apparently on this day we were cowboys.

My 1965
Honda
CB160

When my 16th birthday finally rolled around and
my parents surprised me with my old '53 Ford,
I felt like I had finally arrived.
Alot of good times were had in the old '53.

Maybe the first picture ever taken of me and the GTX. I had no idea at the time how much this car would impact my life.

Finding the GTX pailed in comparison to finding Lynn. This picture was taken on our first Valentines Day together, a mere 5 months after we met and began dating.

Lynn and my '53 Ford on a beautiful fall day.
I held onto the old '53 for a little while after
getting the GTX. This picture was taken just a
few weeks after Lynn and I started dating. A
few months later, on my 17th birthday, Lynn
surprised me with a poster she had made of
this shot.

My 16 year old self next to my '53 Ford.
Taken the same day as the picture
above.

Me sanding on the 1967 GTO project in front of "Ye Olde Auto Shoppe" at Princeton High School.

Two beauties. Lynn standing beside the finished '67 GTO, that she picked the color of. My good buddy Dave ended up buying this car from me. He is still an avid GTO enthusiest to this day.

Me with the GTX and the GTO. I thought it was cool then but it seems even cooler now.

The GTX still sporting some numbers from a drag strip the night before.

This picture of Lynn ran in the local newspaper announcing our engagement.

We did it!

This picture was snapped just before we left the church in our matching blue leisure suits.

As we left the church that beautiful June Day, the GTX served as our chariot, escorting us to the rest of our lives. In the right light, you could read "Just Married" on the hood of that car up until the day we sold it.

My 1971 Kawasaki H1 MACH III.
Greased Lightening.

My nephew James' 1961 Studebaker Lark.

Here is the car as it set at Wayne Cox's farm in Effingham, IL on the day we were reunited with it after all those years.

Pulling back in after taking our old car for a little spin, for old times sake.

On the night Wayne Cox came to town to swap GTX's.
What a sight: three real 1967 440 GTX's in my shop overnight.

Wayne "Spanky" Cox. The nicest guy you'll ever meet.
Shaking on the deal. We are so thankful for the role he
played in re-uniting us with our car.

These keys miraculously re-appearing in my life acted as a sort of catalyst, igniting in me this dream of finding my car again.

While still hunting for my GTX, I painted this model GTX to look just like it. Now here it is, setting on the real thing. It was special to be able to photograph them together. The dream finally becoming reality.

Getting the car back wasn't the end of the story.

It was only the beginning.

Durant man reunited with long lost love

By REGINA PHILLIPS
Staff Writer

Let nothing stand between a man and his life, liberty or pursuit of that first set of wheels that put his fate in action.

Mike Banks was 16 when the outside of a golden 1967 Plymouth GTX caught his eye.

"I was looking for the fastest thing could find for the best price," Banks said.

With these features, the GTX started spinning the wheels of young Banks' destiny.

Since the car was paying for itself one race at a time, he said he still had enough change left over to play the jukebox at the local hangout.

"I punched the numbers on the jukebox, and Lynn and her sister came to me, and Lynn and her sister came to me and said, 'We heard you have a fastest car around. Can we have a ride?'"

He made an impression all right.

Not only did he have Lynn's heart racing, but, to the contrary Mr. Crisp's neighbors, he was unforgettable.

"When Mike would come and pick me up, the neighbors would have to hold onto their windows because his car would shake them." Lynn said.

"And when we would set out in the car, he would leave it running because it was cold. They'd say, 'I wish that Banks boy would let her out and go home.'"

The car was also well known elsewhere. "It had a reputation. People would see that car and really get on it — start squealing their tires and everything," Lynn said, "even when we went to a town 80 miles away."

No wonder Lynn said, "We would run through the quarter every Sunday, before and after church."

That must have given Mike an idea. In between popping the question, he decided to pop the question right there in his car.

On June 28, 1970, at the First Baptist Church in Princeton, Mo., he let the GTX sit still long enough to get married. That's when friends decided to render a detail job. The car awaited the newlyweds, draped in crepe paper and doused with shaving cream.

And that's how the couple drove down the first stretch of their lives together. Mike had both his beauties — the one decked in a matching blue leisure suit and his golden gift on wheels.

Little did Lynn and the road led them on a move to Palmer, pulling Lynn's Volkswagen behind the GTX.

But, in December 1979, when gasoline prices had spilled over $1 per gallon, Mike and his GTX came to a crossroads and had to part ways. Mike sold his treasure to a man in Duncan.

Still, he had Lynn and new daughter Kristen. Later came Charity.

In spring 1997, Mike became interested in tracking down that memorable GTX.

One day in the attic he came across a carbon copy of the car's last Bryan County registration. Aha! A vehicle identification number. He traced it to two different men in southern Missouri, both former owners.

And then he found the little rascal — Wayne "Spanky" Cox, that is, a Plymouth enthusiast in Effingham, Ill., and owner of about 400 vehicles. Some of them are even stored in a heated building — one of which was a 1967 Plymouth GTX.

Spanky said he stumbled upon the car by mistake. The truck driver spotted it while taking a short-cut route and had to go a mile or two before he could turn around to scope it out. Dennis Wilbanks did not want to sell the car at first, but Spanky talked him into it.

The tires barely got settled on Illinois soil when the Oklahoma cat found satisfied them out.

Mike, along with his family, took a summer vacation to go visit the long

TWO DECADES and several states could not keep Mike Banks from rediscovering his first car. He is taking the keys from Wayne "Spanky" Cox of Effingham, Ill., who was the last owner of the car. Banks handed over keys to a twin 1967 Plymouth GTX he located and restored to trade with Cox.

lost matchmaker. He brought along the old set of keys he had found still bound in their leather pouch inside an old recliner.

Mike walked up to the car, new red and decided to give it the test. "I put the key in the trunk, turned it, and the lid popped open. That was all he needed."

"He has always dreamed of going to a car show, walking the keys in the trunk and having it up in the show said, 'When that trunk popped open, there was a moment of silence. It was like, 'Nobody talk. He is one with the car.'"

Well, actually, the car still belonged to Spanky. And he did not want to sell it.

But there is always room for negotiation.

Spanky said he would be willing to trade, one 1967 GTX for another. So, Mike was on a mission to find a twin. A scramble double was located in March and with Mike spent the next year and a half himself to the swap.

Mike and Spanky exchanged a few photos and information through the

mail until their deal came Sunday night to find our Spanky would be in town Monday morning to make the exchange.

"I hate to give it up," Spanky said. "But I know how it is, wanting your old car back."

"He's been like a little kid," Kristen said. And Lynn joked with him about being more excited to get the car than when he took her to the hospital to give birth to Kristen and Charity.

"I thought it was because of me he had to sell the car." Kristen said, then she laughed. "So I thought, when I get rich and famous, I'll have to find it and buy it back." Maybe the automobile angel let her off the hook.

Though the girls never really formally met the machine, they became acquainted with dad's GTX. "It's hard to believe the car is actually here," Kristen said. "It's like a legend. I've heard about it all my life."

Now that her folks' love has materialized, the moral of this story, as if determined through much discussion, is a man will be reunited with his true love will find the road to the Banks.

"And you can take the drive to the Banks.

Phillips, Regina "Durant Man Reunited with Long Lost Love." *Durant Daily Democrat* [Durant, OK] 4 March 2001: 1. Print.

The Durant Daily Democrat ran this article on the front page of the Sunday paper.

DOWN IN THE NATION

A S WE TURNED OFF OF HIGHWAY 69/75 AT the Platter exit some 540 miles from my home, and just seven miles before entering Texas, this move suddenly started to get real to both Lynn and me. As we traveled the four miles down this little country road to a town that actually was no longer a town at all, just a tiny little community of houses, the reality of this move sank in for both of us. We were not just visiting to leave in a few days. This was going to now officially be our home. Neither of us spoke this out loud, but we were both feeling exactly the same way.

For me the search for a job was paramount and I got started on it right away. I decided to look in Texas primarily because it had more business opportunities. Denison, Texas was just across the Red River from our little town of Platter; so I started my search there. I had only looked a couple of days when I walked into the front door of a business on Armstrong Avenue, called Grayson Fire Extinguisher Company. I walked very confidently, and I thought professionally, up to the front counter and asked the lady behind it, "May I speak with Mr. Grayson, if he is in?" She then laughed at me and said, "You're not from around here are you?" I answered, "No," while wondering how she could tell. She then told me, "This is Grayson county Texas." I got the job.

This job required me to contact businesses to check their fire extinguishers or sell them new ones. We had contracts with many of the places I visited. My job was to walk their factory, either once a week or once a month, and check the tags on the extinguishers. I would take the extinguishers that were out of date or had been used back to our shop to be serviced and leave a "loaner" in their place. We also serviced automatic systems in places like restaurants and nursing homes. For this part I had to pass a test in Austin for the State Board of Insurance. My route was entirely in Texas and consisted of Paris on Mondays, Denton on Tuesdays, and Dallas on Wednesdays. Both Thursday and Friday I spent in Sherman, the town bordering Denison to the south. The vehicle I drove was a Ford F150 cargo van with no windows in either the back or side. It also had no air-conditioning, making it very challenging in the hot Texas summers. My training consisted of riding for one week, while my boss drove, and then driving the next week while he rode with me. The week after that I was on my own. Now remember, I was 18 years old and came from a town where it was 25 miles to the closest real stop light, and we were the county seat. The week that I drove and the boss rode with me, after turning too sharply in the long van and bumping up over a curb with the rear tire, embarrassingly for the third time, I said, "I hit another curb," to which my quick witted boss replied, "I think you actually missed a couple of them back there." Elm, Main, and Commerce are the three main streets through downtown Dallas. They go through what is referred to as "the canyon" because of the sky scrapers on each side. Two of these streets are also one way. Within the first few weeks of going by myself, I had the terrifying experience of becoming part of the "I turned the wrong direction on Elm Street" club of Dallas. When I saw what I had done, I ducked into an alley before the first approaching car reached me.

We had moved to Oklahoma at the end of October. By Christmas time I was pretty homesick, having never been away from my family before. Christmas that year was on a Saturday. Lynn and I had planned for me to get off work on Friday, jump into the car, and drive all night Christmas Eve. In those days it was a 12 hour trip back to Princeton, being two lane highway nearly all the way. We would then spend Christmas day and night at home, and leave to go back on Sunday morning, so I could go to work on Monday. On Thursday afternoon when I came in off my route, my boss called me into the office and told me that he and his dad, who was the owner (Mr. Grayson), had talked and they had decided to give me Friday off to travel home. Needless to say I was ecstatic. I hurried home. We threw some stuff into the car, and we drove all night that night instead of Christmas Eve.

I worked at this job only a year, but in that year I put in 60,000 miles behind the wheel of that van. I also got to know the area very well, and seeing the inside of huge factories and how things are made in them, was very educational.

One of the places I called on was the Volkswagen dealer in Sherman, and I always dealt with the parts manager. One day I went in and the parts manager was nowhere to be found. When I asked where he was the man said, "Oh, we fired him. You don't know a good parts man, do you?" Seeing an opportunity I didn't want to miss, I looked him in the eye and answered "me." Once again I got the job.

When we first moved to Platter, we lived for the first couple of months with Lynn's parents in a 10 x 50 trailer house, but in a couple of months we bought a trailer house of our own. It was a 12' x 55', but with only one family living in it, it was plenty of space for me and Lynn. It was on the edge of Platter (If there was an edge of Platter) which was actually about 100 yards from the center of Platter. This trailer house was already sitting on the corner of eighty acres that some of Lynn's extended family owned, and they graciously offered for us to leave the trailer on their property rather than have to find a location to move it. I had great fun as we had the run of those 80 acres. It had a creek with a cable to swing on over it, and was just a beautiful property.

Lynn had two cousins that lived in the Dallas area, and they and their husbands would often come up on the weekends. We were all roughly about the same age and we had great fun together. Their two husbands had both grown up in the city, and they loved to come up to the country on weekends when they could. We shot guns and bows and arrows and crossbows, and lifted weights and had a great time. On one occasion, one of the guys had bought his first ever shotgun. We all took it down in the pasture to shoot. There was a big ditch on this property, and the men that owned it were both in the construction business; they used it to dispose of their building refuse. There was a pile of one gallon paint cans at the edge of the ditch, and it was a large pile with dozens of cans. I was throwing them up in the air, and the guys from Dallas were shooting at them. They weren't having much luck hitting them. This was their first ever time shooting a shotgun at a moving target. At one point I decided to show off, and I had one of the guys throw one of the paint cans up in the air for me. It wasn't very far away and I hit it dead center with the 12 gauge load, and it just turned the can wrong side out. All of a sudden this brown stuff rained down on all of us. Immediately, someone in the group said, "Do you smell that?" It turns out some guy at the construction site had taken a dump in one of those paint cans and put the lid back on it tight. That happened to be the very one I showed my expert marksman skills on.

There is a saying, "You can take the boy out of the country, but you can't take the country out of the boy." I brought our Princeton antics with me to Oklahoma. My wife's sister married a guy who was also from Princeton, one class ahead of me in school, and they moved to Platter also. We were always doing something that the locals deemed crazy. My father-in-law eventually bought a house that had an old store building beside it, and we would work on stuff in it. Some of the local teenage boys would come hang out there to see what we were working on. One day they were talking about a movie they had watched and wondered how they did those cop turns. The brother-in-law said, "Mike will show you how to do a cop turn," but the kid didn't believe I would do it. Lynn had a favorite aunt that was in her 70's and couldn't drive. After Lynn moved there, Aunt Sallie gave $300 for an old yellow Ford Maverick so Lynn could drive her to town. We kept it at our house and used it like our own car. I told that kid to get in and took him down the street at about 40 mph, and did a cop turn. It scared him half to death.

Once Lynn and I were in Platter in her Volkswagen and I went around a corner so fast that the right side wheels came off the ground. Volkswagen suspensions are made in such a way that if you jack up the back end, the tires tip under. When the wheels came back down the right rear wheel was tipped under causing us to momentarily be out of control. We happened to be in front of the post office, and nearly ran into the large, iron, post office box that sat outside, missing it by only inches.

Besides driving that old Maverick around town, like it was the last heat of a demolition derby, we were also famous for ripping through the streets of Platter on a dirt bike, and an old go-kart that I had bought off a couple of kids for $15. It was antics like this that caused Lynn's cousin's husband that lived in Dallas and came up frequently, to start calling me and the brother-in-law the "Dukes of Platter."

Another cousin's husband called me one day and told me he had a 1963 Plymouth Valiant that he had been working on and could not get it to run . The city was forcing him to get it off the street, and if I wanted it, I could have it for the $70 it cost to rent a tow dolly to bring it to me. After I got it, I found he had tried to put a set of points in it, and had removed the distributor, thinking it was necessary to do that to replace points. When he put the distributor back in, he got it in the wrong spot causing the car to backfire and break the teeth of the little gear on the bottom of the distributor.

After that, no matter how many times he pulled the distributor up and put it back in a different spot, it still wouldn't run because of the broken gear. All I had to do was knock out the roll pin in the bottom of the distributor, and replace the two dollar gear, and put it back in time, and I was in business.

I had a ball in this car. Someone had put a shifter in the floor for its three speed transmission, and it had the famous leaning tower of power, the legendary slant six for an engine. It also had one of the ugliest body styles that Mopar, or any other company for that matter, ever came up with—topped off by the fake impression of a spare tire pressed into the sheet metal of the trunk lid.

We lived down a one lane gravel road that dead ended at our trailer house. There were barbed wire fences on either side, making it a very narrow lane. Once going to work in the Volkswagen, the neighbor's bull was out. As I passed him, he felt hemmed in between the fence and the car, and kicked a sizable dent in the front fender. I had been driving the VW to work to save gas instead of the GTX, but now I had my old Valiant to drive to work. Literally every time I left our trailer in that car, I would floor board it leaving our driveway, and run it through all three gears. When I got to the end of our road, I would throw it back up into second gear as I cramped the wheel right, and power slid around the 90 degree corner throwing up a rooster tail of gravel.

Once I was at the dealership I worked at, and I told the service writer I needed a state inspection sticker for my old Valiant. So he wrote me out one and I took it home and stuck it on the windshield. A few days later the Valiant was sitting out the back door of the dealership's garage, and it was backed in facing the large door. The service writer, while walking through the shop, noticed that neither of the front turn signal lenses could be seen on the car, they both were bent up facing the bumper above them. He came over to my counter and said, "Mike, go out there and bend those turn signals down on that car. It has a brand new inspection sticker with my signature on it, and you cannot even see the turn signals." Woops.

I was coming home from work one evening and the old Valiant started vibrating so badly that it was just jumping up and down. I thought a U-joint was about to let go, but just kept cramming it, hoping I could make it home before the drive shaft came flying out. I wasn't really worried about it, I thought it was more funny than anything. All of a sudden something on the front seemed like it exploded, and in fact, it had. The right front tire blew out. That bumping that I thought was so funny was a knot on the right front tire. I now found myself running 75 mph on a raised section of highway, where past the shoulder, the ground fell off for 40 feet, and the old Valiant going all over the road. Thankfully, I got it slowed down without going over the edge.

Another time I was coming home in the VW bug when I hit a huge pot hole in the blacktop road. I criticized myself for hitting it because I knew it was there; I went this way every day. I just wasn't paying attention. As this was happening, I saw movement in the rear view mirror. It was kind of like a streak went by. I pulled the VW over and as I got out, I noticed the left rear hubcap was missing. It was what I had seen streak by; hitting the chug hole had knocked it off. I went over to the side of the road and retrieved the hubcap from the fence row. As I bent down to pick it up, I noticed something lying in it. When I inspected it, I found it to be a cotter pin. I went back to the car and looked down at the axle where the cotter pin belonged. I saw that the nut that held the brake drum and the rear wheel on the car had run out in the absence of the cotter pin to hold it on; it was just about to clear the last thread and fall off. What are the odds of me hitting a hole I knew to avoid and knocking the hubcap off, and then me catching a glimpse of it in my mirror? What are the odds of that cotter pin staying in that hubcap as it bounced along for 40 feet, and then me noticing it to alert me to check that axle nut? Perhaps a guardian angel is the answer to this, and many of the other crazy things I survived. If that is the case I would imagine Mercer County, Missouri is a tough assignment for a guardian angel to draw.

Even though they were not the GTX and were not fast, I had a lot of fun in Aunt Sallie's '70 Maverick, and Lynn's '67 Bug, and a '63 Valiant that a cousin gave me. In true Oklahoma fashion, when I got through with the Valiant, I traded it for a washing machine and a .22 rifle. I tried to get them to throw in a one eyed dog, but they were too attached to him.

GREASED LIGHTNING

S HORTLY AFTER MOVING TO OKLAHOMA, and while still working for the fire extinguisher company, I was checking the fire extinguishers at a garage in Sherman and went into an old store room. I could hardly believe my eyes. There sat a Kawasaki H1 3 cylinder Mach iii. This was the motorcycle of my dreams. When I was a kid, back in my 160 Honda days, my Dad and I were in a motorcycle shop in an adjoining town to buy some parts for my Honda. While standing behind the person that was ahead of us in line I heard a loud wailing like half a dozen lumber jacks had just barged in with chainsaws running full throttle. Then I caught out of the corner of my eye through the plate glass in the front of the store, a motorcycle standing nearly straight up on its back wheel, coming by at what looked like 70 mph, and this was in town, on a brick street. The guy behind the counter said "that is so and so," and called him by name. When it was my turn at the counter I asked the same guy what kind of a bike that was, and he said "A Kawasaki Mach iii." In my head I said, "Uh huh I thought so." You see I had been reading about them in cycle magazines but had yet to encounter one in the wild. I had a magazine at home that had an article where they had tested one. They had uncrated it at a drag strip, and with no break in, it ran

12.70 s at like 112 mph. A simple explanation of what I understand about this model is that Honda had started working on the CB750, a bike which would literally end up revolutionizing the motorcycle industry. Some say Kawasaki had a 4 cylinder 4 stroke motorcycle in the works also, but at some point Kawasaki put a hold on that, and hurriedly developed a light weight 500cc triple cylinder 2 stroke. It was good at one thing, going fast in a straight line from a dead stop, especially while running beside a 750 Honda.

These bikes had startling acceleration. Their power band started at 7000 rpm, and at wide open throttle, when you hit that point you knew it, and you better be hanging on. These bikes had two nicknames: one was "the widow maker" as they were notorious for bad handling and a high speed wobble, and the other was "crotch rocket," and even though that has been a common term in the last 30 plus years, it is the earliest bike that I remember being called that. I desperately wanted one of these and actually test rode a used white '69 model, but I couldn't afford it. Now here I was standing in front of one. It was dust covered and had the heads and cylinder jugs removed. I asked the man in charge and he said that it was his and he had no interest in it anymore. I asked him how much he would sell it for, and he said $35. Now I had less money than I had back when I had test ridden the '69 model. However, with a loan from someone till pay day, I came back after work and got my h1. I brought it home and found that the number 2 piston was burned, which was a common problem on these bikes. The next week I called on a motorcycle shop in Lewisville, Texas, and I asked the guy in charge if he knew where I might find used pistons and cylinders for an h1. He smiled as he reached down under the counter and pulled out a sack with these very items in it. He said that he had just put a big bore kit on a guy's bike in town, and these were the take offs. He wanted $15 for them. So I was in business. At this point we were still living with my wife's parents in their small trailer house that sat on the property of the church my father-in-law was pastoring. The sight had once been the school for this little community until consolidation had put it out of business. The church had built a new building there just a few years before, but the old school building was still on the property also. The church had plans to renovate it into an educational building in the future. When we had moved here, our stuff had been stored in this building as there was no room in the small trailer. This is also where I pushed the old Kawasaki into when I got it home, right there in the entry way. I tore it down there and it wasn't long until I had the engine put back together. This part of the story is kind of a hoot because that church did eventually remodel that building, and whenever I would have occasion to be in it, I would walk into the beautiful vestibule point down at the carpet and say, "I rebuilt a 500 Kawasaki right here."

I got it running and began riding it. Oh what a handful that thing was. It would come over backwards immediately if you grabbed a handful of throttle in first gear. The front wheel would not quit climbing in second. It would lift the front wheel by a foot or two when going to third. I learned when getting on it, to climb to the very front of the seat and lay up on the tank with all my weight to keep the front wheel down. I once put Armor

All on the seat and that was a big mistake. When I would crack it open it would slide me to the very back of the seat, and I would have to let off to keep from flying off. These bikes got horrible fuel mileage—some said as little as 12 mpg. I never checked it, but I did have to push it home twice from running out of gas. I never really rode this motorcycle for transportation. I just road it around in the country, running it through the quarter, and taking people rides to show them how it would run. On one such occasion I invited my father-in-law, the preacher, for a ride on it. He was a veteran, having served in World War 2 before he was a preacher. He had never driven a motorcycle himself, but after he got out of the service his best friend had an old Harley and that's what they used for transportation when they were out carousing around. So he wasn't apprehensive at all when I asked him if he wanted to take a ride. My favorite place to hot rod the bike was straight down the road from his house, it was a country blacktop with a two mile long flat straightaway. I took him down those two miles turned around and nailed it. I had the front wheel off the ground a couple of feet high when shifting and I ran him up to about 90mph. When we got back to his house he was mad, but didn't say it. He just got off and headed for the house. I said, "Pete it runs pretty good doesn't it?" His only reaction was, "Yea boy," which was a southern term used by his generation. I should have had my butt kicked for being that disrespectful. I didn't keep the Mach iii very long, and I don't remember being heartbroken on having to part with it. I think I just really wanted to experience just how powerful they were and I had gotten a good taste of that.

I also had a use for the money it could bring. We had $400 of our wedding pictures to payoff. So I advertised the Kawasaki for sale. I had gotten it looking real sharp. I had someone paint the tank and put a new Kawasaki decal on it. So I priced it for $500. The first guy who came to look at it was a doctor from Sherman who said he wanted the bike to make a café racer out of. This in my opinion, because of their handling characteristics, was one of the worst choices for a café racer—a drag bike yes, café racer no. He offered me $475, and I took it on the spot. I felt like I had made all of the profit in the world and it was quickly used to pay off those wedding pictures.

Probably a year or maybe two later, I was now working at another job in Sherman. While on my lunch hour I stopped by a Honda motorcycle shop where I sometimes hung out. When I drove up, there were a half a dozen guys that had made a circle around a motorcycle. One of them was the owner of the shop, and when I approached he said, "Hey Banks, come over here and ride this motorcycle. It will be the fastest motorcycle you've ever ridden." The guys backed up to let me get a look at the bike, and when I did, lo and behold, it was my Kawasaki, and sure enough it had been given the café racer treatment. It had clip on bars and it had a big mean looking set of expansion chambers that had replaced the mufflers. Also the Honda shop owner said that it had a set of one ring racing pistons (which had replaced my fifteen dollar ones) and it was wearing a pair of 100 dollar a piece tires which was unbelievably high priced at that time. They handed me a helmet, and I took off. He was right. It was terribly fast, although I really couldn't get the full affect even though they had given me a helmet. I had no glasses and every time I would open it up, my eyes would blur so badly that I would have to let off. I am glad I got to experience one of those iconic bikes.

IT'S GONE

ONCE WE MOVED TO SOUTHERN Oklahoma, I found the GTX was not very well appreciated down here as it was in Missouri. I was used to people coming up to me at gas stations and saying "Is that a GTX? Does it have the 440 in it?" I had even had to keep a bicycle lock around the hood latch hidden behind the grill, to keep guys out of it when I wasn't around. Down here it seemed the car was invisible. I also noticed that I didn't see as many muscle cars of any variety per capita as I did back home. What I did see were lots of Chevy pickups. El Caminos were also very popular. This made me feel like an old Indian moved to a reservation, and then finding out there were no buffalo here, but lots of armadillos. But, hey, at least they are easier to catch.

One day while driving in Sherman, the automatic transmission went out on the GTX. Lynn's dad came over and pulled it home for me. I was able to buy a 727 torque flight master rebuild kit for $49.95 wholesale. I also purchased a book on rebuilding the torque flight transmission, and I got my brother-in-law to help me wrestle it out in the dirt beside our driveway. I rebuilt it and put it back in. I drove it and it didn't work right. We pulled it out again, and before I attempted it again, I went and talked to a transmission man. When I described how it acted, he said he was sure I had torn a lip seal in one of the drums. He told me how to use a feeler gauge to shoe horn the little seals in, as the piston went down inside the drum. He then pulled out a drawer on his tool box and gave me a couple of seals for free. I was very appreciative for his help. This time it worked fine.

The only hitch in the transmission job, besides having to do it twice, was our dog Mo. Mo was a full blood boxer and had been given to us by my Aunt Linda and Uncle Bob who raised boxers. Mo had a fancy registered name, but we called him Mo because he came from Missouri. Mo was very smart and very mischievous, and very nosey; he also stole things. Many times when inside our trailer we would see Mo running like a sidewinder down the hall. That was his body language when he was being stealthy. We had learned to follow him, and watch him go hide whatever he had taken from another room. During this transmission job, we had repeatedly had to run Mo off from underneath the car when he got in our way. He would crawl on his belly under the car and stick his head up right where we were working, trying to see what was going on. When we went to put the cross member that holds the transmission in for the last time, one of the four long bolts were missing. These are big bolts, four or five inches long, and we had been careful to lay them right behind the tires on each side as we took them out so they wouldn't get kicked around while we worked. That bolt was nowhere to be found, and I had to round up a regular hardware store bolt, the same length and threads, to replace it. Mo had stolen that bolt, and he very possibly did it during the daytime while I wasn't there. He really got a kick out of that kind of stuff.

Surprisingly, I have no stories to tell about hot rodding the GTX after we moved to Oklahoma. Its heyday was for sure back in Missouri. There was once a couple of boys who had asked if I would sell it, and I had fun taking them down to a twisty road and running into corners pretty fast, then braking, and at the apex of the curve, nailing it and coming out of it sideways. I did this about four times, and they were sure glad for the ride to be over with. There certainly wasn't any instance of racing or anything like that.

Even though my driving doesn't sound like it, after Lynn and I got married, it was like someone flipped a switch in my mind, and I became an adult. Even now, when I hear popular songs from the late seventies, if they are only one or two years after our wedding, I don't consider them songs from my youth even though some of them are from when I was only nineteen years old.

One of the last times we used the GTX for anything other than to go to town and back, we took it to Six Flags Over Texas. We have a picture of it that day sitting in front of my wife's aunt and uncle's house in Grand Prairie, TX. It was a bright sunny day and it looks great in the picture. It's a fitting image of that last trip. It was very hot that day and we had to wait in a long line to get into the amusement park. Although it didn't get to the point of boiling over, the GTX got hot according to its temperature gauge. It had never done that before, but then I had never idled in traffic for forty-five minutes in 100 degree temperature before.

The GTX never quite ran right after that day. I did a compression check on it, and found it to have two side by side cylinders, numbers 2 and 4 on the right side, that were down on compression compared with the rest of the cylinders. I speculated that it had a head gasket leaking between those two cylinders because of the overheating incident. I really couldn't afford to put any money into the car, and even if I could, we really couldn't afford to drive it because of the gas prices. I felt like I couldn't afford to keep it around, which wouldn't be practical, but I certainly was not going to just nearly give it away.

The second gas crisis of the '70's was in full swing, and I had the advantage of working in a Volkswagen Honda Audi dealership. We purchased a 1977 VW Rabbit with only 15,000 miles. It had been traded in at the dealership by a doctor. This was funny for me to wind up with a car like this. Back in Princeton when we were dating, sub-compacts were just beginning to be seen around our area. I remember looking at a Chevette in a Chevrolet showroom in Trenton, and looking through the window down at the pedals in the floor, wondering how a full grown man would even get his feet in there on those tiny pedals. One day while driving around in Princeton, someone was in town in a brand new Volkswagen Rabbit. It was the first one I had ever seen, and I immediately detested it. It felt like hate at first sight. It was somehow a threat to my muscle car soul. At this point the muscle cars were over ten years old, and unleaded gas and low compression was the order of the day. I was already somewhat of a dinosaur, preferring the old muscle cars over the newest, latest stuff. Now this little car to me was a precursor of things to come, and I was not wrong; things were heading south in a hurry. I fell in behind the Rabbit, and followed very closely as though to intimidate it, all the while ranting about the little foreign piece of junk. Lynn teased me profusely and acted like she was afraid if I didn't get a hold of myself, I might lose my cool and ram it. Now I owned one; how quickly things can change.

One day Lynn was coming home in our Rabbit, when I heard her coming down our lane. It was winter time, and quite slick outside, a rarity for down here. I could tell by the sound of the car that Lynn was, true to form, going what I considered to be too fast. I was listening from the vantage point of the toilet stool in our little bathroom, when Wham! There was a loud bang, and the trailer shook to the point I had to put my hand down on the edge of the bath tub to avoid falling off the stool. Yep, she had slid into the trailer house, coming very close to knocking it off of its blocks and me off the throne.

As the old GTX was certainly on its way out, it was eclipsed by a much more important entrance into our lives, the birth of our oldest daughter Kristen Michelle Banks. Kristen's first words of "Dah Daddy" a few months later, were even better than the moan of the four barrel of that old 440. I now had a new title.

As the parts manager of a car dealership, there are, at least in those days, a lot of salesmen that visit you selling various products, like chemicals for your mechanics to use, or detail supplies for your used car department. Also nut and bolt salesman sold things from license plate screws, to fuses, to light bulbs. These guys usually carried a catalogue of their products, which was huge, usually a foot thick. They would come up and hoist it up on your counter, hoping then that the buying would begin. One day, a new nut and bolt salesman came around, and after we went through his catalogue, he wanted to show me a picture of his drag car. In the back of his catalogue, he had action pictures of a Plymouth Cuda on the drag strip. I looked at his pictures with enthusiasm, and since he was a Mopar guy, I mentioned in passing that I had a '67 GTX. His immediate response was, "Would you want to sell that car?" I said that I would consider it. He said he had a brother that lived in Duncan, Oklahoma, and that he collected Chrysler high performance cars. Their shared last name was Petty, and they claimed to be distant cousins of Richard Petty, at the time probably Mopar's most famous customer. He asked me how much I would want for the car, and I told him $1,200. He told me he would contact his brother and let me know. The next day he called and asked if he could see the car. I agreed to drive it over to Denison, Texas so he could look at it. The car still ran pretty good, even with its weak compression reading in those two cylinders. I remember pulling it up into his driveway. He asked if he could drive the car, and I stood in his driveway while he was gone for all of five minutes. When he came back, he went in and called his brother. Then he came back out of the house and bought the car. That quick and it was gone!

Looking back on this, the surprising thing to me, maybe even shocking, is I don't remember having any remorse whatsoever. I don't remember being sad, or reminiscing, or thinking this is the last time I will see or drive the car. I actually feel that much more, writing this now, than I did then, and don't know how I avoided it. I was actually very pleased with the price of $1,200. When I had quoted that price, I half expected him to reject it immediately. What pleased me about the price, more than having the money to spend, was that by buying it for that price, without trying to low ball me, I knew I had found a couple of guys, even down here, that appreciated the car for what it was. When I told the guys I worked with that I had sold the car to a man and the price, they were flabbergasted. What they were basing their response on and what I appreciated was that a run of the mill twelve year old Plymouth was a $200 car, had it not been a GTX.

I will add a warning to anyone with a special vehicle, or anything else for that matter, that you are thinking of letting go. This car is so special to me that forty years later I am writing a book about it. What did we do with the $1,200 that I got for it? I have no idea.

GONE FOR GOOD

V OLKSWAGEN RABBIT'S HAD BEEN electronically fuel injected since their beginning. Volkswagen then came out with a model that was carbureted; it had a small solex carburetor on it similar to the old VW beetles. It got a couple of miles to the gallon better mileage than the fuel injected model, and it also cost less. Its maintenance cost was also lower—a fuel injected Rabbit had a fuel filter which cost $10 at the time (quite expensive) whereas the same filter for the carbureted car cost $.99. Our dealership only got one of these carbureted Rabbits and I traded ours in on it. In those days most foreign cars came without air conditioning, and the air conditioners were dealer installed. I installed a factory VW air conditioner on my car myself to save money. Now this boy, who had hated the first Rabbit he saw, was on his second one.

I had begun to buy and fix up old Volkswagen Beetles, and sell them on the side to make extra money. Because of high gas prices, there was a good market for old, air-cooled VW bugs for people to use for work cars, and for second cars to save gas. For many folks, when they thought of small cars, they thought of Beetles because Beetles were the only small car they had ever been around.

Most of these old Beetles that I was buying had engine problems. Air cooled cars run hot by nature, and the Texas heat took its toll on them. Most had either a burnt piston, or had dropped an exhaust valve on the number three cylinder—the cylinder that ran the hottest. This was usually caused because people didn't think it important to keep the little rubber seals around the spark plug wires in good shape, reducing the cooling air around the cylinders. Another cause was the engine running lean. People would put an extractor exhaust system on without re-jetting the carburetor, or they would come down from Colorado where their carburetor was jetted for high altitude, and then their engine would overheat.

I really was in a good position for this. To add to my auto mechanics class in school, I now worked with two very good mechanics, Calvin Thompson and Johnny Bateman. These guys were nice enough to answer my questions and show me how to do stuff. Calvin was a retired Air Force mechanic and flight engineer and was the only guy I've ever seen that could work on cars all day and never get his shirt dirty. If Calvin's hair was messed up or he had very much grease on his hands you knew he was having a bad day. Johnny was so good and fast, he could pull a VW bug in of a morning, pull the motor out, and take it into our unit room. He would do a complete engine rebuild with new rod and main bearings, new pistons and rings, and cylinders. He also rebuilt the heads, grinding the valves and even replacing the valve guides. He cleaned and painted the sheet metal. He would then reinstall the engine in the car and test drive it, and many times, still had time to draw another job before our 5 PM closing time. Guys like these are good to have around if you're learning to work on cars.

Other "perks" of working in the VW dealership were getting parts at wholesale and having the availability of the lifts in the dealership to use. At home, I also had the use of a building on my father-in-law's property to work in after hours, which worked great, as long as I was working on a Volkswagen. It was the only car small enough to get through the double walk-in doors in the front of the old store building. Even then we had to make a ramp about one foot high in the doorway so we could tilt the Volkswagen up on one side so the fenders could clear the door opening.

One particular Volkswagen, after I had rebuilt the engine, I replaced the windshield and put an entire new interior in. I replaced some damaged fenders with brand new VW OEM sheet metal; also it got a complete paint job. My brother-in-law and I were painting it, and we were trying something for the first time, and that was adding a hardener to the acrylic enamel, causing it to chemically dry sort of like epoxy rather than having to wait days for it to dry. We had no ventilation system at all, and we didn't wear respirators of any kind. It wasn't noticeable at first, but the more we painted the happier we got. Before it was over, even runs in the paint were leg slapping hilarious. Then all of a sudden I had to run out the back door and vomit. It was fun while it lasted.

Once there were three of us young guys in our twenties working at that old store building, and there was a car sitting out back with its front pulled up to a chain link fence. This wasn't a Volkswagen. It was a larger car. It had been sitting in this one spot for months and its tires had made indentations in the ground. Try as we might, the three of us though young and fit, could not untrack those tires and push it out. There was a neighbor of my father-in-law whose back was stronger than his mind. He was an older man, and we had watched him in the past lift some impressive weight. I looked at my brother-in- law and said, "Do you think Hank is awake?" because it was after dark. The guy who was helping us said, "Why? Does he have a tractor?", and we told him, "No, Hank is a tractor," and we all snickered at that. One of us went over and knocked on Hank's door. He pulled on his boots without tying them, and walked out back with us. We said, "Hank, we need help pushing this car." Hank walked over to the car and said, "Which way do you want to push it?" This car was sitting about a foot from the fence in the front, with absolutely nowhere to go. This caused us all three to get tickled to the point that we were bent over laughing, and while we were, Hank got between the car and the fence, put his back against the car, and pushed the car out by himself.

This was a time of a lot of changes in our young family. I changed dealerships and took a job at a Volkswagen, Toyota and AMC Jeep dealership that was 60 miles away in Ardmore, OK, causing me to rack up 120 miles a day and 600 miles per week commuting. At this time Lynn and I found a house we wanted to buy. Just like other things in our life, we felt we had found the perfect one. We weren't looking for a house in Bryan County because were planning on moving to Ardmore. Lynn's sister Jeana had recently gotten her real estate license and was looking for a house for her and her husband to buy. She found three new homes that one builder had built on 2.5 acre lots adjoining one another. They were nearly finished. She took us to look at them because she was very interested in one for herself. While there, Lynn and I fell in love with one of the houses. To us this one house was just a stand out. At one point, Jeana asked Lynn and me if we might be interested in buying one of these houses. We told her, "No." When she asked why not, I said, "Well, the one we would want is the one you're going to buy." She then asked which one that was, and when we told her she said, "Oh no, I want the one beside it, not that one." To get this house, two things had to happen. First we had to sell our nine month old car, which we really didn't need because I was driving demonstrators at this new dealership, and second we had to sell our trailer house. They had to sell in that order because if we sold the trailer but couldn't sell the car, we still couldn't afford the house and would have no place to live.

We started by advertising the car in the weekly shopper and on the daily radio swap shop program for two weeks with absolutely no response. It looked like our plan was over before it started. Then one day we got a single call on the two week old shopper ad. The people were from the next county about forty miles away. We arranged to meet with them the next Saturday at the TG&Y store in Durant. This was early in the week, and the wait until Saturday was excruciating. We had agreed to meet at 10 o'clock and we were there early. We stood out front of the store and waited, but when 10 o'clock came, no one showed. We waited about thirty minutes, and we then dejectedly went inside the store.

We shopped in the store for what seemed a long time, and when we were leaving, we saw a family standing in the foyer of the store. We took a chance and asked them if they had come to look at a car, and they said they had. They bought the car.

I had bought our first Rabbit, a '77 model, when it was only four months old and had 15,000 miles on it. I had driven it two years, and it had 55,000 miles on it when I traded it in. Because of gas prices rising dramatically, I was allowed exactly what I gave for it on trade-in on the brand new '80 model Rabbit. I then drove that car one year and 24,000 miles. Because of buying it at cost and installing the air conditioner myself, I was able to sell it for $500 more than I gave for it. We drove three years and 74,000 miles in one car that was four months old when we purchased it, and another that was brand new and ended up coming out $500 to the good. Maybe I ought to be a car dealer.

We then, with renewed fervor, tackled the selling of the trailer house. We put it in the shopper with pretty much the same results as the car. Lynn would also put it on the swap shop each day. She was beginning to get embarrassed being heard on the air each day trying to sell the trailer. The radio station also had a rule that you could only run an item so many times. How embarrassing it would be she thought to have the D.J. stop her in mid-sentence and say, "Ma'am we're going to have to stop you now; you have put that trailer house on here too many times." Lynn sucked it up and bravely called one more time, but had decided this would be the last time. Just a few minutes after getting off the air, the phone rang. It was a lady who had been driving down the road and had heard Lynn on the radio. She had scrambled to get her purse for a scrap of paper and a pen to write the number down. She had a young son and daughter-in-law that were looking for a trailer house, and when they looked at it, they thought it was perfect and bought it on the spot.

We were now able to get our new home. Our trailer had been 600 square feet, and our new home was 1600 square feet. Kristen just lay in the floor and rolled from wall to wall. The living room with no furniture in it seemed like a gymnasium to her.

I drove the 600 miles per week going to Ardmore and back for eighteen months. It wasn't so bad of a morning when I was fresh and had an hour to myself before facing the work day. I rationalized that if I lived in a city I would have a commute of this long just to get across the city, while having the frustration of stop and go traffic. I would much rather spend an hour driving through the country side. At quitting time, when I was already tired and hungry, having to drive an hour home was much more difficult. It was like living in two worlds; any school, church, or social events were either happening at home or work and there was no mixing of the two worlds.

There was something that I used to break the monotony of my evening drive, and that was trying out the different cars. When I had taken the job, it came with a new demonstrator. The owner had explained to me he could not afford to put as many miles on a new car as I was driving. He said that until I finally moved to Ardmore I could drive used cars—pretty much my choice and that they could benefit by me checking the cars out, and for me to make a list of any repairs that needed to be made. There was a large choice because this was a franchised dealership that was strong on used cars, and our owner bought from the auction, not relying on trade-in's only. He only bought extremely slick and usually sporty vehicles. I never abused these vehicles, but I did have a very heavy foot in those days. There was one blacktop that I cut through as a short cut to my home rather than going around the main highway. On this blacktop there were three spots where big tubes went under this road. These tubes had been put in rather shallow, and this caused three little quick "whoop de dos" in this road a few hundred yards apart. These were steep enough to qualify as, what we as kids in the backseat of the family car called, tickle belly hills and we loved when Dad went over them, doing just what their name implied. The first time this happened I was hurrying home one night, and when I say hurrying I do mean hurrying. As I went over the first of these hills, I heard a strange sound as though the engine revved up. By the time I had heard it for the third time, I realized what the odd sound was; the engine was in fact revving up because this was a front wheel drive car, and the front wheels were momentarily coming off the ground on each hill. I found they did that at just over 100 mph. Many of the cars I drove were front wheel drive, and I entertained myself this way many times.

Once we had a Triumph TR7 on the lot. This was the Triumph that kind of looked like a flying wedge. I had been a big fan of Triumphs, especially the TR6 right before this one. I chose the little Triumph to drive that evening. Every night going home I crossed Lake Texoma which is 1.9 miles wide where Highway 70 crosses it. We locals refer to the incredibly narrow two lane bridge built in 1942 as the Kingston Bridge. I needed a long strait place to try the little Triumph out and the bridge provided that. I managed to get the TR7 up to 117 on the Kingston Bridge.

I had continued buying and selling cars on the side, and I always had a vehicle that I was working on most nights. After supper I would go to the shop and work until at least 10 o'clock, and many times midnight. Then I would get up and go again the next morning. How wonderful is the strength of youth.

It was then that I got the opportunity to become a used car dealer. I had never dreamed of selling used cars as my main business, although I did it all the time. I actually liked the idea of having a wrecking yard, but to deal in late model salvage required too much money. You had to be able to give, sometimes, thousands of dollars for a nearly new wreck, and then to have to wait while the parts sell to realize a profit. I was not thinking about a junk yard, but a late model salvage operation, like I would call on as a parts man when we needed a used transmission or something like that for a nearly new car.

I did in fact become a used car dealer, and at twenty-four years old I was, as my Granddad Dick Callen was fond of saying, so green it's a wonder the cows didn't eat me. It's funny looking back now. I wasn't so much worried about buying or selling the cars as I was how to fill out the paper work. I got the office manager from the dealership I was leaving to show me an example of the paperwork on their car deals. I ordered similar forms from the state and I was good to go!

In my little office on the edge of town in Durant, Oklahoma, I had plenty of time to daydream between customers, and I began to think about the old GTX. After I had been a car dealer for a couple of years and the GTX had been gone about four years, I decided to see if I could find it. I could not find the man in Denison who had bought it for his brother, he had moved and no longer lived in the area. I remembered the last name of Petty because of Richard Petty and I remembered that it had gone to Duncan, Oklahoma. I also remembered something about the man who had bought it owning a gas station. I called information for Duncan, and found a yellow page listing for a Petty's DX service station. I excitedly called the number and Mr. Petty, the owner answered. I told him who I was and that I was interested in what might have happened to the car. At first he seemed a little foggy about what car I was talking about, but then he remembered and said, "Yeah, that car sat out here a year before it sold." He then told me that he had the car painted red, and had the seats recovered, and put a new vinyl top on it. Now I at first thought that surely we were talking about two different cars. My car's paint had been in really good condition except for the faint "just married" burnt into the hood, but it wasn't noticeable unless you were looking for it. The vinyl top had been as good as new and the interior was fine except for the driver's seat. He assured me that we were talking about the same car, and I was finally convinced when he said he had to replace the right cylinder head because it was cracked. There was the answer to my low compression between cylinder 2 and 4 on the right side. He told me he had sold it to a guy in southwest Missouri, and that he would get me his name and number. I called him a couple more times, and each time he promised me the name and number. During these talks he added that the guy owned a lot of Mopars. Finally, the last time I called him he was not interested in talking to me, and said he could not find the guy's name and number, and basically told me not to call him anymore. It appeared like it was gone for good.

GO-KARTS

SOME FAMILIES DEVELOP TRADITIONS, and have a favorite pastime that they enjoy when they get together. Whether it be competing at a favorite board game, a rousing round of charades, or an ongoing ping pong rivalry, this activity is usually the center of any family gathering. One of the most famous is the Kennedys' touch football games that we have all seen home movie footage of. For our family, for a few years, that favorite activity was go-kart riding. It all started when my brother-in-law and I were in Sherman, Texas one day, and we noticed someone had put in a go-kart track. This go-kart track was brand new and when we saw it, we literally swerved the car off the road and into the parking lot. When we approached the gate, it was obvious they were barely open if open at all. We asked if we could ride and they agreed. We may very well have been their first paying customers.

We immediately found out that their go-karts were way too fast for how narrow their track was. In a word, it was perfect. The great thing about this setup was a person, especially a not very good driver, could easily lose control and wreck. This made it easier to disguise the fact that all we wanted to do was wreck each other, and also strangers. Although we loved wrecking people, we only wrecked loved ones, friends, and strangers. We made the twenty-five mile trip several times the first couple of weeks, literally riding as much as we could afford, and ending when we got kicked off, which sometimes didn't take long at all. We were afraid they would consider their track too dangerous and change it, which they eventually did, but they only widened it and thankfully left the karts fast.

The first times we rode these karts, we were the only ones on the track. The track was surrounded with old, used tires around both the inside and the outside of the paved surface. Outside of the tires there was a chain link fence that surrounded the whole thing. On one of those first trips, I hit the brother-in-law so hard I knocked him over the tires and into the fence right at a pole, and he knocked the pole down. Of course I was immediately kicked off. The next time out he knocked me into the fence, but I hit between poles, running my go-kart up under the chain link fencing so far that it took two track attendants to get me out, one pulling up on the fence, while the second one pulled my go-kart out by the back bumper.

We then got our wives talked into riding with us. We now had some new blood in the game and they became cannon fodder. At first they would get out on the track and run fast, and we would come up behind them and spin them out, or knock them into the fence or another rider. After that, they would try to putter around near the inside of the curves, hoping to avoid us, or at least not fly so far when we hit them.

This was not the only track we visited. When we saw one someplace else, we would stop and ride. We especially liked new tracks because we had not gotten a reputation there. Sherman had started placing an employee on the back straight so they could throw us out earlier. Someone put a track on the west side of Durant and we couldn't wait to get out there. This track had used tires stacked two high all around it. Lynn and Jeana had become very savvy by this time, and no longer considered our promises not to wreck them as sincere. This track's operator was brand new and was not prepared for serial go-kart hooligans like we had become. I was licking my chops at the opportunity this new track with an easy operator provided, but Lynn was having none of it. She would literally come to a stop right in front of the front gate and let me roar by to avoid me. When I felt the time allotted for the ride had about expired, I did a cop turn with my kart on the back strait, and came around a corner running the wrong way, catching Lynn off guard and hitting her head on, knocking her completely over the two car-tires stacked on top of one another, and into the infield. After kicking me off, two guys went out in the grass and lifted Lynn's kart back over the tires. That was pretty much the final straw for Lynn being on a go-kart track with me. I do admit to having a fleeting thought of, "What have I done?" when I saw her go-kart flying through the air and over those tires.

After this, we delighted in sharing our new found fun with any family and friends that came to visit us, especially those from north Missouri. When my dad and my brother would come down, we couldn't wait for us all to go for an evening of fun, wrecking one another. Dad and Steve gave as good as they got, and we all had great fun. Lynn's dad also went with us, and he also mixed it up with us; it was a hoot.

One time my brother in-law's own brother came down, and we couldn't wait to get him on the track. The two of them looked very similar and could have passed for twins. That night they were also both wearing blue shirts. After making a few laps, my brother-in-law whacked his brother a good one. Up to this point his brother had just been racing around, minding his own business. When the guy running the track saw him hit his brother, he immediately waved him in to throw him off. When he pulled his go-kart into the little lane where you both got on and off your go-kart, the manager couldn't wait for him to get off, but began leaning over the kart and giving my brother-in-law a piece of his mind. This track was an oval, built on the side of a hill, with the starting line being on the low side of the hill. As I came along the back strait on the high side of the hill, I saw my brother-in-law being kicked off down below. I determined with him gone, the fun would be over. I then came down off the high side at full speed and hit him in the back, while the attendant was still bending over his kart lecturing him. This impact knocked his kart about 30 feet and off the end of the track. I then veered right and took off up the hill. The attendant was so infuriated with me that he took off running across the infield, not waiting for me to come around. He then commanded me to stop the kart where it was, and promptly ejected me from the track. The brother-in-law took this opportunity to drag his kart back on the track, and was innocently motoring around. After catching his breath, the track man remembered that he was in the process of throwing him off. He then mistakenly chose the wrong blue-shirted brother and threw him off instead. This brother had a very bad temper and a worse vocabulary for profanity, and he let the attendant have it at the top of his lungs for five minutes. He was the only one of us that had been totally innocent, and hadn't done anything. He and I then watched from the sideline while my brother-in-law finished the ride with a smile on his face.

Our family go-karting sometimes spread out to other venues, even across state lines. A couple of times we all converged on Branson, Missouri, and each time karting was involved, and we tried several of their tracks. The most memorable one was on a twisty, curvy track that was reflective of the Ozark Mountains it was built on. There were several of the family riding and some watching. The backside of this track was on the down side of the mountain, and could not be seen at all from the front gate, where the non-riding family members were waiting and watching. My brother Steve and I had developed a rivalry over our kart riding over the years, and on this day it seemed to be at a crescendo. Our focus on wrecking one another was so great that our wives were on the track with us, and were hardly getting any negative attention. I was riding with a big handicap because this track had such steep hills. The fact that I was much heavier than the others made my kart no match for their speed; so Steve would fly by me and hit me a glancing blow and motor on. I developed a plan. I dogged along at half-speed waiting for the right moment and position on the track. When I saw Steve across a corner from me, I took the extreme high side of a corner that barreled down a hill. (Going downhill, my weight was an advantage for speed.) I headed for him and caught Steve at the bottom of the hill. I intended to spin him out at the bottom of the turn. Instead of trying to get away from me, Steve met my challenge and turned into me. If it had been filmed, the ensuing crash would have been a Banks go-karting highlight moment. When I hit Steve, my greater momentum, because of my speed down the hill and my increased weight, caused his go-kart to fly through the air at what looked to me like eighteen inches off the ground. Similar to the fleeting feeling I had when knocking Lynn over the pile of tires stacked two high, I remember thinking, "Oh no! I have killed my brother!" Fortunately the kart didn't flip but came down on its wheels. According to the family waiting at the top of the hill, the crash sounded very loud, and three of the track guys took off running to the scene, wildly blowing their whistles in unison. The funniest part was that the next thing they saw was me coming around the track looking very innocent, followed by Steve with the front wheel of his kart wobbling extremely, and making a clanking noise on every revolution of that tire. Steve had a few bruises the next day to remember the crash by.

Once, my wife and I were scheduled to accompany a group of young people from our church to ride go-karts. As the day approached, Lynn asked me one day how I was going to manage taking those kids go-kart riding. My response was, "What do you mean?" She said, "Mike, I have never seen you ride go karts that you didn't get thrown off." I told her I thought that was a slight exaggeration, to which she countered with, "If so, it's very slight." I had to agree to that. We took the kids and I was on my best behavior, maybe better than my best behavior.

PRIMING THE PUMP

A S A YOUNGSTER I HAD BEEN VERY involved in building model cars, and looking at a display of model car kits in a store always brought back a very familiar feeling of what it was like to get to purchase the latest new kit I had been wanting, or better yet, to receive one for a birthday or Christmas gift. After the GTX had been gone for around fifteen years, I was killing time in a store one day looking at a display of model cars, while Lynn and the girls were shopping. I say "girls" plural because a few years before, we had added to our family with the birth of another little girl, Charity Danielle Banks. When Charity was born Kristen was nearly nine years old. We had waited until we thought we could afford another child, but as the years rolled on and we still didn't feel we could, one day I told Lynn, "I don't ever remember hearing anybody ever having a baby repossessed. Let's go for it."

I was excited to see they were making a model of the 1967 GTX, and the girls bought me a kit for Father's Day. I so enjoyed building that model, and Charity enjoyed helping. I can still see her standing in a chair at our dining room table watching intently as I worked. I found as close of a gold color as I could to the original color my car had been, and painted the interior the correct white, with a white top also. It was really good to admire a replica of the car that had meant so much to me, and to be able to show it to my friends. A funny thing happened soon after the model was finished. I brought it to a family gathering, as it was something I was proud of and excited about. My brother was the main one I wanted to show it to, and on handing it to him, a wheel promptly fell off. I then gave him a hard time saying, "Well, you used to tear up my model cars when you were a little guy. I guess nothing has changed."

A while after this, we moved our car lot to a new location and added car rental to our business. One day a man named Robbie came in to rent a car. He had recently retired and was moving from California to Durant. He, as so many had, moved to California during the dust bowl and the depression to find work, and stayed on. Now that he was retired, he was moving back home. He had been pulling a trailer in the move and had been in an accident. He was having to put his pickup in a local body shop and needed to rent a car until it was fixed. He rented the car for a few days, but had to extend his rental several times because the shop didn't get his truck out nearly as quickly as he expected. When he would come in to extend the rental, we would visit. I think he was a little lonesome, not really knowing anyone in town. One day, during our conversation, he said he had to make a trip back to California when his truck was finished. The reason for the next trip was to pick up his 1971 Plymouth Road Runner, which he had bought new in '71, and get it back to Oklahoma with him. I told him about how I appreciated Mopars and about my old GTX. He said whenever he got the Road Runner back here, he would show it to me, and I asked him to please do that.

A few weeks later he pulled up with the Road Runner on a trailer. It was a b5 blue car; it was very slick and it was wearing its original paint. I made over the car and told him how nice it was. About a week later Robbie drove up in the Road Runner, and said he wanted me to drive it. We took it outside of town, and it felt good to be driving and hearing a big block Mopar again.

A few months passed and Robbie came by my office, this time without the car. He told me how he was just sick about the Road Runner because it had been garaged its whole life, and now he only had a carport. He said he had decided to sell it, and hoped I would sell it for him on consignment. I questioned him to make sure that he was ready to give it up, and he assured me he had made up his mind. We drove over to his house and I drove the Road Runner back to the car lot.

When I picked up the car, there was a Road Runner doll standing up on the parcel shelf in the back window. I started to reach in and get the doll out, but Robbie said "No, leave that there." He then told me the story of how he bought the Road Runner brand new in Los Angeles and headed up the coast of California. When he stopped for gas the first time, as he was paying, he spotted this Road Runner doll for sale in the station. He said after purchasing it, he carried it out to the car and reached back across the backseat, and placed it in that very spot, and that it had never been moved since that day.

Another interesting item was the Road Runner had a very unique hood lock right in the bottom of the hood emblem. It looked factory, but I told the man that was the first time I had ever seen that option, which caused him to laugh. It turns out he was a machinist and had fabricated this lock, and drilled and installed it in his hood.

I went with my wife to the grocery store that evening, and as was customary for me, I passed the time she was shopping by looking at the car magazines. This time I decided to try and get some idea of what the value of this Road Runner was, and I purchased a copy of a magazine that I had not been aware of before, *The Mopar Collector's Guide*.

Reading the Mopar Collector's Guide really awakened a lot of old feelings in me. I went back to the grocery store the next time and purchased another magazine; this one was *Performance Mopar*. I learned that there had been a lot going on in the world of Mopar performance cars the last two decades that I had not been aware of. The biggest change to me was the renewed interest in these old cars, in both the area of restoration, and also drag racing. Things like the KOS King of the Street Drag Racing series had started, and I knew nothing of them. My experience with a muscle Mopar was during the first go round, when they were our everyday drivers. One of the most significant changes was the availability of reproduction parts. When I had last worked on Mopars, we had to rely upon NOS dealer inventory or used. I remember looking for a replacement lower seat cover for my GTX, when it was a mere nine years old. I checked every Chrysler Plymouth Dodge dealer in the Texas cities I worked in, to no avail. Most of them laughed when I asked them.

I remember talking to my dad on the phone and telling him about some of the things I had been learning about in these magazines. I had seen 440 stroker motors of well over 500 cubic inches, and pictures of nearly 4000 pound, street legal race cars, coming off the line with their front wheels in the air two feet high. Now that takes some serious horsepower!

It didn't take long for the Road Runner to sell. The best part about the sale was the guy that bought it traded in a 1966 Plymouth Satellite. A '66 Satellite is the same body style as a '67 GTX, the only noticeable difference being the grill, headlights, the tail panel, and the lack of hood scoops. This particular car had been the only car being driven in our area the same body style as the GTX since I had moved down here. This Satellite had sat in front of a local body shop, and I drove by it on my way to work for a few years, but then it had stopped being there, and I had lost track of it.

I now had in my possession a real live '66-'67 B-body Mopar. I really hadn't expected that would ever happen again. This car had the early style 318 polysphere V8. These motors, although only 318 cubic inches, are huge on the exterior; their valve covers are as wide as or wider apart than a 440. The very next year Chrysler came out with the small block LA series 318 V8 which was a totally different engine. I drove the Satellite some, and took my family for a ride in it. I was surprised that even though it was not nearly as stout as even a 383 car, it would lay rubber pretty well taking off, and did seem to breathe pretty good running wide open. It wasn't till probably fifteen years later I was talking to a woman on my car lot, and she told me about the yellow Satellite she and her husband had owned, and how a much respected engine-builder had ported the heads in it, and the camshaft that was in it, and all the modifications he had done to it. She said, "He claimed it ought to be the best running polysphere 318 in the country." It was the same car the man had traded me.

One day a man in a very nice pickup, pulling a trailer, turned beside my car lot and drove up the next road several yards, and parked in front of the business behind me. I just happened to be standing in my office and saw him turn in. He came in to my business instead of the one he parked in front of. When he asked about the Satellite, I knew why he parked as he did; he intended to leave with that Satellite on his trailer, and he didn't want me to know how determined he was to buy the car.

I hadn't kept the Satellite anywhere but inside my shop. I didn't have it sitting out for sale. He had just heard of it by word of mouth, and he was from a town thirty-two miles north of us. He had owned a '66 Satellite when he was a young guy, and was excited to find a replacement for it. He bought the car and I got to see another person get a long sought after car.

Before we sold the Satellite a woman came in to our business to get her car cleaned up. We had added a detail shop to our used car and rental car business at that point. As she was picking up her car she said, "I have a couple of cars similar to that one in my backyard that I would sure like to get rid of." Trying to hide my excitement, I asked her where I might see these cars. The cars turned out to be a 1968 Road Runner 383 4 speed car, and a 1967 Dodge Charger. She wasn't very proud of the

Road Runner. It was ugly with peeling paint and a bad interior. It was also stuck between two gears so it wouldn't move. She wanted a lot more for the Dodge, as they had started to restore it and quit. It had the whole front suspension out from under it, making it hard to load and move. That early Charger body style with the fastback styling is not very appealing to my eye, but I love Road Runners. I bought the Road Runner and, to get it loaded, my nephew James and I had to fight off a bunch of red wasps that were very upset about their home being disturbed.

When we got the Road Runner back to the shop, I pulled it into one of the bays. My friend Gary was doing the detailing of the cars at this time, and his brother Ernie was there visiting with us. When they saw the old Road Runner they swarmed it. Ernie and Gary were both shade tree mechanics, and they just automatically decided to see if they could make the old car run. The lady who I bought the car from had to go to another location to get the title. So she had agreed to bring the title by the office and I would pay her, and she would sign the title off. While Gary and Ernie were working on the car, she came in the door at the same time I heard Gary and Ernie start grinding on the starter of the old Road Runner, which I hadn't told them to do. I began to hear the engine start to hit, and I was afraid if it actually started the lady might not want to sell me the car, or she would go up on the price. I quickly excused myself and stepped through the door between the office and the shop, and gave them the sign an umpire makes when you're safe, moving my flattened hands back and forth across each other to tell them to cease and desist cranking on this car. They got the message, and we finished our deal in the office.

I came out in the shop and told Gary and Ernie that they could resume their efforts to resuscitate the old car. It was summer time and the roll up door was up on the shop bays. I was standing outside the building about ten feet behind the Road Runner, when all of a sudden, it backfired. The Road Runner had straight exhaust pipes coming out under the rear bumper. A wad of something blew out of the left tailpipe, right in front of my feet. It was a mouse nest with about six to eight little pink mice about an inch long, and a very fat momma mouse, surrounded by what had been their home. The little guys didn't make it, but momma mouse shook herself and ran off, deciding to only reside in Chevrolet tail pipes from then on.

These first three cars had pretty much fallen into my lap. I now began to look for Mopar muscle cars in earnest, for the purpose of reselling them. I also began looking for one particular kind of Mopar muscle car, and that was a 1967 GTX, and if I found that, it would not be to resell.

GROWING OLD MOPARS

I NOW BEGAN TO GIVE MORE ATTENTION to the old Mopars. I had feelers out actively looking for them, plus these first three sitting around at the car lot had alerted people of my interest in them, and had caused many conversations which yielded many leads.

One day when our local trade paper called *The Shopper* came out I saw an ad for a '68 GTX not far from my house. I knew of this car and had been to the owner's shop and looked at it. I couldn't believe he wanted to sell it. He had talked like it was a car he was building for himself to keep. I called him and then went right on down to look at the car. He had painted it himself, using two-stage basecoat clear coat paint, which was somewhat new to all of us at the time. He had done a great job on the base color coat, but had gotten a lot of runs in the clear coat. The car also had developed an engine problem, and didn't run as strong as it should. I think all of this together had made him grow frustrated with the project. I suggested he ought to hang on to it until he felt like taking another shot at it, but he assured me that he was through with it. I paid him the asking price and came home with a Plymouth called GTX. This was a good start and I was happy.

I decided to try color sanding the car to remove the runs, hoping that would work and I wouldn't have to repaint the whole car. It was risky because there was no way of knowing if the clear coat was deep enough to remove the runs without sanding all the way through it. The experiment worked, and I then buffed the sanding scratches out, and it came out beautifully.

Now I tackled the engine. He had told me what camshaft he had put in it, and I felt that it was too high of a lift, and too long of duration for this application. I ordered a Mopar performance camshaft, one step down, for it. When I pulled the old cam out of it, I found out it had a lobe worn off because of a mistake in installing it. I put the new cam in, and it screamed after that.

Buying that GTX was not the only good thing that happened during this time. There was a location on Main Street in our town that had become empty, and I felt it would be a perfect location for our car lot and car rental business. There were several people wanting this location, and the landlord let us know we could have it— the same week as we got the '68 GTX.

Moving to this new location would require some new signage. There was a local beer distributor going out of business, and in the auction advertisement it had listed two brand new, never-installed, backlit signs. I knew, if they went cheap enough, I could have new plastic pans made for these housings that advertised my businesses, giving me some really nice signs at a fraction of the cost of new ones from a sign company.

On the day of the auction, while looking through the merchandise, I noticed a cardboard box with a t- shirt lying in the top. I decided to move aside the t-shirt and see what else might be in the box. When I moved it, I saw that the box was filled with antique beer cans. Most of these cans were what were called cone top beer cans, and they had a distinguishing cone on the top rather than being flat. They looked more like an old brake fluid can than a beer can. These cans were made this way because when beer was first offered in cans, the company capped them like a bottle, using the equipment they already had. I knew these cans had a good collector value because my dad collected beer cans. I quickly tried to assess how many cans were there and their condition, without drawing the attention of other bidders to them. I knew whoever prepared this stuff for sale cared nothing for these cans by the way they were stuck in the bottom of this box of junk, covered by a t-shirt. My experience was that boxes like this usually don't bring but a couple of dollars max. When the bidding started, there was one other bidder who recognized these cans had value (he might have been the one who put the t-shirt on top.) When the bid was at fifty dollars I was just about to my max, but decided to risk five more dollars, and I got them for fifty-five dollars. Money was really tight right then, and I called my wife and said, "Mrs. Banks, I just made you some money." When she said "How?" I responded with, "I just bought some old beer cans." She then asked, "How much?" thinking I would say, fifty cents or a dollar. When I told her, "fifty-five dollars," she was, as always, trusting but surprised and curious.

I took the box of cans immediately to the truck and locked them inside. Then I went back into the auction and bought my two signs I had come for. When I got them home, I found out I had twenty-two cone-top Schlitz Vitamin D beer cans, four flat-top Pabst Blue Ribbon cans, and two flat-top cans with a label that read ABC St. Louis. This was a Saturday, and that evening the girls needed to go to Sherman, Texas to the mall to get a dress for a school function. While the girls were shopping, I went into a bookstore to see if they had a book on beer can collecting. I quickly found a book on the subject, and as I was thumbing through it, I saw a picture of the ABC St. Louis cans that I had. It turned out that the ABC stood for Anheiser Busch Company, and they were some of their earliest cans; they were valued in this book at $450 each. The Schlitz Vitamin D cans were from 1936, the first year beer was ever put in cans. It must have been quite a sight for the other folks shopping in that small bookstore to see a 250 pound man doing cartwheels down the aisles.

I bought the book and took it home. In the back of the book was a list of prominent collectors with their addresses and phone numbers. I picked three collectors from three different parts of the country and contacted them to see who would offer the most money for the cans. When talking to the collectors, they called this a significant find on the Schlitz cans, and said that they had to be careful because a find like this could change the market value. They, of course, began asking me the condition of the cans. I had purposely pulled out the only three cans that weren't perfect of the twenty-two Schlitz cans, and gave Dad one of the good ones. I didn't want to have to explain about any rusted, dented, or defective cans of any kind, but just about nearly perfect ones. I billed them to the collectors as eighteen Schlitz Vitamin D Beer cone top cans, three Pabst Blue Ribbon cans, and two ABC St Louis flat top cans. These guys would ask me how much rust was on the seam down the side of the Schlitz cans, and I would answer, "None." They would say, "You mean it is bright silver still?" and I would say "yes." They then would say, "Turn the can upside down. How much rust is there?" I would answer, "None." "Ok, what color is it?" they would ask. "Bright gold color with numbers in ink stamped on it," I would reply. I remember thinking that had someone sat these cans in their kitchen cabinet in 1936, I could still not imagine pulling them out after 61 years and finding them in this good of condition. They were pristine. The guy I sold them to asked me how I got a hold of them, and why I wanted to sell them. I told him that I had gotten them at an auction and was not interested in them, as I didn't drink. His response was, "Oh my, I don't drink either. I just love to collect beer cans." I didn't get the retail prices listed in the book, but after giving my dad two cans, and keeping the three in the worst condition for myself, I received a cashier's check for $1300, and I was happy.

Years later, after eBay came along, I pulled out one of the cans with rust on it and put it on eBay. It brought over $400. I calculated that if I had sold those cans years later on eBay they probably would have brought about $9,000.

During those years I was also buying old motorcycles and working on them myself, and reselling them—mostly large Japanese bikes like Yamaha Viragos,

750 Hondas and 4 cylinder Kawasaki's. This didn't turn out to be a very profitable venture. The truth is, if someone gives you an old Japanese bike that doesn't run, and hasn't been tagged in a few years, by the time you put an ignition box, a pair of tires, and a cable or two on it, and bring the registration up to date, you have as much in it as it is worth. These old motorcycles were still fun to ride around on until I sold them, but not terribly profitable.

The next Mopar purchase was a 1969 GTX; it was a project car having no motor or transmission in it. The man I bought it from said that it had a notorious past in those parts, and had been used back in the day to run both illegal booze and marijuana out of Mexico. Some years back, its motor and transmission had been pulled out at the start of a restoration. Somehow, they had gotten separated from the car, and they were long gone. The best thing about this car was that it had been a southern Oklahoma car its whole life and had zero rust. I remember being a little tense bringing it home because it only had two remaining lug nuts on each of the wheels on the left side. I was using a car dolly in those days to tow cars with; so I had to have one end of the car or the other on the ground. The reason for the missing lug nuts was the studs were broken off. The reason for the studs being broken off is that old Chrysler products used to have right-hand thread lug studs and nuts on the right hand side of the cars, and they had left hand thread studs and nuts on the left side of the car. It was common for some gas station jockey, not familiar with old Mopars, to twist the left ones off while trying to remove them, turning them the wrong way.

While on the subject of quirks of old Mopars, one of them is the Chrysler Pentastar emblem on the lower right hand fender. They only put one on the right, not the left. Some restorers assumed that the car should be symmetrical, and drilled holes in the left fender and installed a Chrysler Pentastar. When you see a car at a car show that is a Dodge, Plymouth, or Chrysler, and it has a little gold Pentastar on both front fenders, behind the front tires, you know it was probably restored by someone without a lot of previous Mopar experience.

These old Mopars sitting around my car lot always drew a lot of attention. I once had a classmate of mine from north Missouri stop in. He said that he was going down the road and saw the Banks sign on the building. He knew that I had a car lot in the south, but told himself that there were possibly lots of people named Banks in the car business. However, he told me that as he approached and saw all the old Mopars around, "I knew that had to be you". Another memorable time, I was out in the shop and a guy walked into one of the Stalls, looking at one of the old cars sitting there. I asked if I could help him, and he said, "No, I just wanted to look at the old cars." I said, "Are you a Mopar man?" His answer was, "No, Pontiac. I had a GTO, but you guys always out ran me." I noticed that if I would be fooling with a car with open headers, and would crank it up in a stall, setting the timing or something, guys would start showing up drawn like moths to a flame.

Once a man came into my shop and he said in earnest, "Where do you get all these old Mopars?" to which I answered, "I grow 'em." He said, "What do you mean you grow em," to which I said "I just go out back and plant left handed lug nuts and wait for them to pop up."

FOUR DREAM CARS

ONE OF THE MOST FULFILLING THINGS that I have ever done concerning cars is to make my two daughters' and my niece's and nephew's dream cars a reality. Just like with finding my car when I was a teenager, we had to work within a strict budget, but for all four kids the end results were cars much nicer and cooler than what most people would have thought possible.

It all started when Kristen, my oldest daughter, was about 9 years old. I was looking at a magazine and I saw an advertisement for a new roadster that Mazda was soon to come out with. There hadn't been any roadsters sold in the United States for about ten years. All of the roadsters we had enjoyed in the past, like Triumphs, MG's and the like had been discontinued. In fact, all convertibles had gone away in the late '70's. It seems the consensus by the higher-ups in the car companies was that they were too unsafe. This new roadster design was inspired by the famous traditional roadsters of the past. In fact, the advertisement I had run across had a picture of a red Miata in the foreground. In the background was a black and white image of James Dean standing in front of a vintage Porsche roadster. I showed this advertisement to Kristen and asked her if she would like a car like that when she got old enough to drive, and she said that she would. From then on this became Kristen's dream car, and she talked of it often. When Kristen actually turned sixteen, Miata's were still very expensive. So, her first car was a very slick little Pontiac Grand Am coupe with body damage that I had traded for and then fixed it myself. As Kristen was learning to drive, even before she got her license, I felt like she should know how to drive a stick shift. I felt every driver should know that even if it wasn't their preference to own one, they should have the knowledge of how to drive a stick, in case of an emergency where the only vehicle available was a stick shift—kind of like knowing how to swim in case you fell in water over your head. I took Kristen out in various standard shift cars and trucks, with the end results being us pulling up in the driveway with Kristen jumping out of the car crying, running into the house and slamming the door. She would then run right past her mother and go to her room, again slamming the door. When I came in the house, I was greeted by my wife asking what I had done to Kristen. I never was able to teach her to drive a standard. The summer before Kristen's senior year I was at the auction one day, and a red Miata came into the lane. It was the perfect car, and I felt it even before I knew all the particulars about it.

The first Miata's were 1990 models; so they were produced and began being sold in 1989. There are a few subtle differences in those 1989 delivery cars made in the first two or three months of production. This car was an early production 1989 delivery car. It was a one owner car that had been traded in at a luxury car dealership, and they had brought it to auction because they didn't feel they had a market for that type of vehicle as a used car. It had all of its books and records, and only 74,000 miles. Best of all, it had the optional removable hardtop which was a very rare and expensive option. With the hardtop installed it looked like a totally different car than a regular Miata, and the first time we took the hardtop off we found the soft top in like new condition; very possibly it had never been raised. I brought the car home that afternoon and surprised Kristen with it. It was as close to the car in that picture she had looked at as a 9 year old as you could get, and was probably within a few hundred cars of it on the production line. She was of course excited beyond words, and I told her this is your car if you can learn to drive it. It was a 5 speed. She was driving it around in three days, and was teaching her friend to drive a stick in two weeks. She got to go to school the first day of her senior year in her dream car.

I remember after we got the Miata, taking Kristen out one day for some instruction. I felt that many inexperienced drivers panic in emergency situations, and figuratively if not literally, just throw their hands up in a skid. This was before anti-lock brakes, and I wanted Kristen to know what a car in a skid felt like. I explained to her about pumping the brakes to keep the tires from locking up; but even for the best drivers I explained to her, sometimes locking up the brakes is unavoidable. I then told Kristen to hang on tight as I ran the car up to sixty and then slammed on the brakes, locking them up and keeping them locked up until we'd slid to a complete stop sideways in the middle of the road. I said, "Now you know what it feels like, and if you ever find yourself in that situation, maybe it won't be so terrifying." Kristen became a very good driver. I feel safer riding with her than anyone else now.

The second dream car was for my nephew James. James had very unique taste, and he saw near his grandparents' home an early '60's Studebaker Lark, and he fell in love with that body style. He especially liked the front grill of the car; to me they vaguely resemble an older Mercedes grill. James would say that was the kind of car he wanted, but could get no encouragement from anyone that he would be able to acquire such an old and obscure model of car, especially one in good enough condition to drive. Of course we stopped and asked about buying the car he had seen, and the people were not at all friendly. They made it clear they would not sell the car. Finally, one day James was talking to me and he mentioned how someone had told him he might as well give up on the idea of getting an old Studebaker, that this was simply not going to happen. After hearing that, I decided then and there that I would find him a Studebaker Lark or know the reason why not. I felt empowered like Jimmy Olson had just told Clark Kent that someone was picking on him. I needed a phone booth to change into my Superman costume. I then started to shake the bushes searching for a Studebaker Lark.

I called on an ad for a 1961 Studebaker Lark near Grapevine, Texas. When I talked to the man on the phone, he told me he was selling it for a friend of his, a woman who was a flight attendant. She had been living in the area and flying out of the DFW airport, but she had moved to Florida several months back, and had been renting a storage unit to keep the car in. She needed to sell it so as not to have to keep paying rent at the storage facility. From the man's description of the condition of the car, it sounded just perfect. He said it was in good mechanical condition and ran and drove well, with good tires. The things it needed were paint and interior work; I knew we could easily handle that. There was one problem, the asking price; they wanted three to four times what money James had available to him. Before getting off the phone, I told the man that I was looking for a car for my nephew and that this price was out of reach; it was not even within bargaining range. He then said, "Look, she really needs to get rid of this car, and she is more interested that it go to someone who will appreciate it and not tear it up, than she is the money." He said the car had been a shared project of the woman and her boyfriend, and that they were driving it and restoring it together when they broke up. She put in for a transfer to overseas flights and moved to Florida, and that the car was just a painful reminder of their relationship that had ended, and she no longer had any interest in the car. He said I should call her, and he gave me her number.

I called the flight attendant, and she was very nice. I asked her some history of the car, and she said it was a one owner car when they found it. They had seen it sitting beside a house, obviously not being driven, and they had found the owner to be a very sweet old man. They had fallen in love with both him and the car, and she didn't want his car to be neglected. I think they had made him promises that they would only improve the car. I assured her that she had found both a family that could finish the restoration of the car, and a young man who would cherish it. She asked me what he could pay. I apologetically told her the amount, and she without hesitation, said she would accept that for the car. I thanked her for being so gracious, and assured her she had been a part of making a young boy's dream come true.

We made arrangements to meet her friend at the storage unit. He believed that the car was probably up to the task of making the 100 plus mile trip to Oklahoma. James, his mom Jeana, (my wife's sister, the same one who punched the juke box buttons that night, way back there in Princeton), and I went in my pickup to get the car. When we got there we found an awesome little Lark Cruiser VIII. It had the 289 V8 with an automatic transmission, which has a quaint unorthodox shift pattern, with drive at the bottom. It also had an interior that had little Larks woven in the fabric. To top it off there was a clear glass dome in the center of the steering wheel with a little Lark floating in it. It was easy to see why the previous couple had fallen for it. This thing was loaded with character. We paid the man and headed back towards Dallas on our way home.

We were traveling East on the LBJ freeway when we got to Dallas. So far the car had been running great. I was driving it; James was riding shotgun; and Jeana was following in my pickup. When we crossed the bridge over I-35 it was rush hour, and the highway right there was five lanes on each side. I was traveling in the middle lane when the car just died. I of course tried to restart it, with no success. The car had been performing so well. I theorized that even though the gas gauge showed plenty of gas, that perhaps it didn't work right and we possibly had run out of gas. If that wasn't the case, then we were in a mess that could not be easily remedied. There were two lanes of cars on each side of us, flying by just a few feet away, and they were all going 70 or faster. If you have ever driven in Dallas, you know what I mean. Literally, before I could do anything, a big rollback wrecker pulled in front of us and stopped. The driver stuck his head out the window and yelled back at me, "Do you need my help?" I said, "I will know in a couple of minutes." I put my back flat against the car and worked my way back to the pickup, where I had a can of gas I brought along just in case of a situation such as this. I grabbed the gas can and made my way back to the car, and hurriedly poured the gas in the old Studebaker. I then jumped back inside and tried the starter; it still wouldn't run. It wasn't out of gas; so I told the driver to load it up. I got in the truck with the wrecker driver and James hopped in my truck with Jeana. The wrecker driver asked me where to take the car. I told him to take us north to McKinney, which would get us through Dallas and out of the traffic to a safe place to leave the car. I didn't want to pay to have the car towed all the way to Oklahoma. I planned to go back home and get a trailer and come straight back and get it. After we got to McKinney, the car had been unloaded and the driver had been paid, I decided to turn the key in the starter one more time for good measure. Lo and behold, as they say in the south, it started. I then knew exactly what had happened; it had vapor locked because of the Texas summer heat, and during our 30 minute trip to McKinney, it had cooled off enough to run again—vapor lock was a common problem on cars of this age. We were then able to get it on home just having to stop a couple of times on the way home to give the old girl a breather.

When we pulled into the car lot back in Durant, I was surprised to see that James and Jeana didn't pull up to the office, as I did in the Studebaker, but instead pulled my pickup right up to the door of the cleanup bay of our three bay shop. As my family came out to admire James' car, I noticed in the background Jeana and James had the water hose out, and James was feverishly scrubbing the floor of my pickup with a scrub brush. Thinking this was an odd moment for a quick detail of my truck, I ambled on over for an explanation.

It turns out, as Jeana and James were following the wrecker down in the heavy traffic of Dallas, Jeana, who has always been famous in our family for having a bladder the size of a walnut, determines she has to pee and can't wait. Here was the dilemma; we had no cell phones at that time and we were not headed for any particular destination. I had told the wrecker driver I would pick a parking lot that looked good when we got to McKinney. Jeana and James were to simply follow us and didn't know where we would be stopping. If they pulled off now, they wouldn't know where to find us, and would not be there to pick me up when the wrecker driver and I stopped to let the car off. Jeana tells James she can't wait any longer, and to grab the wheel so she can scoot underneath him, and they will swap positions in the truck. James was not even close to being prepared to drive in this heavy traffic as he was just beginning to learn to drive. As terrifying as suddenly finding yourself in heavy traffic as a new driver is, what Jeana was about to try to do, was by his own testimony, about the scariest thing a young boy could experience. That was to be in the same pickup cab as your mom as she tries to pee in a pop can. The fact that this is almost an anatomical impossibility is the reason for the frantic scrub brushing of my pickup floor board that was taking place. This had just happened when they had pulled up behind the wrecker at McKinney, and they were both glad I hadn't noticed James was driving. They were then able to switch back positions when they got back in the truck to come on to Durant. When I found this out, I did remember them looking a little sheepish back there at McKinney. As the old saying goes, "all is well that ends well," although I think James does suffer from slight PTSD because of that experience. And for me, from then on, as long as I owned that truck, if I dropped my powdered doughnut on the floor, as much as I love powdered doughnuts, I just let it go.

We then attacked the restoration of the Studebaker with fervor. James stripped the complete car to the bare metal. It was a rust free car and required only minor body work of a few small dents. On the day I painted the car, about half way through the job, the ancient old compressor in the corner of the shop quit working. I determined it was the 240 volt contactors that turned the compressor on that had failed. I then stationed James across the shop with a paint stick in his hand to push the contactors together when I needed more air. James has become an extraordinary painter, and has paint jobs that have won best of show in prestigious car shows, and it is funny for me to remember his part in the first paint job he was involved in, turning his head and closing his eyes, being afraid of the sparking as he pushed those contacts together on my command.

The paint job turned out great! We then began restoring the interior. We retained the door panel fabric that had the little larks woven in, and we had a local guy who is very talented recover the seats in red vinyl to match the factory red dashboard, and red and black door panels. They looked great, with its shiny new Herman White Paint job, the factory color which is a creamy white.

The weekend before the first day of school we were all looking forward to James driving his car to school. James' little sister was a cheerleader and she was practicing her cheers on the carport near the Studebaker, when accidentally, she somehow spun around and kicked the plastic taillight on the old car, and as it was old and brittle, it shattered. We now had a dilemma in that even though reproductions were available, you could not go to AutoZone and get a taillight for a '61 Studebaker. Nor could you go to a Studebaker dealer which hadn't existed for nearly 40 years. I gathered up the pieces of the taillight from the carport, and took them to my workbench. I was determined to get that boy to school on Monday in that car, if at all possible. It really wasn't the red glass that had broken, but the housing of the taillight was also plastic, and it was one piece with the lens; fortunately, the housing was painted silver. With a lot of fiberglass and a few of the collected pieces, I fabricated a left taillight for James' car. After sanding and painting the silver part, it looked so good that when the pair of reproductions came in weeks later, he didn't put them on for a long time; the one I made was doing great.

The end of the story is we waved as another one went off to the first day of school in his dream car.

Next in line was Jodi, James' little sister and the aforementioned cheerleader. Jodi had watched her bigger girl cousin drive a Mazda Miata, and she also hoped to get a Miata for her first car. That was easy enough except for one thing; she wanted a purple one. Here was the problem; Mazda didn't make the Miata in purple, but Jodi could not be derailed. If she got a Miata, it needed to be purple. Once again I was at the car auction, and an incredibly clean and nice '93 Miata came through the lane. It happened to be white, which would be the easiest color as a base for a color change. The car went for a price that was within' the amount she had to purchase a car, so I bought the car and brought it home. Now I am no fan of purple for a car color, but I made a deal with Jodi that I would change the color on the car to purple, if I could pick the purple. At this time Ford was making the Ranger pickup that they called the Splash. They came in vibrant colors, and had been made somewhat famous by yellow ones on the TV show Bay Watch. We had recently on the car lot had a Ranger Splash that was purple, and it really was a pretty color. Actually, Ford's name for the color was a blue, but it appeared purple to everyone. I showed Jodi the color and she liked it. James played a great part in changing the color on this car; he took every piece off the body that would come off, like moldings and mirrors and lights. We jammed the car, meaning we painted inside the door jams, under the hood, and inside the trunk so it didn't appear that it had been painted. I really painted above my head on this, as I had never done a complete paint job with the then fairly new, two-part basecoat clear coat system. I borrowed a gun from a body man friend of mine, as my old gun was not suitable for the base clear paint. The paint job turned out beautiful, with the only flaw being a dime sized ripple in the paint, right behind the right headlight, from a drop of sweat that dripped from my forehead onto the car. I called that my signature. James actually did most of the hard work on this car in removing everything, and then putting it back together; he even removed the convertible top.

There was one final detail to complete the car. Kristen's car had alloy wheels as an option. This car had only the steel road wheels. The alloy wheels on Kristen's car were a dull aluminum from the factory. One day a guy came by my shop and asked if we would be interested in buying some Miata parts; he had wrecked a car and was parting it out. One of the things he had to sell was a set of alloy wheels, identical to the ones on Kristen's car, except they were chrome. Of course, we had to have those. Now Jodi needed some chrome wheels for her car too. As I began searching for a set of wheels, I could not find anyone who even knew what I was talking about. I could find the dull aluminum ones all day, but could not find a reference for chrome ones, even from Mazda. In my searching, I also learned that the '93 model alloy wheels for Jodi's car were actually a different design than Kristen's '90 model wheels, but they still were only available in dull aluminum. I finally solved the mystery; back when these cars were new, some dealers sent the wheels out to a chrome shop and had them plated, but they never came from the factory that way. I began to call chrome shops and wheel shops to get prices. One day I called a chrome shop asking what he would charge to chrome-plate a set of wheels, if I found some and brought them to him. He said that a long time ago a guy had brought him a set of Miata wheels to chrome, and that when the job was finished he never picked them up. He offered them to us for the price of the plating job only. The best part was they were the correct wheel for Jodi's '93 model car. These wheels were just the icing on the cake. We were selling a lot of Miata's on the car lot back then, and people would come in and tell me about that sharp looking purple one running around town. The end result was another youngster driving around in her made to order car. That's three down and one to go.

My youngest daughter Charity's dream car was, once again, a car that I had shown her years before she was old enough to drive. I remember being at the Dallas Auto Auction and being in the snack bar, looking out through the window at the auction lane below at a roadster that was about the coolest looking car that I had seen in a long time. It had a very aggressive looking long hood, and then I realized that it was one of those new BMW Z3's that I had been reading about. This one was a black one and I was impressed. BMW had decided to throw their hat into the roadster market ring, and had come up with, at least to my eye, the best one yet. I began pointing out Z3's to Charity, and she soon loved the Z3. She actually looked at several different models of cars, and finally settled on the BMW. Apparently even though I was a dyed in the wool American muscle car guy, I must have a repressed love for foreign roadsters, and was attempting to live vicariously through my daughters.

A BMW was a bit more of a challenge to find within our price range. At this time, I had bought in a local estate auction, a car for $200 that they could not get started, but I was sure that it, in fact, would run. It was an old Chrysler K car and it was pea green. I had become famous, at least in my family, for driving cars like this back and forth from our home ten miles from our business. Just before this I had bought a pair of Ford Escort station wagons, only giving $150 for one, and like $300 for the other. Even though our car business was known for late model, low mileage cars, I loved driving these almost free cars, and could care less what anyone thought of me driving around in them. All of this meant when I took Charity to school and picked her up most of the time, I would be in the K car. The K car was truly ugly and not at all "with it" and some of the kids teased her that this was what she was going to get for her first car. She blew them out of the water by saying she would appreciate any car her dad gave her, and if it was the K car, that would be alright with her. I was so proud of her attitude. In talking with her closer group of friends, when they would talk about their dream cars, Charity innocently named the Z3 as her dream car, and they immediately told her, "You might as well forget that; your dad is not going to get you one of those." She came home and told us about that conversation, and I thought, "Excuse me for a second; where is the nearest phone booth?" Charity's favorite color for a BMW Z3 was black, with her second choice being dark blue. Once again, at the car auction I found a 1996 BMW Z3. It was also a one owner trade-in at a luxury car dealership. I brought the Z3 home to Charity two weeks before the start of her senior year, and once again we sent one off to the first day of school in their dream car.

DID YOU KNOW YOUR CAR IS ON FIRE?

C. W. MCCALL IS A SINGER THAT HAD A lot of funny songs that my crowd enjoyed in the 1970's. One of my favorites of his is a song called "Classifieds." This song is about him answering a want ad for a 1957 Chevy pickup and is similar to a lot of experiences that I have had. The song starts out, "I was thumbing through the want ads in the Shelby County Tribune when this classified advertisement caught my eye."

Well I was thumbing through the want ads of *The Dallas Morning News* when an ad for a 1968 Road Runner caught my eye. I called the guy on the phone, and by his price and description, I didn't think I could go wrong. So I asked him to hold it for me. By this time my nephew James had gotten old enough to go with me on some of these excursions, and James and I, with the car dolly in tow, headed for Dallas to go get the old Road Runner.

Starting with bringing his Studebaker home, for a period of time it seemed every time James and I had an outing that had something to do with cars there was some kind of adventure. Once we went to Dallas to a swap meet, and all the way there my pickup had gotten more and more down on power. On the way home it got to where it couldn't even run the speed limit. Finally, in the middle of nowhere, it died. I coasted down the next exit and into the gravel driveway of a country beer joint. I went inside and asked the lady tending bar if she had any tools I could borrow. She rummaged through a big junk drawer and came out with the only tool she could find, a claw hammer. I had an idea of what had happened to the truck; so I slid underneath it and beat a large hole in the catalytic convertor with the claw end of the hammer. I took the hammer back in and thanked the lady. I went out and cranked the truck and it ran better than it had in weeks, but it sounded like a dirt track car. James was impressed.

Another time we parked our truck at a swap meet on a grass area that had at least fifty cars parked on it. There were "no parking signs," but there were so many cars already parked there that we had to look hard to find an open space. When we came back our truck was nowhere to be found in the line of vehicles. We found out the police department had all of the vehicles towed, including ours, but since then the entire grass area had filled back up again. Mom used to say, "If everybody jumps off a bridge, are you gonna jump off it too?" Lesson finally learned.

Still yet another time we were again going to a swap meet in the spring time, and the weather was very threatening. James and I were trying to figure out which way to go to try to get out of the path of the storm. We had one problem. The radio in my truck wasn't working and we weren't able to get a weather broadcast. I had recently purchased a replacement radio at a wrecking yard, and it was behind the seat in the pickup. A lot of good that was gonna do us. But, I had an idea. I leaned forward in the seat and had James fish the radio and some tools out from behind it. He then scooted over into the middle of the seat and took the plastic dash off the truck. I pulled the dash back and held it right behind the steering wheel while James unbolted the old radio, reached in behind it, and unplugged its wires and antenna. He then put the other radio in where that one had just come from, and screwed the dash back on. All this was done while driving 70 down I35. Even NASCAR teams don't work on their cars while they're rolling.

Now back to the '68 Road Runner. As in these previous outings, having challenging episodes when James and I and a truck were involved, this trip was to be no exception. When we got to the location of the Road Runner, we found a car that had a good straight rust free body. It had an interior that had been the home of several generations of mice. The inside of the car was also alive with fire ants, making sitting in the seat an impossibility. Under the hood it had its numbers matching 383 magnum, but that was all you could say for it. The engine was missing its cylinder heads, intake and carburetor, and it also had two rods thrown so badly that they were in pieces. I remember saying, "When this thing came apart it wasn't idling." The engine was nothing more than a big old rusty hunk of junk. Aw, just what we were looking for! We loaded it on the car dolly and headed back to the nation. We had been on the east side of Dallas in Garland, Texas and we were traveling on the same LBJ Freeway that the Studebaker had conked out on us, but this time we were headed the other direction.

We were driving along and everything was going very smoothly when something that appeared to be a scene out of a gangster movie happened. A very long black four-door luxury car started to come around us on the left. We were driving in the inside lane as we didn't want to pull the old car very fast. Instead of passing us by, the big car matched our speed, and for a few seconds, ran right beside us making me wonder what they were doing. The windows on this car were the darkest possible tint; so I could tell nothing about who was in the car. All of a sudden both windows on the car that were facing us started to come down, and when they got about halfway down, I saw four men in the car. When the windows got to the bottom, I was dreading to see those Uzi's come out, but instead, the man in the front stuck his head out and yelled, "Did you know your car is on fire?" I hollered back, Thank you," and headed for the shoulder.

We bailed out of the pickup and ran back to the car. Black smoke was really billowing out by this time. Although there was tons of smoke, I could not see any flames. I knew what must have caused this. The car probably had a bad wheel bearing, which can create enough heat to cause a car to catch on fire. I really needed to see under there to see if there were any flames visible. I cautiously stuck my head up under the car, right beside the gas tank, and I remember thinking, "I don't guess there's anything under here that could hurt me." I never saw any flames; it was just the grease burning off inside the brake drum because it had gotten so hot.

We were right at a ramp, and after it quit smoking, we pulled the car very slowly up the ramp into a convenience store parking lot. We had one problem we had to address. The car had only two tires that weren't flat, and they were on the back. We now had to take the car off the dolly and turn it around, then swap all four tires from front to back, and then winch the car back on the dolly. It was over a hundred degrees outside and we were drenched in sweat when we finally got it reloaded.

When we got the Road Runner back to the shop, we sprayed the inside with insecticide to kill the ants, and then pulled it into our first bay of the shop. By the next morning the whole shop and office building smelled so bad you could hardly stay in there. I told Ernie, "Dig around in that old car and see what's causing all of that stink." I figured the car had a dead animal under a seat or in the trunk. He yelled at me a few minutes later to come over there, that he had found the stink. What he had found was that the car had a full to the brim tank of gasoline that was several years old, and had gotten skunky. The top of the fuel tank was completely rusted out with holes several inches across, and that gas was just sitting there, as if in an open bucket. All of this was within a few inches from that red hot brake drum, backing plate, and axle on the day before. That sure made me remember sticking my head up under there, because I had decided there wasn't anyway that could be dangerous.

I was able to save the numbers matching block, by having the two cylinders that were damaged by rods trying to leave the premises, sleeved. One of the biggest selling points of a Road Runner when they were new was their low price. These cars could be ordered through the PX, and many military boys in Vietnam ordered their cars, and picked them up in California when they got off of the boat from Southeast Asia, and drove their new hot rod home. Rare for a Road Runner, this car had been ordered with the premium interior, and it was a really nice two-tone cream and gold color. We replaced the entire interior from headliner to carpet, including the door panels and seats. This car was also very close in color to my GTX, and it had been just making me more homesick for my old car. This Road Runner made a gorgeous car. James and I had towed it home on Labor Day weekend, and by Christmas time, we had it ready to sell.

While I had this car on my car lot for sale, one day a man brought his young son in. The boy was probably about ten years old. The man was a very well dressed, soft spoken man. He asked if I would take him and his son a ride in the Road Runner. We got in the car and headed out of town, and as we drove the man said, "I have a strange request if you would do it." He said, "I would like to see what a car like this can do." He continued on and said "I would like to know what it would feel like, for instance, if you were drag racing someone." Can you imagine him asking me to do something like that? I found a place to turn around, and stopped the Road Runner in the middle of the road. I then did a short burnout to clean the tires. Next I pulled the car up to the imaginary starting line and loaded the torque converter by placing my left foot on the brake and bringing the rpms up until I could feel it start to pull against its own brakes, just as I had learned in the old GTX so many years before. I then nailed the throttle while releasing the brakes, and ran them up to 100 mph.

On the way back to the shop, the man thanked me very genuinely, and said, "How do you learn how to do that." I said, "Aw that's just a sign of a misspent youth."

I sold that car to a man who owned a business in a nearby town and then lost track of it. Many years later I was showing a couple of cars in a local car show, and a man came up and asked if I was Mike Banks. I said, "Yes." He then said, "You sold my brother-in-law a Road Runner several years ago." I asked him a couple of questions to make sure what car he was talking about. He then said that "this Road Runner is now in Stuttgart, Germany." It turns out his brother-in-law sold it to a collector car dealer in Dallas when he was done with it. They in turn had sold it to someone in Stuttgart. Years later, the German owner had tracked down his brother-in-law that I had originally sold the car to, wanting to ask questions about the history of the car. I would imagine by the time the guy in Germany got his car home, he had a considerable amount more invested in the car than what I sold it for those years before.

ONES THAT GOT AWAY

T HERE'S A SAYING AMONG COLLECTOR car people that says on desirable models you can't give too much, you can only buy too early. Over my years I have seen this play out many many times. When we were looking for the GTX when I was young, we found a guy who had two Shelby GT 500 Mustangs. They were pristine examples with dual quad intakes. He was asking ten thousand dollars each for these cars, and my dad and I were absolutely blown away that a Mustang, any Mustang, would be considered at that price. For anyone who has the vaguest interest in collector cars or Mustangs in general, this might have brought tears to your eyes.

In the early '80's I attended a Kruse Collector Car Auction. In those days it was quite a fancy event with the ring men and auctioneers wearing some semblance of a tuxedo. I remember overhearing a guy talking to a group of men about a 1957 Chevrolet car he owned that had extremely low miles, something like under 10,000. He was telling these men that several years earlier he had given $10,000 for this car, and how his buddies and many others in the old car trade, thought he was nuts. This is the amount it took to acquire the car at the time, and he realized that when the market said this was an acceptable amount, that the car would not be available to him. I then continued listening as he told of a man a few years later coming to his motel room with a briefcase with $40,000 cash in it, even though he had been told at the car show they were both attending, that the car was not for sale. He didn't sell. He told how the local Chevy club would ask to come to his place because they had to settle an argument of whether a particular nut on a '57 Chevy was supposed to have a flat washer or a lock washer under it. What a bargain that '57 would be for $40,000 today, let alone the original ten thousand he paid.

Early on as a used car dealer, I was visiting my wife's parents in southeast Arkansas. Each day I would leave my wife and daughter at her parent's house to visit, and I would go a different direction each day to hunt for a source of wholesale cars. One day I was in western Mississippi and stopped at a GM new car dealership. This was a small dealership and I noticed several DeLoreans mixed in with the other cars. Two of them were wearing red paint, a real odd thing for a stainless steel car. When I went in I was able to talk to the owner of the dealership. After inquiring about any of the models of cars and trucks I was interested in purchasing, he asked if I would be interested in some new DeLoreans. At this time DeLorean motor cars had been out of business for a while, and these cars were a couple of years old but were still being sold as new cars, with no miles and an MSO[2] instead of a title. He priced these new DeLoreans to me for $10,000 each, quite a significant deduction from what their original cost was. Although I wasn't interested, I asked how come two were red, and

---

[2]A Manufacturers Statement of Origin, or MSO, is what new cars come with before they are titled.

he said they had had them etched and painted with special paint to stick to the stainless steel, in hopes they would sell better with a color on them. My next question was how did, he as a GM dealer, end up with Deloreans, and he said he got a special deal on ten of them. I said, "How many do you have left?" and he only answered "several." As I was walking back to my car I counted ten Deloreans on his lot.

It's always surprised me how overnight something can seemingly go from common to collectable. I remember standing at the Dallas Auto Auction and seeing a '70's Trans Am Pontiac bring $5,000. I was astounded someone would pay that much for one, and remember saying and feeling the same way when I observed a 1972 Chevy short bed pickup also bring $5,000. A newer body style of that truck in a comparable condition wouldn't have brought this much. Sometimes it seems a vehicle jumps from used car status to collector status nearly overnight. At some point VW bugs did the same thing.

When we started handling the Mopar muscle cars I was only interested in true muscle cars, and personally only big block cars. Consequently, I passed on several vehicles that I would love to have another chance at now. One day a young man from twenty-five miles away drove a '69 or '70 Baracuda with a 318 in it in and he wanted to sell it for $1,300. It had a clean body and ran well, but I didn't buy it. I'm not very proud of that decision. Another time I was called about a 1969 Dodge Charger they wanted to sell for $600. I went across town to look at it. It was a complete car although it didn't run. It was also a 318 car and was a dark gray color.

Underneath the gray primer the car was Dukes of Hazard orange. Yea, I passed on that one too. I'm going to stop with these stories before you question my IQ, but understand, the idea of cloned muscle cars was fairly new and I wasn't on board. I'm kind of an old school guy. In fact they tore down my school when they built the old school.

THAT'S WHEN I LEARNED WHAT A ROAD RUNNER WAS

W HILE IN A RUSH ONE DAY TO GET somewhere south of town, I was going by a local veterinarian hospital when something caught my eye. It was a 1968 or 1969 Plymouth Road Runner parked in the parking lot. Seeing a Road Runner out on the road and not at a car show is rare. Seeing one used as daily transportation, like taking your cat or dog to the vet, is extremely rare. This sighting was extraordinarily rare because this car looked completely unrestored. The most amazing part was it still had its original stamped steel wheels and dog dish small hubcaps. These cars usually didn't make it much past the next weekend from their original purchase before those wheels were replaced and a popular set of mag wheels were installed. These days you will sometimes see a Road Runner with those original wheels and hubcaps, but that is usually only after a full-bore OEM restoration, the kind where every detail is correct for the build sheet/fender tag. The mud splatter and dead silver paint made it obvious that this car was not a detailed restoration. I was so curious about this car but had no time to spare to investigate. I told a few of my friends about it and that was the end of it, or so I presumed.

One day when traveling home from a car auction in Dallas I was driving through Sherman, TX and there in a large parking lot sat the same Road Runner. I quickly pulled in and parked close to the Road Runner and called my wife back at our car lot. I knew Lynn was expecting me back around a certain time and I let her know that I might be delayed because I was going to camp out beside this Road Runner until its owner came back. No matter how long that took.

Fortunately I didn't have to wait long. In a few minutes an elderly gentleman exited the store and came walking towards the car. He was a tall slim man and was dressed very dapper with a tweed sport jacket and a fedora hat. His clothing was definitely something more commonly seen in the '60s or '70s than at that current time.

I approached the old fellow cautiously so as not to put him on guard. I told him that I had noticed and had been admiring his car and asked if he was the original owner. He answered that his late wife had been the original owner. He then proceeded to graciously relate the whole story to me.

He said that he had a good job with an airline company in Dallas at the time, and he felt that they were doing pretty good financially. He decided to bless his young wife with a new car. He took her to a local Chrysler Plymouth dealer and they went in the showroom. The first car they came to was this very Road Runner and he sat in the driver's seat and his wife sat in the passenger seat. He said after he got done checking out the dashboard controls and the feel of the seat that he climbed out. When he climbed out his wife then slid across the bench seat to where he had been sitting. He said she grabbed the steering wheel with both hands and exclaimed "I want this one!" He was totally surprised by this as he had planned on them looking at these cars in the showroom and then proceeding outside and ultimately looking at dozens of cars before they chose. He then asked her "Are you sure?" "Yes!" she replied "This is the one I want!" He said he then rationalized that he had brought her here to pick out a car for herself and if this is what pleased her then this is the one he was going to get her, so he bought it on the spot.

This next part of the story is priceless to me. He said they had owned the car for a short while but he had never driven it. One day on his day off he had to run an errand so he decided to take the wife's new car instead of his. He was in city traffic and as he was coming up an on ramp the traffic was heavy and there was a car approaching really fast so he pushed the accelerator on the wife's Road Runner to the floor to get ahead of the oncoming car. "I thought the thing had exploded" he said "There was a loud booming noise and squalling and screeching and I immediately veered off on the shoulder, put the car in park, got out, and opened the hood." He said when he opened the hood, the car just sat there idling calmly and everything was just perfect. He then proclaimed "That's when I learned what a Road Runner was" I was so glad I persisted until I got to hear this great story.

THE HUNT

A S WE WERE DABBLING IN SELLING Mopar muscle cars as sort of a sideline to our business of selling late model used cars, my desire to have another '67 GTX to replace the one Lynn and I used to have began to grow. I began to look at Auto Trader Publications, Hemming's Motor News, and the Mopar Collector's Guide searching for one. I called on a few but they were mostly very non-original. Most of them had their engines changed out through the years, and the super commando 440 was long gone. The few that were nice, original, or restorations were sky high in price. I remember each month, when the Mopar Collector's Guide came, going straight to where a 1967 GTX would be listed, hoping for the best. As I would read these want adds, I would share with Lynn what I was finding, and sometimes show her a picture of one of the cars. She seemed very interested and asked a lot of questions.

One day, sort of out of the blue, while talking to Lynn about one of the cars, she just kind of blurted out, "I think we can find our old car." I said, "You mean the very one?" and she said, "Yes, the very one." She said, "Yes, I really feel like God is going to give us your car back." I was kind of surprised and excited at the same time. I knew that Lynn didn't throw statements like this around lightly, and that her intuition was usually right on, especially the spiritual kind.

Lynn suggested that we go up in our attic and drag down all of our old paperwork to see if we could find the VIN (vehicle identification number) of the old GTX. We had moved from our trailer house to our new house only two years after selling the GTX, and very likely there would still be some paperwork history on it. This was a great idea, and it paid off very quickly. We pulled down containers and boxes with many years of dust, and within the first ten minutes, Lynn said "Here it is." She had found the last registration where we had tagged the car. We now had a serial number to identify the car we were searching for. This happened on a weekend, and I could not wait until Monday morning to get started looking for my car.

The first place I went was to our local tag office, which I dealt with constantly being a car dealer. They put the VIN number into their system, but it returned with no results. This didn't surprise me since their search was only in Oklahoma. I didn't expect it to still be in Oklahoma, since the old man I talked to years ago told me he sold it to someone in Missouri. My next stop was a friend in the local police department, who also didn't find any reference to it. He made the statement to me that his search was exhaustive, and that the car was long gone, probably totaled out and in a wrecking yard years ago. Fortunately, I was not discouraged by any of this. I knew that my car was recognized as collectible and purchased as such all of those years ago, and I also knew that collector vehicles are rarely wrecked and certainly not junked, even when they are wrecked. I knew it might have been several years since it was tagged and driven, possibly stowed away somewhere in a garage or warehouse. Also I had Lynn's word to go on; so I soldiered on.

My next step was to get out one of my copies of the Mopar Collector's Guide. I had become acquainted with it back a few years ago when trying to determine the value of that first '71 Road Runner that the old fellow had left with me to sell on consignment for him. I called the Mopar Collector's Guide, looking for help locating my car. Back when I had last talked to the man in Duncan years ago, he had told me that the person that bought it was from southwest Missouri, and that he was a collector with a lot of Mopar muscle cars. I naively asked the person on the phone at Mopar Collectors Guide Magazine for a list of their subscribers in southwest Missouri. They quickly told me they were not allowed to give out that kind of information, but they did tell me that the largest Mopar muscle car wrecking yard in the world was located in southwest Missouri, and if the guy I was looking for was a Mopar collector in that area, rest assured they would know him. They said the name of the wrecking yard was R & R Salvage in Aurora, Missouri, and they gave me their phone number.

I immediately called the number, and the phone was answered with "R&R Auto Salvage. This is John." I said, "John, my name is Mike Banks, and I am calling you from Durant, Oklahoma." I then continued on with, "In the late 1970's I had a gold 1967 GTX that I sold to a guy in Duncan, Oklahoma, and I am searching for that car." I had much more details to give him, but at that point John interjected into the conversation, "I owned that car." I thought I must have gotten a hold of some kind a nut who would agree to anything. I said to John, "Now hold on a minute," to which he said, "Yea, I know what you're gonna say; the color of my car was red alright, but I'm tellin' you: it was gold underneath that red." I said, "What kind of transmission did it have?" and he said, "An automatic on the column. I said, "What about the interior?" He said, "It was white with the little buddy seat." Once again he stopped me and said, "Listen to me. My grandma lived in Duncan, Oklahoma, and one year my dad visited her for Christmas, and when he came back from the trip, he said, 'there is a 1967 GTX sitting out for sale in Duncan,' and he and I went back down to Duncan and I bought it and drove it home." He said, "In fact, it was my daily driver for a few years." He then said, "I know what you're gonna ask me next, and I have good news and bad news. The good news is, "Yes, I know who I sold it to; the bad news is he didn't have it very long and I heard that when muscle car prices went through the roof in the late '80's, that it went to California and it sold for big money." He then proceeded to tell me the name of the person he had sold it to, and the name of the town he lived in. The town had one of those names like you commonly find in the Ozarks, like Bug Tussle. John said it was about thirty miles from where he was. He didn't have a phone number for him, but he would try to get it for me. After a couple of weeks and a couple of calls back to John at R&R, he said he was unsuccessful at coming up with a phone number, and I was on my own.

I called information for the small town, and found six or eight people by the last name I had been given, with phones in that area. This was a very small town with only a few hundred people living there. I began to call the numbers for that last name one by one, and asked if they knew this person. When they would say, "no," I would say, "I am not a bill collector or anything like that. I just want to talk to him about a car he used to own," but after going through the whole list, not one person would agree to knowing him. I always left my name and number anyway, saying just in case they found someone who knew him. Several days went by and one day I got a phone call, and the man stated his name and said, "My mom said you called about a car." I had been talking to his own mother at one point, and she wouldn't even admit to knowing him. Wow!

This guy was not hesitant at all to tell me the whole story of his involvement with the car. He said after buying the car he had intended to keep it forever. He had a son who was young at the time, and that he intended for him and the boy to enjoy it together right then, and that eventually it would become his son's car. He said that after owning the car for only a few months, a semi-truck stopped in front of his house, and the driver came to the door asking about possibly buying the car. He said he remembered that it was Super Bowl Sunday of that year, and that he was trying to watch the game. He said that he told the trucker that the car was not for sale, but that the trucker was very persistent and they were finally able to make a deal. The part about the car going to California was not correct; the trucker was from Effingham, Illinois, and he had a building that housed many Mopar collector cars. Once again, he didn't have his phone number or his name, but assured me he had it written down somewhere, and would find it and call me in a couple of days. He didn't. After a week I called him, and he said to give him a few more days; he had some other places to look. After another week I called again; he had not been able to come up with anything more. So all I had to go on was a Mopar guy in Effingham, Illinois who had a lot of them.

I began to call everything car related that I could think of in Effingham, Illinois. I called the Chrysler dealership. I called the auto parts stores, and even though they didn't know anyone with a building full of old Mopars, I would ask them to suggest someone who might. One of the fellows who they put me onto was the president of a large Corvette club, but even he had not heard of my Mopar guy. This went on for several days with no breakthrough. Late one afternoon, while sitting at the car lot, just watching the clock, waiting for closing time, I got an idea. If there was someone out in the country side of any county that had a ton of collector cars sitting around, or in a large building, surely the deputies of the county sheriff's department would know about it. I just didn't know if they would be sympathetic to my cause. Once again I called information in Effingham, and asked for the Sheriff's department. A very pleasant female dispatcher answered the phone, and as nicely as I could, I explained what I was doing, and asked her if she might know of such an individual. She said she didn't know anyone who fit my description, but that there were several deputies in the station right then, and if I would give her a minute she would ask them all if they might know who I was looking for. After about five minutes she came back and said that none of the officers could think of anyone fitting the description either. She then asked me, "You wouldn't by any chance have the serial number of the car you're looking for, would you? I told her that yes in fact I did. She said, "Give me a minute and I will run it against the county tax records." When she came back to the phone, she said, "The owner's name is Wayne Cox. Would you like his phone number?"

SPANKY

AFTER GETTING OFF THE PHONE WITH the Effingham, Illinois dispatcher, I took a deep breath and contemplated if I had finally found the person who owned my car now. Up until then this whole process of dreaming about finding the car and the excitement of tracking it down had been fun. Now I was apprehensive. I was finally standing before the door and I didn't know what I would find on the other side. Would it be like *Let's Make a Deal*, and the door had my dream car behind it, or would it be like when Geraldo opened Al Capone's vault, full of let down and disappointment. Sometimes the anticipation of a thing turns out to be more intense than the fulfillment of the thing. In this case, my dream of finding this car had been intensifying for a couple of decades. I have mentioned trying to locate it after it had been gone only a very few years, but after that, there was an incident several years later that had fueled my passion for this long lost love even more.

When Lynn and I were newlyweds, I determined she needed her own set of keys for the GTX. Looking back now I wonder if that wasn't a part of me beginning to fulfill my wedding vows—you know, kinda like "what's mine is yours and what's yours is mine." (Hey, this was not a small thing. Some newlywed couples have a hard time combining their bank accounts.) Many of my friends had begged just to drive this car, and I wouldn't let them. When Lynn and I started dating, they would get mad when, on the rare occasion, they would see her driving my car. Now possibly, unknowingly, I was bestowing on my new bride the co-ownership of my most precious worldly possession—the beloved muscle car. If you don't buy all of that, okay, I went to a hardware store and had an extra set of keys made for the GTX.

I gave Lynn the original Chrysler Corporation logo keys that had come with the GTX new, and I kept the reproductions for my pocket. Lynn kept her keys in her purse in a little leather key fob that said, "Jesus is love" on the outside; it had a snap so you could fold its flaps over the keys. Along with the keys to the GTX, she also had the key to our VW rabbit, and the keys to our mobile home. One day Lynn's keys went missing. She had used them to drive the VW home and to unlock the front door. So we knew they had to be in the house, but we could not find them to save our lives. We suspected that the keys were down beside the cushions in our small recliner that sat beside the front door, because Lynn had a habit of throwing them down in the seat of it when she had her hands full of groceries, or some other items. I stuck my arm down on both sides of the chair's cushions and even turned it upside down, but could not make it give up the keys. We then suspected Mo our dog had stolen them as he was accustomed to do, but after checking all of his hiding places that we knew about, no keys were found. We reasoned the keys would turn up somewhere in the house eventually. We never found them. It was easy for me to make the VW rabbit keys in my own key machine at the dealership I worked at, and we also easily got a key for our home reproduced. We didn't replace the GTX keys as we were no longer using it for our main transportation, and Lynn really didn't need them anymore.

Later when we moved into our new home about six miles away, the recliner that we had suspected held the keys was moved with our other furniture. In a few short years the recliner mechanism broke, requiring us to throw it away. I loaded the recliner in my pickup truck and took it to a private dump ditch on some friends' property. I backed the pickup right up to the ditch and climbed up in the bed. Being young and strong, I unnecessarily hoisted it over my head. (It was a small recliner.) I could have easily just pushed it off the tailgate, but I picked it up and threw it just for fun. When I got it over my head, I heard a clank as something hit the pickup bed floor as I released the chair, projecting it deep into the dump ditch. When I looked down, lying at my feet was Lynn's long lost key fob. I couldn't wait to get back home and show the keys to her. We marveled at how they had remained hidden all those years. For years after that I would daydream about attending a car show or collector car auction, and having the forethought to bring the old set of keys with me. In this reoccurring daydream, I would walk to a red 1967 GTX and try the keys, and to my amazement, the lock would turn and I would realize that I had found my car.

I dialed the number the dispatcher gave me. After a few rings a machine answered and said, "I am not able to answer your call right now. Please leave a message after the beep." The phone then continued to beep for at least twenty times. I have never before or after that heard an answering machine that had that many messages recorded. So I left my name and a short message about wanting to talk to him about a car. Then once again, I waited.

After more than a week I still hadn't heard back from the message I had left, and the tension was mounting. On the morning of Memorial Day we had slept late, and I was lying in the bed awake but had not gotten up yet. The phone rang and I reached over to my night stand to pick up the receiver. I said, "Hello.", and a very pleasant and cheerful voice said, "Mike this is Wayne Cox, but my friends call me Spanky. You wanted to talk about a car?"

As I began to talk to Wayne, I was so relieved that he exhibited no bad attitude at all about me having hunted down a car that he now owned. Anyone who has ever stopped and asked about an old car sitting on someone's property, no matter how neglected it might look, knows the hateful reaction this often causes to the owner of said car. Many times their reaction would be more fitting to a question like, "Could I sleep with your wife?" or "Could I dump the holding tank to my RV in your front yard?" than simply asking if a car might be for sale. I felt no such thing from Wayne. He truly seemed to be happy to talk about the car, and he had more questions about it from me than I did for him. With that said, it was also clear that Wayne truly loved this car. Wayne told me that he had between one and two hundred cars on his property at that time. Several dozen of them were stored inside. Of those he mentioned, a select few he drove and showed often, and mine was one of them. He had personalized Illinois license plates on my car that read '67 GTX. Wayne asked me to send him some pictures of the car when I had it, and also to write about my owning it. Wayne also got my address and said he would send me pictures of the car now.

When I got off the phone to Wayne, I had mixed emotions, although much more good than bad. On a scale of one to ten, I felt this was a seven and a half experience. Most of the good experience was that Wayne was such a nice guy, and that he also was a real deal car guy. I was glad that the car still had its original engine and drive train. I was also glad that it had not undergone a high dollar restoration, putting it out of reach for me ever to purchase it. The negative was that from this conversation, it was obvious that Spanky, as he invited me to call him, had no intention of ever turning loose of that car.

I was excited I had found the car, of the condition it was in, and the personality of the owner. Charity, who was nine years old at the time, had assumed that finding the car meant we were automatically getting it back. So when I hung up the phone, she in all honesty said, "So when do we get it?" and I had to explain to her the reality of the situation. Even though it would require patience and some time, I still had an underlying confidence that someway, somehow, we would someday get it back, and for now I was so happy that it was found.

REUNITED

A FTER OUR ORIGINAL PHONE conversation, Wayne was good to his word and sent me some pictures of the GTX with a short note. I in turn sent Wayne pictures of the car when I had it, and included a short history, beginning with my purchase of the car, and ending with me selling the car. When Wayne received my letter and pictures, he called me. Wayne said he had an idea. Why didn't my wife and I come up to Effingham, and meet him and see the car. He said if we chose to do that, he would loan us the car for an evening. We could take it out on a date for old time's sake, and return it to him the next day. I was very impressed with his trust and generosity, and told him we would consider it.

Of course, during this time, my mind often went back to the subject of this car. As I would think about it, I would always come to the conclusion that I hope only finding the car is not the end of this story; surely there will be a way to get it back. One day, while sitting at my desk in my car lot alone, I gave myself a pep talk. I said, "Mike, come on. You're a car dealer. Surely you could come up with a late model vehicle that would be enticing enough that Wayne would want to trade your old car for it."

So I picked up the phone and dialed Wayne. After some general conversation I said, "Wayne, I'm a car dealer and I was wondering if you were looking for any kind of used vehicle. " His response was, "Well yes, in fact I am." He said that he was a truck driver, and that the company he drove for was based in Chicago. So he had to drive into Chicago to get his truck each time he went out on the road. He said he was looking towards retirement in a few short years, and was planning on buying a new pickup then. For now, he needed to replace his old truck with one to bridge the gap between now and retirement, and he only wanted a Dodge.

Nothing could have been more perfect. Just a couple of weeks before this, a young man pulled into the car lot in an extremely slick Dodge pickup. I immediately noticed this truck didn't fit the driver. It was a very slick, single cab, long-bed old man pickup. When the guy came inside, he said his father had recently died, and that he had inherited this truck. He said his father had bought it new, and that it was in very good condition with low mileage, but that he didn't want to keep it, and just needed to turn it into money. He and I agreed on a price and I bought it. This truck fit me perfect. It had a V8 engine and it had rubber mats instead of carpet, which I love because when I get them dirty I can take a water hose and wash them out. The truck was equipped with a very-rare for the day, granny low four speed transmission, especially since it was only a half-ton. I began driving it for my daily driver. While using the truck one day, a funny thing happened. Charity wanted me to take her somewhere in town and we went in my truck. When she got inside she said, "Oh no. I hate this truck. Do we have to go in it? I don't like it when mom takes me in this truck." I didn't pay a lot of attention to her. I figured her little girl mind could have any reason not to prefer this truck, from the radio to the color or the feel of the seat. On the way back, Charity said, "Wait a minute! This truck didn't do today what it does when mom drives it." She said, "When mom takes off it goes like this" and made gyrations with her body like she was riding a bucking horse. I got a good laugh out of that, and later questioned Lynn about it. I didn't realize that Lynn didn't know that low gear is actually second in a transmission like this, and that first is compound low, used only for towing or hauling heavy loads. I can still see Lynn's neck-snapping departures from stop lights, depicted by skinny little grade-school Charity, and it always makes me laugh.

I told Wayne about this truck, and he indicated it was a perfect fit for him; so he asked me how much I wanted for it. I said, "I would want to trade it to you for my old car." "Oh my, no," Wayne said. "The car is not for sale, but what do you want for the truck?" I reluctantly told him, and he said, "I will take it." In all my years of being a car dealer, I don't think I have ever been less excited about selling a vehicle. Wayne said, "I will mail you a check, and just hold the truck for me. I have a brother in Tulsa which is not that far from you. I will have him come and get it for me."

I received the check promptly, but the truck sat beside the building for a couple of weeks before the brother arrived to pick it up. We had a good visit with Wayne's brother, and told him the whole story. When I told him that I really wanted to trade this truck for the

GTX, Wayne's brother said "I am surprised you have not made him mad. Those cars are like kids to him. Wayne doesn't sell his favorite cars."

Wayne and I continued to talk on the phone that spring and early summer. We visited about the MOPAR nationals that were being held in Indianapolis that year. Wayne was a regular at this event, and it was an event that I had really wanted to get to attend. We decided on a trip to the MOPAR nationals in August, with a stop at Wayne Cox's farm on the way up to see the GTX and Wayne's other cars. The plan was, after our stop at Wayne's, we would continue on to the nationals, and Wayne would come up also, and he could show us around while we were there.

On the way to Effingham and Indianapolis, as we were traveling on I 44, we stopped in Rolla, Missouri, and visited Callen grocery, which was my great uncle's (my granddad's brother's) grocery store. We talked with my aunt and uncle and their youngest son Dave. While at their home, I remembered when I was very young visiting their home, and that Eldon, one of Dave's older brothers, had an MG TD. I remember riding with my dad in it. The things that stick out to me were its large flat steering wheel and the side mount spare tire. I think it might have also been right hand drive.

We spent the night in Rolla, and the next morning headed out for Effingham, Illinois, and our long anticipated reunion with our old car. For Lynn and me, it was all about the memories, and was symbolic of our early relationship and marriage. To the girls, it was a chance to see the legendary thing that they had heard so many stories about.

As we came through St. Louis, Missouri, we were running along on the interstate and admiring the Gateway Arch. A truck pulling a trailer pulled along beside us, and on the trailer, was what looked like a brand new 1967 GTX; it was silver in color and I doubt that it even looked this good brand new. This year of the Mopar Nationals, the 1967 GTX was being honored as their featured car on its thirtieth anniversary. It turns out this heavy hitter was headed for the Nat's as well.

After arriving in the city of Effingham, Illinois, I then pulled out of my wallet the instructions Wayne had given me to continue on to his farm outside of town. The last leg of the trip was down a gravel lane, taking us to Wayne's home.

As we pulled into the driveway there was no dramatic unveiling of the GTX, for Wayne had it pulled out and waiting for us, backed up against a fence that surrounded his quite large parking area. Wayne had parked it where it was the first thing we saw when pulling in. We drove right passed it and parked beside the blue Dodge pickup with the Banks Motor Company sticker on it.

Wayne's house was directly in front of us. His large shop was to our right, and the GTX was to our left. The large door was open on the shop building, and you could see several Mopar beauties nestled inside there. After exiting the car, I walked over to the shop expecting to find Wayne, but no one was inside. There was a radio playing, but no Wayne. We all then walked over to the GTX and began circling it and admiring it. I was surprised to see a set of keys hanging in the ignition switch. I didn't dare touch those keys. This car belonged to another man, and something I had learned from a boy concerning a gun or a car, you didn't touch it unless invited to. On my second trip around the car, I did allow myself one long awaited liberty. In my right front pocket was that lost then recovered set of Lynn's keys, still in their Jesus is love key fob. I slipped the keys out and selected the round headed one, and stuck it in the trunk. As I turned it slowly, savoring every degree of rotation, all of a sudden there was a very lively pop, and the trunk sprang up a few inches. The car seemed to have been anxiously awaiting this moment of being reunited with its old owners, represented by this set of keys, as much as we were.

In a short while, Wayne rolled in. We greeted one another and he said, "Well, how did she drive?" Once again I was impressed with Wayne's trusting nature. Wayne explained he had to run to town to get some parts, and had left the keys in the ignition so we could drive it, if we got there before he got back.

We then did all pile into the car for a short ride out in the country. The feeling of the car was so familiar. The most obvious was the way that you sat down deep in the car, with the door to your left being higher than most cars. The steering wheel is also distinct in that the thickness of it is thinner than modern day cars. All of these things were saying, "Yea, this is my car alright." I was very respectful of this car belonging to Wayne, not me, and consequently, I didn't get on it. Oh what an embarrassment it would have been had I have taken the car out because of Wayne's graciousness, and broke it. With that said, if cars had a consciousness, I'm sure the old GTX would have had a hard time believing it was really me behind the wheel. If someone would have reassured it that, "No this really is Mike," I'm sure it would have said, "That can't be him. Aliens must have taken over his body because my pedal hasn't even gotten close to the floor, and he's been driving me at least ten minutes."

Once while my Granddad was visiting me from North Missouri, an old man traded in a pickup truck. While we were doing the deal, my granddad and the old fellow began to visit with one another. They talked about farming and the different crops grown in their own areas. Granddad was the kind of guy that never met a stranger, and they had a great time visiting. This man buying the truck was at least as old as granddad was, if not older, and he was very slow geared. He moved about by shuffling his feet and was also slow speaking. Soon after we got our deal done and the man left, I got a call from a person telling me that they had decided to buy a car that they had been talking to me about. This was a car that I had to pick up in Dallas, and it was already afternoon. In those days I pulled cars out of Dallas with a car dolly that I pulled behind my pickup. On that day, I had the engine apart on my truck, rebuilding it. So I jumped in the old man's trade-in and hooked the car dolly to it. I invited Granddad to go with me, and he was more than happy to ride along. This was a Friday and a holiday weekend, and the traffic was horrendous. I was in a great hurry to get to Dallas, and get this car loaded, and get back out of there. So the speed limit was somewhat compromised. We reached the place where the car was, and I paid for it and loaded it. I then began to come out of Dallas headed back to the nation, just as fast as I had come down, only with a car tagging along in tow. Granddad was not used to this kind of traffic and the speed everyone in Dallas was driving. He had been pretty quiet up to this point, just taking it all in. All of a sudden Granddad blurted out, "Well, I'll tell you one thing. I'll bet this truck thinks somebody turpentined that old man!" If you don't know what "turpentined" means, ask somebody from the country, preferably the south, who is over eighty years old. You might get lucky and get an explanation. So also must my old car have thought that its former driver had experienced a life changing event.

I couldn't have been happier with the condition of the car. I had known for decades of the color change and the interior being re-covered, but outside of that I found most things just as I left them. The odometer showed 20,543 miles compared to the 11,000 it showed when I sold it; of course both of these figures were plus 100,000. The engine was still painted red; the correct color for a '67 GTX 440 engine is turquoise. When we had rebuilt the engine in the seventies, I thought turquoise was a very un-cool color; so I painted it Chrysler red. I wasn't too crazy about how dark the red was, but it was certainly better than turquoise. Under the back bumper, the two factory original chrome exhaust tips still hung. They were used on only the 1967 GTX and not even found on other Plymouths, or the Dodge sister car the Coronet R/T. These tips are very unique as they are oblong and somewhat bologna-sliced at the same time, and at that time had not been reproduced. Ever since I had bought the car, the left exhaust tip had a nickel-sized hole burnt in it, and after getting down on one knee to check, there was the tell-tale hole. 1967 GTX's came with a Carter AFB carburetor (which stands for Aluminum Four Barrel) on them. A common upgrade for hot rodders was replacing the AFB with a 1968 and up, Carter AVS, which stands for air valve secondary. Most guys felt they outperformed the AFB. I was a little disappointed when I found the correct AFB on top of my old 440, because it had been updated to an AVS when I had owned it before, but within a few short minutes, while exploring in the trunk, I saw a gunny sack (if you're from north Missouri, or a toe sack if you're from Oklahoma) and when I opened it, there lay a carter AVS, probably the same one I had heard moan so many times in the past. Overall it seemed to me that the last three owners of this car had been just keeping it preserved for me. It felt good.

We then took a tour of Wayne's buildings full of cars. We saw his other favorites and his current projects. As we were dismissing ourselves to leave, Wayne said, "Oh, you can't leave without seeing all my cars." He then brought out a large four wheeler, and my whole family piled on it. While I drove, Wayne instructed me where to go out in his pasture, to go up and down his rows of vintage tin.

Wayne had one more treat in store for me when we got back up to the home and shop area of his property. Wayne owned a 1966 Plymouth Belvedere II, factory equipped with a 426 Hemi engine. This car was completely original with only 41,000 miles. It was a very rare and valuable muscle car that would have been right at home in the high dollar section of a car show, with velvet ropes keeping the crowd back. Wayne said, "Hey Mike, I need to put the old Hemi car back in the building. Why don't you get in it and drive it down to the end of the road, and turn around and come back, and put it in its stall. A very generous man Indeed.

MOPAR NATIONALS

N OW IT WAS ON TO INDIANAPOLIS AND the Mopar Nationals. To see this event was a dream of mine, but certainly not on the scale of the dream I had just had come true, of finding the old GTX. We arrived in Indianapolis and decided to go out to Indianapolis Raceway Park to survey the show before we went to our motel and checked in. We were very impressed with the size. We later learned the show cars numbered in the thousands, and there were something like 800 race cars registered. Each one of these vehicles was required to be either Mopar or Mopar-powered to get in the gate. AMC vehicles were also admitted because they had been purchased by Chrysler earlier, and were now under their corporate umbrella.

The first thing I noticed was the sound coming from the drag strip. What caught my attention was what I wasn't hearing. I had been to different drag strips many times and loved the sound, the louder the better, with the fuel cars being the best. This was different; this was the sound of two potent muscle cars with loud mufflers, but not open headers, leaving the starting line side by side, with their tires loudly squalling, as they frantically fought for a bite on the pavement. There was the sound of both car engines screaming to their individual redlines, and then the distinct shift points accentuated by another loud yelp from the tires. This was the sounds of my youth. You could close your eyes and be standing beside a blacktop road, or sitting in the front seat of a muscle car with the windows rolled down on a hot summer night. Just as amplifiers and electric guitars have never made acoustic instruments obsolete, I am here to say that horsepower measured in the thousands, and clutches that won't let two-foot-wide slicks slip, has not made the sound of a street race obsolete to this guy. The tension of my business back home and the logistics of taking my family on this trip just got caught up with the smell of burnt rubber and blew away.

The second morning we met up with Wayne Cox, and began walking around with him. It seemed like Wayne knew about every other person we came to. One man in particular I stood and listened to as he and Wayne talked about their cars, particularly one this gentleman owned. After we moved on from this man, Wayne said, "Do you know who that was?" and I said, "No." He said, "That is the guy that owns the Silver Bullet." The Silver Bullet was arguably the most famous street race car of all time, and it just happened to be a 1967 GTX. It was owned back in the day by a guy named Jimmy Addison; Addison had connections to Chrysler and the guys who were working in research and development for their high performance cars. This particular GTX had been a test mule for their high performance goodies, and when they were finished with it, Addison had ended up with it. He built a wicked Stroker Hemi for it and replaced several body panels with fiberglass, and consequently became the king of Woodward Avenue Drag Racing. Several car magazines did articles on the car in the early seventies, making Mr. Addison and the nicknamed Silver Bullet famous.

The car was eventually sold by Jimmie, and his engine and the car were separated. The color was also changed, and for the most part, the car was lost but not forgotten. The man we had been talking to had found and restored the car to its former glory and specifications. He then found Jimmie Addison and gave him a job traveling with the GTX to car shows, and setting up in a nearby tent or meeting room, and telling stories about the street racing glory days of him and the Silver Bullet. Wayne had asked the man, "Why isn't your car here today?" and he had replied that he and the promoters hadn't been able to agree on a price; so I knew he owned something special, but it wasn't until he walked away that I found out what it actually was.

The Mopar Nationals provided many more interesting things to experience. John Schneider, better known as Bo Duke of *The Dukes of Hazard*, was there and he had brought along an original General Lee that he had retained after the show ended. There was also a display with the white Challenger from Vanishing Point. Charity got her picture sitting on the tailgate of the original Little Red Wagon wheelie pickup. The KOS (King of the Street) drag racing group was there. They were an all Mopar crowd whose cars had to be street legal, with a valid license plate, lights, etc., to pass inspection, but outside of that, it was no holds barred. They ran in the 8.80's at 154 miles per hour. They were quite impressive grocery getters.

We stopped by the Mopar Collectors' Guide's booth, and found out they knew Wayne too, and had featured some of his cars in their magazine.

While strolling through the show field, we came across the 1967 GTX we had seen on the trailer, traveling on I44 through St Louis, Missouri. It looked even better up close than it did on the highway. I got to talk to its owners, and took many pictures of it inside and out, including the engine and trunk. I took these pictures in faith that someday I would use them for reference when I was restoring my own GTX. We later learned this car won its class in the show.

Of all the neat things we experienced at the Mopar Nationals, the thing that stands out to me the most shows how much of a dad and a family man I had become. Charity, who was nine years old at the time, hadn't eaten anything since we had left home. She had a nervous stomach and was a little off her feed from being out of her element. At the Mopar Nationals McDonalds had a mobile location, and after begging I finally got her to eat half of a poor quality, too expensive quarter pounder. I considered it a big victory; I had been so worried about her.

Now it was time to get back down to the nation, via a short stop at my hometown in Missouri to tell my family my good fortune of seeing and driving my old car.

GREAT NEWS

N OW FINALLY THE FIRST 1967 GTX CAME into the fold. I found out about a car in northern Tennessee and contacted the seller. He sent me a VHS video of the car. It was an unrestored 1967 GTX 440 4 speed, and to make it better, it was gold with a white interior. After seeing the video, it scared me that I had waited for the video to come in the mail. You know that feeling when you pull a puppy out of a box of puppies and look it in the eyes, and you just know you have to take this one home. Yea, that's what it felt like.

I was the first person to drive this car on the street since 1973. The man I bought it from said he found out about this car that was rumored to be in a warehouse in the early '80's. When he finally tracked it down in the city, he met the owner in a very sleazy warehouse district. When arriving at the warehouse and the door was opened, there was no GTX to be seen. This made him worried that he may have been lured there to be robbed or something. The guy then began unstacking boxes, and the old GTX was underneath. It had an old blanket lying on the deck lid, and when they pulled it up, the deck lid was covered with surface rust because it had drawn moisture under the blanket. Except for that surface rust, the only other rust was a quarter sized spot in the left quarter. The guy's story was that his dad was a well-to-do business man, and that he had gotten the car when it was new. He was a very wild kid, and by 1973 he had blown up the 440 so badly that the main bearing cradle had broken off the lower part of the block. The man I got it from pulled it out of the warehouse and took it home. He replaced the 440 with one out of a 1969 GTX that was a real good standard bore block; he freshened it up with new rings and bearings, and a new Mopar performance 484 lift purple shaft cam. The car already had headers. It had just been an old street fighter in the late '60's and early '70's, and it looked the part, with early speed equipment, hood pins, and cheesy do-it-yourself pin stripes.

The man I was purchasing it from said that after he replaced the motor, he backed out of his driveway and went around the cul-de-sac he lived on, and back in the driveway, but never drove it out on the road as it had no brakes. He then stopped working on the car and had lost interest in it four or five years before.

After getting it home, I immediately replaced the whole brake system and got the car road worthy, and found out that it was a beast. It had blown out mufflers behind the headers, and would set the car alarms off on the cars on the lot when we backed it out of the shop. I was taking one of my friends for a ride in it one day and showing off. I feathered the throttle out of the hole, as it was like it was on ice. When I hit second gear, it laid two very loud squalling black strips of rubber. Thinking we were done laying rubber, I wound it out in second. When I hit third, the back tires broke loose again, and the car went sideways; I nearly lost it. It is definitely a handful and loads of fun to play stab and steer with.

My girls and my nephews have been very impressed with this car. When you invite somebody to get in it while its running, the thing is vibrating and the exhaust is causing the floor boards to groan. The doors and windows are rattling, and you get this feeling kind of like climbing down on a bull in the chute; when I slip my foot off the clutch, the chute opens and it tries to throw you out through the back of your seat and both doors at the same time. The ignition switch is worn out, and after getting on it, when you go to turn it off you have to fish the keys out from under the seat, where it threw them. The kids love that part. Kristen says it best. We have had many fast cars: Z28's, Trans Ams, a SVT Cobra Mustang, and Corvettes. Once while explaining to her how fast this particular Corvette was, she stopped me and said, "Dad, I hear what you're saying, and I can feel those late model cars are fast, but your old Mopars scare the crap out of me." 'Nuff said.

During this time Wayne Cox and I had continued talking to one another on the telephone. It was coming up on a year since we began, when I got a phone call from him. He started out saying, "Mike, I have been thinking about you wanting your old car back, and I have decided what I would do. If you will find me a 1967 GTX that I like as well as yours, I will trade with you. It must be red in color, and it must be in a condition where I can just transfer my personalized plates over to it. I don't want any money to change hands at all, just a car to car trade. If you can find me a car like that, I will trade with you and you can have your old car back."

I was now a man on a mission. As stated before, I was already looking for 1967 GTX's, but now I intensified the search. I considered turning the gold 4 speed car I had just purchased into a suitable trade, but I just didn't have the heart to change the color on this original old car, and also Wayne wasn't particularly interested in a four speed car.

It wasn't but a few weeks until I got a hit on my 1967 GTX trade candidate radar. There was a car in Little Rock, Arkansas that seemed to fit the bill. I talked to the guy on the phone and it sounded very promising. Lynn and I jumped in my pickup with car dolly in tow, and headed for Little Rock. We met the man at a storage building he owned in Little Rock. When I walked up to this car, I knew immediately that it would not work. The guy who was selling it was a nice guy and an honest guy, but he was not a car guy. Much of this car had been redone, and it had all been done wrong. Just to give an example, he had told me it had a new headliner. When I looked inside, the headliner they had put in it was a little foam backed board like modern cars had in them, not the correct bow type the car was supposed to have. The car had stuff all over it that made as much sense as a screen door in a submarine. I have never driven so far to be so disappointed in my life.

I had gotten real excited about getting my car back soon, and hoped this car in Little Rock would be the one to make that happen, but it turned out that once again, I had to practice patience until I found the right car for Wayne. Seems like this is becoming a thing! On the very bright side, I had a promise from Wayne Cox, and finding cars is what I do so...Time to resume the hunt.

I WANT THE RED ONE

I HAD NO IDEA THAT IT WOULD TAKE AS long as it did to find a GTX to trade to Wayne Cox. On my part it was not for lack of trying. I was shaking the bushes with a fervor. I remember saying and I still believe it to be true, that I probably knew of the whereabouts of more '67 GTX's than anyone in the country at that time. I had several video tapes as well as photographs guys had sent me of their cars I had inquired about.

I had a pretty narrow bracket that this car needed to fit in. It had to be a red 1967 GTX, or one I would make red, and it had to please Wayne; neither of these things were unreasonable. The price and condition of the car, as well as its originality, were the big issues. The car I was replacing was a daily driver category of car. Its color had been changed, and this paint job was over twenty years old. It had a lot of rust repair in the lower quarter panels and driver's floor board, using metal from an old Dodge pickup hood when I had the car painted in the '70's. The interior was reupholstered with non-original material and the drive train was solid, but hadn't been freshened in thirty years. Even with that said, this was a car that you could be proud to drive in a parade, and from my point of view, it was beautiful. I was not interested in the condition; I was interested that it was mine. I always intended to trade Wayne a better car than it, and one that he liked better than it. The dilemma was there were hardly any cars for sale close to this condition. There were plenty of restored cars which had big prices I couldn't afford; there were a lot of non-original cars that didn't have their high performance 440 still intact; and there were also field cars that were too far gone and needed everything. I even bought one of those cars that hadn't been driven for years in the great state of Mississippi. It was a real by the numbers '67 GTX, but it was in too bad shape to bring back quickly or affordably enough. I bought it only because I thought it was too cheap; it also came with a 1966 Satellite parts car.

A full two years had passed since we had gone to Effingham and looked at and drove the GTX. We had finally come into the computer age, and I incorporated this new tool in my search for a suitable car. One day I saw a brand new add pop up on a Mopar website for a 1967 GTX in the state of Delaware. It sounded like it was in a very comparable condition to Wayne's car; it ran and drove well; it had its original engine; and it had its original interior still intact. The owner said it had previous rust repair in the rear quarter panels that needed to be redone. The pictures of the car looked great, and the best part was it was a red car originally.

While I was talking to the man in Delaware, telling him I would take the car and would get back to him on coming to get it or have it transported, my wife had been talking to some customers on the car lot. They had come inside to ask the price on a cheap old trade in that was sitting beside the building. When I got off the phone my wife asked how much I wanted for the old car and I said, "$800" The customer said, "How about we go get that car for you?" He had overheard my conversation on the phone. He was driving a big diesel Dodge dually and said he had a goose neck trailer. I asked him how much he would charge to go to Delaware and bring the car back, and he pointed out the window at the car they were looking at to buy, and said, "We will go get it for that car." So we had a deal.

When they pulled in with the car in a couple of days, it was a big deal for my family because we were finally moving forward again in getting our car back. When I saw the car I had mixed feelings; I had hoped it would be a short and relatively inexpensive job to make the car presentable to Wayne, but after seeing it up close, I could see that this would not be the case. The rust repair in the quarter panels had not been done correctly at all, and the paint itself, although looking good in the pictures on the internet, was not something I could feel proud to present to Wayne Cox. I could see this would be a more lengthy and costly endeavor than I had hoped for. The bright spot about this car was its history and story. I got all the information with the car about its previous owners, and called and talked to them. The original owner was no longer living, but the second owner told me this great story. He said that he was a Pontiac GTO enthusiast, and that he worked for the city of Baltimore, Maryland. He said that one day while talking to a coworker about cars, this guy said, "I'll tell you where there is a GTO in a shed right here in town." His coworker then proceeded to tell him of a certain location in Baltimore. The man I was talking to said that he knew this neighborhood well, and knew exactly where the old man lived. He even remembered the shed there because he said, "There is no car in that shed; it is not big enough to hold a car." Even though he didn't believe his coworker, now his interest was aroused. So he went to the old man's house and knocked on the door. He soon found out he had been wrong about there being a car in that shed, and when the old man opened the door to it, there sat not a Pontiac GTO, but this red 1967 GTX. The old man told him that in the summer of '66 he had been at the Plymouth dealer, and had been excited about their new muscle car, the GTX, and before he left he ordered a blue one. Several weeks later he got a call that his GTX had arrived at the dealership, and he excitedly jumped in his car and went down there. When he pulled in, there were two 1967 GTX's on a car transport, a blue one and a red one. When his salesman came out to meet him, his first question was, "Is that red car sold?" and when the salesman answered "No", he said, "That's the one I want, the red one instead of the blue one." I thought that was a great story, and appreciated how hard it is to find an old car with its history intact. I even found the original build sheet still in the car.

We then rolled up our sleeves and tore into the car. Fortunately, this car had been Z Barted or some similar product when new, which is a rust protection that is sprayed on the body and frame underneath and inside the doors and fenders. So this had been protected from the harsh New England winters and road salt. What had been affected were the places these models normally catch and hold water, like the lower quarter panels, the lower front fenders, and the trunk floor because of the deck lid seal leaking, and things like that. We began by removing the bumpers, grille, and every molding and piece of trim, including the door handles. Then with the help of my nephew, we took this car down to the bare metal; we literally took every speck of paint off of it. We then cut out the places on the bottom of the quarter panels and everywhere else that rust was present. We even removed the vinyl top because there were a few places you could see rust bubbling under it. I then bought aftermarket rust-replacement lower quarter panels for the car.

I commissioned a good friend of mine that had a body shop and a great reputation, to take the car from here. He mig-welded in the new panels, as well as the spots we had cut out in the trunk floor. He even took the headliner down and cut three or four one inch holes where rust had pitted underneath the vinyl top. All of these places were repaired by welding in new metal, not fiberglass or bondo. The places where rust was repaired were then treated with a product called POR 15 to seal it off for the future, and then the car was primed and painted.

We then took the car back to our shop to reassemble all the moldings, trim bumpers, and grille and tail panels. We also had a trim shop install a new headliner and vinyl top. When the car was finally done, it had been seventeen months since we had bought it in Delaware. It was three years since Wayne Cox had agreed to trade if I found him the right car, and it had been forty-five months since finding my car and talking to Wayne on the phone the first time.

I called Wayne and told him the car was done about five minutes after turning the last screw into place. I fully intended to take him the car in Effingham, but once again, showing how gracious he was, he said, "No I'll bring your car down to you and trade there. I'll see you in a couple of weeks."

WOO HOO

FTER WAITING ABOUT THE SAME AMOUNT OF time, that it feels like to an eight year old between Christmases (a week or two), one Sunday night at home the phone rang. It was Wayne. He said he was sitting at our shop in Durant with the car. Charity says that I pumped my fist in the air and let out a shout of "Woo Hoo!" when I got off the phone. Lynn has always joked that it was the most excited she has ever seen me including the birth of our two babies. Our home is ten miles south of Durant. We all jumped in the car and headed back to the shop. By the time we greeted one another and got the car unloaded it was getting late. We certainly had not wanted the car to sit out all night on the trailer. So we put it straight into my shop. I took a picture that still makes me smile inside every time I see it. At this location we had a three car shop. In the first bay was the red car we had brought back from Delaware and worked on for seventeen months and were proud to present to Wayne. In the middle stall was the Gold 440, 4 speed car that I had gotten from Tennessee. It was the correct color that my car had been. I had had it four years and was still in love with it. In the third stall was MY CAR, wow. There were three 1967 GTX's in the same building. All of them ran and drove well. All three had interesting stories. This was rare indeed, and all of them meant something special to me. If you want to know how special these three cars were to me, the car that got bumped to allow all three GTX's in the building was a 1964 Impala Super Sport with 71,000 actual miles and original paint. It was a red car, a 327 automatic. Its original silver bucket seats were often assumed to be reproductions, but they were not, and it had a dealer installed rosewood steering wheel, which at that time were selling for $800 on eBay. When I had made the deal for the car and agreed on a price the owner had said can I keep my trophies. The trunk was chocked full of trophies.

The next morning we met back up with Wayne at our shop, and he test drove his new old GTX. We then had a photo shoot much like the ones you have to wait forever for after a wedding, while eating those little green mints that are only found at weddings. We took pictures of the cars together, and Wayne and I exchanging titles and shook hands. We had some of the whole family in front of the two cars, and then tons of pictures of just our car with us. No one fed cake to each other, but the newspaper was there. Unbeknownst to me, my daughters had alerted a reporter from the Durant Daily Democrat that this trade would be occurring soon, and had called her at the newspaper office that morning. So she came on over to the car lot. She asked a lot of questions about mine and Lynn's history with the car and Lynn got out a photo album and showed her some old pictures of us back in the day. She also interviewed Wayne Cox.

A really interesting coincidence happened that day. A man walked in the office and my daughter Kristen was seated at the front desk. The man asked Kristen "Who is the owner of this business?" Kristen answered him "My dad Mike Banks." The man said "I think I might know him. I might have gone to school with him." "Probably not," Kristen said "He is not from around here." When he asked where her dad had gone to school and Kristen replied "North Missouri." The man just smiled. Just then Lynn walked back in the office, looked up, and exclaimed, "Well, Danny McClain!" She then looked down at the picture album lying open on the desk in front of Kristen, and pointed to a picture of Danny in a tuxedo in our wedding, and said "There you are on our wedding day and now you're here." Danny McClain was a truck driver and he had been traveling south bound on highway 69/75 going through Durant. We had just recently painted a fourteen foot by twenty-eight foot mural on the end of our building. It was a giant license tag that said "Banks Motor Company." It was a blown up, exact replica of our advertisement front license plates that were on the front of every vehicle we sold. I had made the design years before and had chosen the colors yellow on a purple background because the two colors were a great contrast and they clashed with everything so they really stood out. This giant Banks tag was very visible from highway 69/75. The Banks sign caught Danny's eye. He knew I had moved to this area shortly after high school and thought this might be me. So he found an exit and turned around and came back. When he pulled his semi in on the east side of the building, Lynn and I were outside on the west side of the building and didn't see him arrive.

It was so fitting that someone I had run around with when I originally owned the GTX was here for this reunion with it. Lynn and I and he and his girlfriend had double dated in it. She was Lynn's neighbor whose family had to assign someone to hold their palm against their picture window while sitting in their living room when the old GTX was idling away in Lynn's driveway across the street. When Danny was in high school he drove a '63 Chevy. So he and I and Wayne Cox took my '64 Impala and went to lunch in it, and Danny drove.

Wayne had told the newspaper reporter that he really didn't want to part with his car, but he knew what it was like to wish you could have back a car you had when you were young; we were so glad he had felt that way, and had been unselfish towards us. We loaded his GTX on his trailer and bid him farewell as he set out for his home in Effingham.

THE BEGINNING

O N THE DAY THAT WE TRADED CARS WITH Wayne Cox, after he and Danny McClain and the newspaper reporter left, there was still plenty of the afternoon left. Just as I had harbored the dream for all those years of using the old set of keys to verify I had found my car, there was one other thing that I always knew would be the first thing I would do when I actually got the GTX back in my possession. I backed the GTX into the first stall in our garage, over the lift, and I ran it up in the air, to the point the bottom of the front bumper was at about the same height as the top of my head. After doing this, I called my family around and told Charity to have her video camera ready. The radiator support extends down below the bumper on this body style of Plymouth, and is painted black to blend in with the underside of the car. When I was in high school, I noticed that this would be a perfect place to paint my name; so I did that in two inch high white block letters against the black background. Can you imagine how cool this looked seeing my car coming down the road at you proclaiming that this car is owned by this cool guy MIKE BANKS. Yea, that's what I was afraid you would think. After a couple of weeks I came to my senses and realized this was too cheesy even for me, and painted over the MIKE BANKS. It had been a dream of mine to sand the black topcoat off of the lower part of the radiator support, exposing my name underneath. Having the availability of a lift, I could now do the unveiling of this bit of history in style. I began sanding and Charity's video camera began rolling. Sure enough, after a few minutes, here came the white letters that I had put there in my youth.

The next thing on the agenda for welcoming the car back home was a quick trip to our local tag agent. I took the Illinois title that Wayne Cox had just signed off to me a few hours before. I was determined to make it official that this car belonged to me again. I had started working in new car dealerships one year after high school, and began driving demonstrators. Even when I bought a new car, the dealership agreed to pay for my gas and insurance, requiring me to leave the title in the dealership's name with only a power of attorney to protect my ownership. I went from working in the new car stores to my own used dealership, and consequently had titled every vehicle I had owned since then in the name of Banks Motor Company. Even though these cars were all mine, the GTX was the first car in decades which the title now showed was my personal car.

I was proud of my new license plates and could not wait to put them on my car. When I squatted down to screw the plates on the old GTX, I noticed two ugly, ragged holes in the rear bumper in the spot that is normally covered by the license plate. These holes were obviously not factory, but had been put there by someone. They were not round at all but were just, to use a southern Oklahoma term, kind of wallered out. I thought to myself, "Some idiot has ruined this bumper.

Do they know how much one of these bumpers is worth?" I certainly knew how much one was worth, having been involved with restoring these old cars. Just as I was thinking this, a scene flashed through my mind: it was in my mom and dad's driveway in Princeton, and I was sitting cross legged at the back of the old GTX. I had in my hands a small quarter inch drill of dad's. I was making the holes to attach a trailer hitch to the GTX so we could pull Lynn's VW bug, when we would leave bright and early the next morning to move to Oklahoma. I didn't have a drill bit large enough for the holes needed to put the bolts through for the trailer hitch. So I did the wallerin'. I guess that's a north Missouri term as well.

When I got the car back, it had a cassette tape player installed in the dash. I could not stand for this. Fortunately, in my cache of MOPAR goodies, I had an original Plymouth AM radio, which was correct for this car. I removed the old cassette player and noticed that it was powering a pair of speakers in the back window shelf only. I fitted the original type AM radio in the dash, and was plugging in the power terminal from the wiring harness to the radio, when I noticed a green wire dangling off the old original mono speaker that was mounted in the top of the dash. It had not been hooked up in years, maybe since I first sold the car. I looked up at that wire dangling there and thought, "Surely not, surely it wouldn't still play." I already had the car's switch in the accessory position, but didn't realize that the radio knob was also in the "on" position. When I, just for fun, connected the green speaker wire to the radio, the speaker blurted out the words "Jeremiah was a bullfrog." I ran in the office and got Lynn. I said, "Lynn, Three Dog

Night have been trapped in that old speaker all these years. I just let them out."

A couple of weeks after we got the car back, on a Sunday morning, Kristen drove her car down to the highway, to the box where the paper carrier left our newspaper. When Kristen pulled the Sunday paper from the box, she could see a picture of Lynn and me on the front page. We had been watching for the article every day, but assumed it would be a small article on a back page on a weekday. Our article was the whole bottom half of the front page. The title read "Durant Man Reunited with Long Lost Love," and had a picture of Lynn and me in the front seat of the car on our wedding day, as well as one with Lynn and me and Wayne Cox in front of both cars on the day we traded. The writer did a great job on the article. Lynn had told her the story of how we met, and how we had found the car. She did mix up the fact that the guy I bought the car from had raced it for money, and attributed that to me, but that was an honest mix up.

I was really impressed with the response from the community to this article, and it really confirmed to me the soft spot in their heart that most people have for a car from their youth, especially if it was a sporty model. People especially like to relive their experience with a muscle car from this era, either theirs or a friend's. I would have people come on the car lot and I would greet them; I would then follow them around the lot, not being able to get anything out of them, when finally they would ask, "Is that car here? Could we look at it?" I would run into ladies in town in places like the post office and they would stop me and say, "We read your article all the way to the end, thinking it was a romance story, and after reading the whole thing, it ended up being about a stinking car, not a woman that you were reunited with." When I took Charity to school, a couple of the teachers and the principal came out and congratulated us.

This all happened right before our twenty-fifth wedding anniversary, allowing us to drive the car to dinner on this special occasion, and we brought the whole family with us. Those were joyous days, Lynn and I getting to go out and just cruise around in our old car again. On one such day, a beautiful and sunny afternoon, Lynn and I dismissed ourselves from the business and drove the car around town. We had no particular place to go, we were simply driving to enjoy it. We were coming down a residential street in Durant, one where the streets are lined with older modest houses. As we came in front of their home, there was a couple sitting on their front porch. They were strangers to us, but when they saw us approaching, they recognized the car. They then got up out of their chairs and applauded for us as we drove by. It felt like these total strangers were confirming what a miraculous blessing us being reunited with this car was, and at the same time, giving us a wonderful send off for the beginning of the rest of our lives together.

ACKNOWLEDGEMENTS

I want to take a moment to thank all the people who gave help or assistance in the writing of this book. Thanks to Kathy Weiner, Linda Lee and Joey McWilliams for all of your editorial support and expertise. Thank you to my family, Lynn Banks, Kristen Banks, Charity Banks, Jeana Crisp and James Clark for all of the work you put into this book, and for your support and encouragement.

I wrote all of these stories as if I were telling them to a close friend. Everything I have written is true to the best of my memory. If there are any inconsistencies they are the effect of time and not intentional.